ADVANCED PRIVATE INVESTIGATION

ADVANCED PRIVATE INVESTIGATION

A Manual of Advanced Investigative Skills for the Private Investigator

Edited by

WILLIAM F. BLAKE, MS, CPP, CFE

CHARLES C THOMAS • PUBLISHER, LTD.
Springfield • Illinois • U.S.A.

Published and Distributed Throughout the World by

CHARLES C THOMAS • PUBLISHER, LTD.
2600 South First Street
Springfield, Illinois 62704

© 2011 by CHARLES C THOMAS • PUBLISHER, LTD.

ISBN 978-0-398-08652-7 (paper)
ISBN 978-0-398-08653-4 (ebook)

Library of Congress Catalog Card Number: 2011001171

With THOMAS BOOKS *careful attention is given to all details of manufacturing
and design. It is the Publisher's desire to present books that are satisfactory as to their
physical qualities and artistic possibilities and appropriate for their particular use.*
THOMAS BOOKS *will be true to those laws of quality that assure a good name
and good will.*

Printed in the United States of America
MM-R-3

Library of Congress Cataloging-in-Publication Data

Advanced Private Investigation : A manual of advanced investigative
skills for the private investigator / edited by William F. Blake
   p. cm.
  Includes bibliographical references and index.
  ISBN 978-0-398-08652-7 (pbk.) -- ISBN 978-0-398-08653-4 (ebook)
  1. Private investigators–United States–Handbooks, manuals, etc. 2.
Investigations–United States–Handbooks, manuals, etc. I. Blake,
William II. Title.

HV8093.M34 2011
363.28'9–dc22

           2011001171

CONTRIBUTORS

Lynda J. Bergh, MS
L. J. B. Investigations
Coto de Caza, California

Ms. Bergh has over 35 years' experience as a private investigator and as a law enforcement staff member. She has provided training to law enforcement and private investigation in insurance fraud, workers' compensation, child custody issues, and due diligence matters.

David G. Duchesneau, CFC, CII
Standa, Inc.
Milton, New Hampshire

David G. Duchesneau is a former retired New Hampshire State Trooper, serving 20 years in investigative and management positions, as well as 19 years in the private sector, totaling 39 years of investigative knowledge and experience. He is a member of the New Hampshire League of Investigators, ASIS International, United States Association of Professional Investigators, Council of International Investigators, and Intellenet. He is a Certified International Investigator, and a Certified Fraud Consultant.

Steven L. Kirby, BS, CFE, CII
Edward R. Kirby & Associates
Elmhurst, Illinois

Mr. Kirby has over 35 years of investigative experience and is a Certified Fraud Examiner and Certified International Investigator who specializes in polygraph examinations. He is a member and past president of several professional investigative associations. He is a former Fire and Police Commissioner for the city of Elmhurst, Illinois.

William F. Marshall, MA
Veritas Intelligence, LLC
Fairfax, Virginia

William F. Marshall served for six years as an Intelligence Analyst with the Drug Enforcement Administration and has 23 years' experience overall in government intelligence and private sector investigations. He specializes in competitive intelligence, background investigations, litigation support, and insurance claims investigation.

S. Beville May, BA, JD
Prevent Claims, LLC
Exton, Pennsylvania

S. Beville May is a former practicing attorney who now consults with clients to help them prevent and resolve lawsuits. She conducts claims prevention programs, investigations of claims, negotiations, and mediations.

Kevin W. McClain, AA, CCDI
Kevin W. McClain Investigations, Ltd.
Centralia, Illinois

Kevin W. McClain has been a professional investigator for 16 years. He is a Certified Criminal Defense Investigator and a national trainer He is president of Kevin W. McClain Investigations, Ltd., licensed in Illinois, Indiana, Kentucky, and Missouri, and specializes in death penalty investigations.

Reginald J. Montgomery, CLI, CPP, CFE, CST, CFC, CP
R.J. Montgomery Associates
Allendale, New Jersey

Reginald J. Montgomery has over 40 years' experience as a private investigator and law enforcement officer. He has given over 100 presentations on private investigation and security management issues to professional associations, educational groups, and civic organizations around the world.

Harvey Morse, JD, CMI, CFL
Locators International, Inc.
Daytona Beach, Florida

Harvey Morse is a sworn law enforcement officer, a state certified training instructor. He has over 40 years of investigative experience. He is a graduate of Boston University, the Florida Police Academy, attended Suffolk University Law School, is a public speaker, and conducts seminars for lawyers.

George Michael Newman, CFE, CII
Tactical Investigative Services
San Diego, California

George Michael Newman has over 30 years of investigative experience and is a member of Intellenet.

Dana Picore, PHD
Picore Worldwide
Calabasas, California

Dana Picore has a Doctorate in Clinical Psychology with an emphasis in Organizational Psychology and is a licensed private investigator and psychotherapist. She is a former law enforcement officer and field and academy training instructor. She specializes in threat assessments and management and prevention of workplace violence.

Nancy Poss-Hatchl, MS, CPI
Helios Investigations
Santa Ana, California

Nancy Poss-Hatchl is founder and president of Helios Investigations of Santa Ana, California. She has been a Certified Professional Investigator since 1982. She is a member of CALI, CII, and Intellenet.

KEVIN J. RIPA, ENCE, CDRP, CPT
Computer Evidence Recovery, Inc.
Calgary, Alberta, Canada

Kevin J. Ripa is president of Computer Evidence Recovery, Inc. He also serves as Computer Forensics Coordinator for CanPro Global Services Worldwide, Advanced Surveillance Group in the United States, and Premier Shield Pvt in New Delhi, India. He has been conducting computer computer forensic investigations for 12 years, and sits on the boards of the Alberta Association of Private Investigators, Canadian Association of Professional Investigators, and the International Intelligence Network.

Alphonse V. Ristuccia
Larsen AVR Group
Los Angeles, California

Alphonse V. Ristuccia had a 22-plus-year career with IRS-CID where he was a Special Agent and Supervisory Special Agent. For the last 15 years, he has been engaged in private investigations specializing in serious fraud matters where the search and recovery of assets has been an important aspect of those investigations.

Fred W. Rustmann, Jr., BA
CTC International Group, Ltd.
West Palm Beach, Florida

Fred W. Rustmann is a 24-year veteran of the CCIA and author of *CIA, Inc: Espionage and the Craft of Business Intelligence.* He is chairman of CTC International Group, Inc., a West Palm Beach-based provider of business intelligence.

Barry Ryan, BA, CFE
Information Network Associates, Inc.
Harrisburg, Pennsylvania

Barry Ryan served four years as an FBI Agent. He was a security director for both the GTE Corporation and Spalding (A.G.) Company. He has been a private investigator for more than 25 years and is owner of INA, an investigative and technology-based computer forensic company.

Daniel P. Ryan, CPA, Cr.FA
Information Network Associates, Inc.
Harrisburg, Pennsylvania

Daniel P. Ryan is the CEO of Information Network Associates (INA), a Harrisburg, Pennsylvania-based private investigative company specializing in forensic accounting and computer forensic matters.

Stefan Salmonson, PPS
Protective Services, Inc.
More, Minnesota

Stefan Salmonson has over 30 years' experience as a private investigator and law enforcement officer. He specializes in executive protection services and investigative and security management training. He is a nationally recognized speaker on numerous investigative and security matters.

Jeffrey Stein, LPI, BA
ELPS Private Detective Agency
Exton, Pennsylvania

Jeffrey Stein has over 20 years' investigative experience, has conducted over a thousand internal and external interviews during the course of his career in the private sector. He is currently president and founder of ELPS Private Detective Agency and PA Digital Surveillance Systems. He is a licensed professional investigator in Pennsylvania and holds a BS in Criminal Justice from West Chester University. He has advanced training in interviewing and interrogation techniques.

Michele Stuart
JAG Investigations, Inc.
Gilbert, Arizona

Michele Stuart has over 20 years' experience as a private investigator and is a monthly contributor to *PI Magazine* on internet subjects. She has presented numerous seminars and presentations in law enforcement and security personnel.

Barbara W. Thompson, MS, JD, CFE
The Worldwide Investigative Network
West Chester, Pennsylvania

Barbara W. Thompson is a retired attorney and has 15 years of investigative experience specializing in due diligence investigations. She is Managing Partner and Director of Research and Analysis of The Worldwide Network, LLC.

PREFACE

Today's private investigator comes from two primary sources: (1) law enforcement agencies and (2) from academic environments. As a result, the experience gap varies widely. Those coming from law enforcement normally are retirees with an average of 20–25 years of experience as a law enforcement officer. Their experience as an investigator is frequently much less and what experience they do have may have been restricted to a particular investigative area, such as narcotics, robbery, etc. The investigations they will conduct in the business environment will be significantly different. Those coming from the academic world have the advantage of exposure to the latest in investigative techniques and legal knowledge but lack practical experience in applying the information that they have learned. The academic's investigative knowledge is normally restricted to an introductory course where only the most basic of investigative skills are discussed. Each group comes with a different outlook, perspective and set of values. To be successful as a private investigator, they must learn the more complicated skills required in the world of corporate investigations.

The purpose of this book is to provide a basic understanding of some of the more complex matters faced by the private investigator. Real expertise in the advanced level of private investigations comes from expanding this basic information into a more comprehensive working knowledge of the issues. Each area discussed in this book could easily be expanded into a single subject book. This expanded knowledge can result in expertise in a niche business model with considerable personal and business success. It is not our purpose to make an individual a highly skilled private investigator in every conceivable investigative arena. Our intent is to whet the interest in areas not normally encountered in law enforcement or the academic environments. A general minimum knowledge in these areas will be valuable when it is necessary to employ an especially skilled subcontractor to support the primary investigative matter.

The authors of this book are a very unique group of professionals. Each author has a minimum of ten years of investigative experience and many have at least 35 years of experience. The majority of the authors have investigative experience with large law enforcement agencies, in military service, or at all levels of government. The professional certifications earned by the authors demonstrate their quest for professionalism and current knowledge due to the requirements for continuing professional education. Many of the authors have advanced academic degrees such as PhD, Juris Doctor, MBA, and similar degrees.

The following chapters outline some of the specialized areas in which the experienced private investigator may be involved. Each author has written about his or her specialized area based on personal experiences. This tactic eliminates the inconsequential and concentrates on primary issues.

Success as a private investigator is influenced by two different business options. An individual may pursue his activities from a business perspective and provide investigative services for all possible clients through the use of his own skills, augmented by the investigative resources of qualified associates. Second, an individual may rely strictly on current skills and operate within a limited scope of activities which will impact business income and success.

William F. Blake

INTRODUCTION

The world of the private investigator has evolved from a very simple to a very complex business. In our early history, the private investigator primarily operated in a law enforcement officer mode but was employed by an individual or corporate entity. The basic qualifications of the early private investigator were being able to find people who may or may not have committed a crime, and when the circumstances required, be able to shoot first and accurately. There were very few legal restrictions on the activities of investigators and in some cases, their activities were clearly criminal violations of law. There was no public outcry for restrictions on their activities as there was a general public opinion that the perpetrators probably deserved what happened to them. There was also a common opinion that a person had a right to protect his personal reputation and business interests by any means possible. This attitude was portrayed in the early western movies where John Wayne, Hopalong Cassidy, and Gene Autry portrayed the white hat savior of the common person being persecuted by the black hat bad guys.

The expertise of the early private investigators was primarily derived from the survival skills they learned as a hunter and trapper. Tracking a prey and accurate shooting was a necessity for the majority of the early settlers. The so-called private investigator honed these skills to a finer degree if he or she wished to be successful. Only history knows how many of these individuals were literate enough to document their activities.

Over time, business enterprises were organized to provide more comprehensive investigative services over a larger geographical area. One of the more prominent companies was the Pinkerton National Detective Agency, which is still a prominent international investigative service to this day. At the company's zenith, it employed more private investigators than there were members of the United States military services. Intimidated by their size, the State of Ohio outlawed the agency due to fears it could be hired out as a private army or militia. Some of their earlier activities would be illegal under current laws.

As customer needs evolved, similar businesses were organized and engaged in the apprehension of wanted persons, strikebreaking, and protection of dignitaries, as well as protection of valuable shipments of gold, silver, and other valuable commodities. Many private investigative companies were held in contempt and disrepute by the general public because of their questionable activities.

The activities of the private investigator have changed considerably over the last 100 years. The successes as well as the problems of earlier private investigators have had a great influence on the modern-day private investigator. Most state governments have instituted legal requirements for private investigators, among which are minimum experience, insurance, and educational requirements. These actions were taken to protect members of the public. Current and pending legislation at all levels of government also impact what can be accomplished by the private investigator. These restrictions have been a result of an outcry for personal privacy and the inappropriate and highly publicized criminal activities of a small minority of private investigators.

The role of the current-day private investigator primarily encompasses those areas which are not criminal in nature or of sole interest to the business community, such as internal matters and civil litigation. There are also situations where the private investigator may become involved in criminal matters because of jurisdictional problems and financial and manpower limitations of public law enforcement. This has created a wide variety of business opportunities for the qualified private investigator with knowledge and experience with more sophisticated investigative matters.

Because of the ever-increasing public outcry and governmental legislation, the private investigator must develop a recession and legislative proof of business niche to remain a viable business entity. This will require exploring investigative matters not normally encountered by law enforcement agencies. One example is the current and pending limitations on obtaining personal information from public records. The private investigator whose business is primarily based on obtaining personal information will find every increasing difficulty in obtaining the desired information. Now is the time to reevaluate business opportunities and identify goals for the future. At this point, the individual is no longer just a private investigator but a business person who provides investigative services. The emphasis for survival is on "business."

ACKNOWLEDGMENTS

I want to express my sincere thanks and appreciation to all of the authors who took valuable time out of their work day to assist with this project. Each author is a member of Intellenet and an experienced professional. This project was undertaken following numerous comments and discussions, and in some cases, complaints, about the problems encountered in transitioning from positions as investigators in various agencies where there was no need to be concerned with marketing, developing clients, and other business activities. We never worried about these issues—work always came to us, sometimes in far greater quantities than we could control.

The business world is in a constant state of fluctuation, causing some traditional concepts to be unworkable, requiring many changes to remain solvent as a business. Technology, especially the computer and the Internet, turned our business world upside-down. As an example, the increased access to information caused computer forensics to be a very necessary resource. This became a very lucrative business niche for some who were able to sell their services to other investigators and the public as a whole.

Other investigative areas became more complicated through the advances in computers and the ease of obtaining information through the Internet. Legislative actions by state and federal authorities also complicated our business strategies. Currently, the need to develop a unique business investigative niche requires many hours of effort to understand the nuances of legislation and more complex investigations.

The authors have all found a unique business niche where they can provide expert services to others. It is incumbent on all private investigators to identify and become experts in a particular area. The days of the "one size fits all" general investigator is heading to oblivion and will be relegated to history.

William F. Blake

CONTENTS

ADVANCED PRIVATE INVESTIGATION

Chapter 1

ASSET SEARCH AND RECOVERY

ALPHONSE V. RISTUCCIA

There are many, many facets of the private investigation's profession. A "newly minted" private investigator will certainly start out as a generalist; that is, doing everything and anything that comes in the door. After all, it's human nature to not want to turn away business and not want to refer business to some other firm, particularly when one is first starting out. It's human nature to want to begin to build a solid book of business as soon as possible. So, saying no to a client, particularly a new client, is not easy to do. Therefore, instead of saying no, a person new to the private investigations profession, and those who have been around for a while, should say, "yes, if."

What is meant by "yes, if" is: I can do it if the following conditions exist. As an example, people are always asking "can you obtain bank records?" The answer is always "yes, if." And the "if" is: if a court order is obtained; if a subpoena is obtained; if the holder of the account gives permission. So it goes with a client or prospective client who asks, "Can you locate assets?" The answer should be "Yes, if." The "if" in this case is: If you (the client) have the funds to pay for the services needed to locate assets. How assets are located can, and usually does, relate to the amount of budget that is available and the legal process that is available to properly undertake the project. As this chapter progresses, the issues of budget and legal process will be interwoven into the information relating to how we locate assets and how we recover the assets that are located.

Victims of fraud and those who prevail in lawsuits or obtain other legal remedies are continually seeking monetary and other retribution in connection with their issues. This presentation will focus on the investigative techniques used to trace (identify, locate) assets in connection with fraudulent activity. How assets are identified and located could be determined by the nature of the proceedings which give rise for the need to trace assets held by fraudsters or their third-party accomplices. Certainly venue (where proceedings are held and where the assets to be recovered are located) has an impact on tracing and recovering assets. The impact may take the form of inherent challenges in actually identifying and recovering the assets, and/or the financial investment it would take to do both. Identifying and locating assets, hidden or not, is a function of hard work, investigative perseverance, resourcefulness, and some luck. Weaving in common sense to this equation is also a must.

It is very important, at the outset of the investigation, to identify, locate and recover assets, strict confidentiality as to the investigation should be maintained. This is particularly necessary when attempting to trace assets in connection with a fraud matter. It will be difficult enough to trace assets held by seasoned fraudsters or their third-party accomplices who are expert in constructing asset fortresses to protect their assets. If a fraudster learns of an investigation that may result in depriving him or her of these assets, steps will be taken to place the assets further beyond the reach of the asset pursuers.

DEBRIEFING THE CLIENT

It does not matter what type of investigation is being conducted or has been conducted that gives rise for the need to search for assets, it is always a good idea to begin the asset search by completely and thoroughly debriefing the client. This is particularly true if the client is the victim of a fraud and the search for assets is directly related to the fraudulent activity. It is important to document what the target said in explaining what it is that the client/victim was investing in or otherwise getting involved in. Obtain copies of any and all written documents provided to the client/victim by the target. An essential initial step in tracing assets is to completely debrief the victim or victims of the fraudster whose assets you are seeking to trace and recover. It is important to obtain from the victim any and all information regarding the nature of the fraud. It is also important to obtain from the victim copies of checks, wire transfer advices, or other such documents that relate to the transfer of funds from the victim to the fraudster. Also, it is essential to obtain from the victim any and all correspondence of whatever nature between the victim and the fraudster. In addition, it is vital to obtain all telephone numbers and addresses that the victim used to contact the fraudster. This information will assist in identifying places to begin looking for the fraudster and the assets to be identified, located and ultimately recovered. Also, this information will be useful if surveillance activity and/or an undercover operation are contemplated. It is important to determine the current relationship between the victim and the fraudster in order to determine the possibility of an introduction by the victim to the fraudster if an undercover sting is contemplated. If the victim believes that he or she is still on reasonably good terms with the fraudster, the victim should be advised to maintain that relationship, but certainly not provide any additional funds to the fraudster. The victim should be further cautioned not to initiate contact with the fraudster unless so instructed by the investigator. In connection with this, and in an attempt to perhaps "prime the pump," the victim should be instructed that if the fraudster initiates contact, the victim should certainly not mention the fact that investigators are now involved in the matter. Also, the victim should be instructed to ask the fraudster if he is still taking investments and if so, could the victim obtain some consideration by referring an "investor" (undercover agent).

All of the information that is received from the client, both verbal and documentary, should be completely analyzed. It is extremely important to analyze the items that reflect client/victim funds being transmitted to the target. If wire transfers are used, knowing where the funds were sent that were provided by the client/victim to the target can provide leads to follow the money trail. In the case of checks, the endorsement information should be reviewed to determine where/ how the checks were negotiated. Were the checks deposited to a bank account or were they merely cashed? If deposited, to what account, located at what financial institution. If cashed, where? If checks are cashed in amounts that are in excess of $10,000 ($10,000.01), a CTR should have been prepared and filed with the Detroit Computing

Center by the financial institution that cashed the checks. If the checks were cashed at a check cashing business, the check cashing business should have also filed a CTR if the amount of the checks cashed was in excess of $10,000. If the target was provided a series of checks, each in amounts just under $10,000 (like $9,500 or $9,800, etc.) and these checks were cashed at a financial institution, the financial institution should have filed a Suspicious Activity Report with the Detroit Computing Center.

In all probability, a private investigator would not have access to the information maintained at the Detroit Computing Center without a court order. But, if the matter proceeds to the point where litigation is initiated, a court order may be obtained for this information. In addition, if bank accounts are identified as a result of examining the endorsement information on the checks issued by the client/victim to the fraudster, or information appearing on wire transfer advices, here again a court order can be obtained for the records relating to that bank account. Further analyzing of the information obtained from financial institutions relating to bank accounts can lead to assets, items purchased, or other bank accounts to where funds are transferred.

One of the other byproducts of initially thoroughly debriefing the client is that the investigator should get a feel for how extensive the investigative activity will necessarily be to identify, locate, and recover assets for the client. Although a complete road map may not present itself after the debriefing of the client, the investigator will at least get an initial understanding of what may lie ahead. In this regard, the investigator should begin to get a feel for the type of budget that may be required to pursue the matter. If it becomes obvious that a monumental effort may be required to adequately pursue the asset investigation, the investigator should begin to consider conducting the investigation in phases. This approach should be conveyed to the client. It should be suggested to the client that, as a first step, a comprehensive public records search should be conducted to "kick off" the investigation. The investigator should be able to give the client an idea of the budget requirement for the initial phase (database research) of the public records research. The client should then be advised that the next phase of the public records research will be determined by the results of the initial phase and the budget requirements for the next phase will be determined when the details of the next phase are determined.

PUBLIC RECORDS SOURCES

As a first step in researching public records to identify assets, the investigator should conduct research using several commercially available databases: Lexis Nexus, IRB, Merlin, and others. These databases usually provide a wide range of research capabilities that will, with one stroke of the computer key, provide indications of real property ownership, business affiliations, vehicle registration information (cars, planes, boats), court actions (both civil and criminal), bankruptcies, liens, judgments, and other useful information. One of the most essential items of information provided by these commercial databases is residential history. Learning where a person currently resides and where the person has resided previously are good leads in searching for assets. A word of caution: Never, never, ever rely solely on the results contained in database research. It must be understood that oftentimes, the information is not completely up to date nor is it always accurate. It's a place to start but never, ever a place to end the research. The database research should provide the investigator with an initial road map as to where to start the search for public records.

Most civilized countries in the world maintain public record documents that identify the ownership of real property, the principals of business entities, and the parties in legal disputes and provide other essential information that could be used in the search for assets. Always know that many times seasoned fraudsters maintain an asset protection fortress that serves to seemingly separate the fraudster from the ownership and/or control of assets. But, also know that fraudsters seldom get very far from their assets. There are various means to breach the asset protection fortress, but first the assets must be identified, located, and determined in what name they are vested. We have found that fraudsters frequently vest the ownership of real property and other assets in the names of close associates, family members, or business entities such as trusts, foundations, and corporations. Fraudsters also vest title to accounts in financial institutions in a similar manner. Determining who has signature authority on these accounts from which to draw and/or transfer funds is certainly essential, but not always a legal or practical undertaking prior to judicial remedies being employed. However, in some instances, judicial remedies can be pursued prior to litigation being initiated.

If a target of an investigation resides outside of the United States, the initial phase of public records research may not begin with database research but in fact begin with "on-site" public records research in the appropriate venue.

At some point in the public records research phase of the asset investigation, there will be a requirement to obtain and review public records, no matter how they are identified. Reviewing real property transaction documents, litigation documents, business formation documents, UCC filings, and other documents that are filed in a public records depository is an essential part of the asset identification and location process. How these documents are obtained and reviewed is sometimes dependent on the available budget to do so. If the budget for this phase is limited, the investigator may consider retaining the services of a public records retriever who only provides these services: knowing where public records are stored and obtaining copies of these records. Public records retrievers are expert at locating and obtaining copies of public records and their fees are usually quite modest. However, it must be understood that in most cases, public record retrievers are not trained investigators. Therefore, what the investigator gains in controlling costs by retaining a public records retriever can be lost if the investigator wants the public records retriever to review the documents and make the decision as to what is or is not important to the investigation. The investigator must know exactly what is needed and then retain a public records retriever to merely identify where the documents can be obtained and then obtain copies of the documents. If an on-site review of public records documents is required to determine what documents are needed for the investigation, the investigator should personally conduct the on-site research or subcontract the services of a local investigator to conduct the on-site research. Again, budget considerations will play into whether the client will want to incur the travel expenses associated with sending the investigator to wherever the public records are to be reviewed or to retain the services of a local investigator to conduct the research. It may also be easier on the budget to have a public records retriever obtain copies of everything that could possibly relate to the investigation and send those copies to the investigator.

A thorough review of the public records that are retained is also an essential element in the process of identifying and locating assets. Real property transactional documents can be a gold mine of information as to real property owned by the target of the investigation and/or held in the name of a third-party conspirator, be it an individual or business entity. Grant deeds, quitclaim deeds, etc. are the documents that reflect the conveyance of real property from one party to the next. A quitclaim deed is usually used to convey ownership of real property from one party to another when no monetary consideration is involved. Usually, quit claim deeds are used when transactions occur between family members: parents giving real property to their children, as an example. The "Grantor" who is identified on these deeds is the person or persons who is conveying ownership of real property to the "Grantee," the person or persons in whose name(s) the property will be vested when the deed is executed. Trust deeds are documents that secure loans on property. So, if someone buys real property and finances the purchase through a financial institution or other individual, usually a promissory note is executed reflecting the amount and terms of the loan and a trust deed is also executed securing the promissory note. So, in essence, the filing of the trust deed holds the property in trust until the loan is paid off. When a property is sold and a trust deed is on file regarding that property, the loan that exists on the property must be paid off before the trust deed is released (reconvened) and the ownership of the property can be conveyed to the new owner. It is important in asset investigations to thoroughly review all trust deeds, promissory notes, etc. pertaining to real property to determine if there is any equity in the property to make it a financially worthwhile effort to pursue real property as a means of recovering assets for a client. It is also essential to determine if trust deeds and promissory notes relating to real property of interest are in fact representative of actual encumbrances on the property or are merely a smoke screen to discourage the pursuit of property.

Reviewing UCC's is also an important step in identifying and locating assets for recovery. UCC's are a form of liens placed on business property such as inventory, accounts receivable, furniture and equipment, etc. to secure loans and/or lines of credit extended to businesses by financial institutions. As in less than legitimate trust deeds placed on real property, UCC's are sometimes filed to discourage the pursuit of business assets to satisfy claims, judgments, etc.

SURVEILLANCE ACTIVITIES

The extensive use of surveillance and related covert activities are also useful tools in attempting to identify, locate, and recover assets relating to a seasoned fraudster who has constructed a complicated asset protection fortress. It should be always remembered and pointed out to the client that surveillance activity can be one of the most expensive investigative activities that may ultimately provide little or no useful information. On the other hand, it may be the most productive investigative technique that is employed that could yield valuable information. One never knows how surveillance activity will turn out until it is undertaken.

The surveillance agents have to be careful not to be "made" and yet be close enough to the target so as not to lose the target during a moving surveillance. Be sure to note license plates of the vehicles used by the target and a description of the vehicles. If the target has a driver, and is dropped off in front of locations, it is important that the surveillance agents have the ability to park their vehicles and begin to surveil the target on foot. If the target enters a financial institution, it could be very useful to have a surveillance agent walk in behind the target and observe the target's activities inside. Remember, what is gathered during all aspects of the investigation, including surveillance activities, can be very helpful in establishing facts that can be used in an affidavit to support court orders to financial institutions and other third-party record keepers to provide records, freeze accounts, etc.

It is very important for the surveillance agent who has followed the target into a financial institution or other business entity to make copious notes of the target's activities inside of these locations, including a description (name off of name tag, if possible) of every person that the target speaks with. If the target is escorted behind the counter of a financial institution, perhaps to the safety deposit box area, it is essential that every detail of what the target can be observed doing must be documented in notes as quickly as possible before details are forgotten.

Take as many photographs and/or video footage as possible during the surveillance activities. If possible, have covert video equipment available to take video footage inside locations without being detected. Remember, a picture is worth a thousand words. It is always easier to describe activities, places, and things if those activities, places, and things are documented on video footage or photographs. And, a much more compelling argument can be made for court orders if the assertions of the surveillance agent can be bolstered by video footage or photographs. Certainly, video footage of a target driving a Rolls Royce that he/she has backed out of the garage of a residence can go a long way in convincing a court that the target may have a proprietary interest in that vehicle. And, if the target is foolish enough to testify that he has never driven such a vehicle and/or has no interest in that vehicle, video footage reflecting the target driving the vehicle can serve to blunt the target's assertion. This also rings true if there is video footage of a target giving directions to construction workers working on the construction of a palatial home and the target tries to convince a court that he has no interest in this home. When the surveillance detail is added to public records research and other information that is developed, compelling arguments can be made to successfully convince courts to rule in favor of the victim/client.

TRASH SEARCHES

Hand-in-hand with surveillance activity is the use of trash searches. Trash searches are legal in virtually all states in the United States but not always in foreign countries. In the states where trash searches are legal, the key to legally obtaining trash is where the trash is located. If the trash is placed on public property (the street) for pickup by the trash collector, it is then legal to take the trash as it is considered abandoned property. Certainly, a first step in determining the feasibility of taking trash is determining the legality of doing so in the jurisdiction where the trash to be taken is located. Remember, "trash talks." As an example, trash can be (and has been) taken that a fraudster left in a trash container located outside of and down the hall from a hotel room that he occupied. The fraudster routinely deposited torn paper documents into this container and his trash was routinely taken from this container. When the torn documents in the trash were reconstructed, correspondence was found that identified banks where funds of the fraudster were maintained. Also travel plans of the fraudster were identified which made it possible to set up surveillance teams in the locations where the fraudster planned to travel. In addition, envelopes bearing other addresses (other than the address of the hotel) were reconstructed making it possible to identify other parcels of real property that were owned by the target.

COURT ORDERS

Depending on the circumstances and the venue in which you are operating to identify and locate assets, prejudgment (and sometimes prelitigation) judicial remedies may be available to help identify and locate assets. In countries that subscribe to English Common Law, Norwich Pharmacal/Bankers Trust orders can be obtained from a judicial officer compelling third-party record keepers to produce records. These orders can be wrapped in gag orders, preventing the parties that are served from notifying the holders of accounts whose records have been ordered to be produced. Criminal remedies are attached to these gag orders, if violated. Being able to decipher and follow-up on the information contained in the records obtained is an essential ingredient in the successful tracing of assets. As an example, if records are obtained from an accountant, being able to follow the debits and credit transactions in the books and records provided is crucial. If bank records are going to be requested, knowing what to ask for in the order is certainly important. Equally important is knowing how to interpret and follow up on the information contained in the documents provided. This is where employing a CPA or person with CFE credentials can be time saving and very productive. In a fraud case that was based in Canada, we identified a Chartered Accountant (CPA), banks and brokerage firms utilized by the fraudster during our surveillance activities. We were able to serve orders on these entities and the documents that we obtained and analyzed provided extensive information that led to the assets associated with our target. The records from the Chartered Accountant actually contained a written illustration of the asset protection fortress employed by the fraudster.

In addition to a Norwich Pharmacal/Bankers Trust Order, also available in English Common Law countries is an Anton Piller Order. This court order is essentially a civil search warrant authorizing the search of a location for specific documents. Civil search warrants are also available in the United States, but they have been usually obtained in connection with trademark and copyright infringement lawsuits. We were successful in one case in obtaining a civil search warrant from a Florida court in connection with a fraud matter. This civil search warrant allowed us to search the target's residences (hotel, rented condo, and rented mobile home) and several storage units that we identified during surveillance activities and during trash searches. Our searches, pursuant to the civil search warrants, identified bank accounts and other holdings.

How assets are recovered, hidden or not hidden, is almost always a function of where the assets are located and what the assets are. To start with, once assets are identified and located, it is important to make sure that assets that can be moved are not moved. Assets such as vehicles, boats, planes, etc. can be moved from one jurisdiction to another, frustrating recovery efforts. Also, funds in bank accounts can be moved with the stroke of a computer key. Here again, English Common Law countries have a judicial remedy in the form of a court order called a Mareva Injunction. When issued, this order freezes assets so they can't be moved. This order is recognized worldwide, including the United States. The U.S. Supreme Court has held that in the United States, this order cannot be used in a benign debtor/creditor dispute, where, for example, a debtor defaulted on a promissory note. It is available in the United States to creditors who are defrauded or deprived of assets due to criminal activity. This remedy is a pre-litigation tool where it can be shown that assets are likely to disappear when the target learns that a lawsuit has been initiated and/or when a judgment against a target is obvious.

Certainly, any effort to recover assets, hidden or otherwise, is directly tied to the decisions of the courts of competent jurisdiction. In the United States, assets are recovered through judgments obtained by the creditor and the accompanying writs of execution, liens, levies, etc. In most off-shore locations, judgments from a U.S court are not widely recognized as such. Most off-shore courts recognize claims as a means of securing financial remedies for wrongdoing. When pursuing assets in the international arena, claims cross borders more easily and, for the most part, are sufficiently recognized in most legal systems. Securing a claim does not preclude obtaining a judgment. It merely sets forth the issues of a contemplated court action and it provides tools to trace and freeze assets that may ultimately be needed to satisfy a judicially decided issue. In rare but appropriate situations, claims, freezing orders, etc. can be obtained in an *ex parte* proceeding. In a case involving a $240 million dollar fraud perpetrated on a South American bank by a Nigerian fraudster, we obtained from a U.S. court in *ex parte* proceeding orders freezing funds held in bank accounts in the United States.

REALISTIC PROSPECTS OF RECOVERING ASSETS

Attempting to determine the realistic prospects of recovering assets in connection with a fraud is seldom possible at the outset of an asset investigation, although it can be. Certain basic investigative steps have to be undertaken before an informed decision can be made and discussed with the client regarding the prospects of recovering assets. A fundamental and essential ingredient directly relating to the realistic prospects of recovering assets is the financial commitment that the client is able to make to pursue the tracing and ultimate recovery of assets. In many cases, the client has been financially wiped out by the fraud and therefore not in a position to fund an asset investigation. This type of situation can, and oftentimes is a deal breaker unless the investigator is employed directly by a law firm that can provide services to the victim on a contingency basis. If the victim is unable to fund an asset investigation and there is no viable alternative for funding an asset investigation, it can be determined very quickly that there is no realistic prospect of recovering assets.

In most cases, the tracing of assets with a view towards recovery is a long and involved process. This is certainly true when dealing with a seasoned fraudster who is expert at constructing an asset protection fortress. In most large cases, it is advisable to conduct the asset tracing investigation in stages and determine a budget at the outset of each stage. As stated above, attempting to determine the realistic prospect of recovering assets is seldom possible at the outset of an investigation unless it is readily obvious that the financial resources are not in place to fund the investigation. Certain basic initial steps should be taken and then an assessment of the results of these initial steps should be conducted prior to proceeding. As an example, a first step may involve the complete and thorough debriefing of the victim and obtaining and analyzing all documents in possession of the victim relating to the fraud. It may be determined after assessing the information developed during this first step that a financial commitment in excess of the capabilities or willingness of the victim is necessary to pursue the tracing of assets. As an example, if these initial inquiries determine that an off-shore investigation is required to adequately trace assets and the victim does not have the financial resources for this geographically extended investigation, it may be unrealistic to continue to pursue the matter. Or, it can be determined from the initial debriefing of the victim that it is likely that the fraudster's assets are located in places where it may be extremely difficult or impossible to recover those assets. These issues determined at the early stages of an investigation can provide the ingredients to abandon any thoughts of pursuing assets.

Additional investigative steps may be necessary to determine the realistic prospects of recovering assets. As an example, after debriefing the victim and reviewing documents provided by the victim, public records research in logical areas of the United States may be necessary to make a determination that assets are out there to recover or not. If assets, such as extensive real property holdings are identified, it's appropriate to determine if there are liens against the properties that are identified that would effectively make the property worthless to the recovering party. In today's real estate market in the United States, real property can be "underwater" in connection with the market value compared to the existing loans on the property. It may be unrealistic to recover real property when faced with a financial institution holding promissory notes secured by trust deed that are in excess of the market value of the property. It is also necessary to attempt to identify any and all judgments or tax liens that may be filed relating to the fraudster. This information will identify whom your client will be competing with for the recovery of assets to satisfy the loss experienced by your victim client. Here again, the confidentiality of the asset investigation is essential in the event an asset is discovered that others who could lay claim to do not know about. Certainly, litigation records, if identified, should be reviewed for leads to assets and the likelihood that the assets identified in the litigation records have already been spoken for. As an example, if a fraudster has been, or is in the process of being, prosecuted criminally, there may be a restitution component in the sentencing if the fraudster is convicted. It is sometimes appropriate to attempt to coordinate the matter involving your victim with the matter for which the fraudster is being prosecuted. In this case, contact with the prosecutor is an option to consider.

As stated at the outset of this presentation, this dissertation merely scratches the surface of the subject of asset tracing and associated investigative techniques. Additional volumes can be and have been written on each aspect of the subjects covered in this chapter.

Chapter 2

COMPETITIVE INTELLIGENCE: KNOWING THE ADVERSARY

WILLIAM F. MARSHALL

The need and the ability to develop information about one's rivals in today's marketplace through lawful and ethical means have never been greater. Failure to stay abreast of competitors' technological advances, product research and development efforts, pricing changes, product redesigns, changes in marketing strategy, and countless other moves made by one's adversaries in a highly fluid commercial environment can be the death knell of a company. At best, such laxity will lead to moribund growth for the derelict corporation.

The sources of information available today through industry trade publications, supplier and buyer data, blogs, market surveys, government regulatory bodies, industry analysts, media reports, licensing authorities, and a myriad other open source repositories are countless. Not only is it prudent for senior corporate management to watch the competition in order to gain a competitive advantage, it has a fiduciary responsibility to their shareholders to observe their competition and know the challenges that confront them. Too often, client companies conduct competitive intelligence only after their competition has so far outstripped them, that efforts to catch up are costly and time-consuming, and sometimes even futile. These firms could often have maintained their competitive advantage merely by paying attention to their rivals and to changing market conditions through a robust CI program.

Defining Terms

"Business intelligence" is an amorphous term which means different things to different people, often depending on their role in an organization and their ideological predisposition. Some terms often used interchangeably with "business intelligence" include market intelligence, market research, and predictive analysis. Perhaps the most frequently used synonym for business intelligence is "competitive intelligence," and for the reasons cited below, it is competitive intelligence that is the focus of this chapter, as it is most apropos to investigators.

Some practitioners differentiate business intelligence (BI) and competitive intelligence (CI) as two distinct disciplines, and this is a useful dichotomy.[1] "Business intelligence," they assert, involves the use of various technologies, processes, and applications to analyze primarily internal corporate data and systems to enable better business decision making by corporate executives. Applications and techniques such as data mining, client relationship management software to identify common contacts among company employees (social networking), and Crystal Reports are used to leverage in-house knowledge for business development purposes, improvement of operational efficiencies, and cost-savings.[2]

"Competitive intelligence," on the other hand, focuses primarily on the gathering and analysis of external information, that is, market data, such as rivals' pricing, the strengths and weaknesses of competitors' products, planned roll-out dates for new technologies in one's industry, potential clients for one's products and services, and similar information in the marketplace. In the case of both BI and CI, it is important to note that simply gathering information and storing it is not sufficient to categorize either as "intelligence." A mechanism must be in place for analyzing the information in a methodical way, distributing the results to internal consumers, using it for the organization's advantage, and thereby converting information into intelligence.

Investigators would typically be used to a greater extent in CI, rather than BI. Those involved in BI typically would comprise marketing specialists, information technology engineers, and financial ana-

---

1. Jan Steyl, "Business Intelligence vs. Competitive Intelligence," Toolbox for IT, June 22, 2009, available at http://it.toolbox.com/blogs/bi-ci/business-intelligence-vs-competitive-intelligence-32441.
2. Ibid.

lysts. CI practitioners, on the other hand, would generally consist of in-house and outside investigators, receiving direction from a company's marketing, research and development, and legal departments.

STAYING WITHIN THE LAW

An important aspect of both BI and CI is that it be conducted within the bounds of the law and the accepted corporate policy of the organization involved in it. Unfortunately, competitive intelligence is a term often equated in the minds of many with industrial espionage, theft of trade secrets, bribery, and other unethical or illegal practices. This connotation stems in part from Hollywood characterizations in movies such as *Wall Street,* and the biases held by many, who assume that competitive intelligence is an inherently nefarious field. Sadly, however, that stereotype is often reinforced from all too frequent incidents of actual illegalities reported in the media, wherein marketplace information is gleaned through bribery, theft, or other unlawful means.

One of the more recent and high-profile examples of information-gathering which may have broken the law is the case of Raj Rajaratnam, the founder of the $3 billion high-tech hedge fund, Galleon Group. Mr. Rajaratnam was charged with four counts of conspiracy and nine counts of securities fraud; specifically, he has been accused of insider trading relating to the stocks of Advanced Micro Devices, Hilton Hotels, Google, Clearwire, and Akamai. Mr. Rajaratnam was arrested, along with five others (including executives of IBM, Intel, McKinsey & Company, and the hedge fund New Castle Partners), on October 16, 2009. According to the government's criminal complaint, Mr. Rajaratnam allegedly traded inside information he held on certain technology companies to others charged in the conspiracy, who would in turn allegedly supply Mr. Rajaratnam with inside information they held on certain technology companies. Each party would then allegedly execute trades to their advantage using the confidential information obtained from the other, reportedly resulting in millions in profits to their companies.[3]

---

3. A copy of the government's complaint is available at http://dealbook.blogs.nytimes.com/2009/10/16/hedge-fund-executive-is-charged-with-fraud/. It is important to note that Mr. Rajaratnam has not yet been tried or pled, and is therefore presumed innocent at this time.

Such behavior, if true, would not be condoned by CI professionals. The Society for Competitive Intelligence Professionals, a leading association of CI specialists, has studied the issue of ethics in the competitive intelligence arena extensively. Writing in the March-April 2006 issue of SCIP's in-house publication, CI professional Chuck Nettleship offers a number of useful insights to organizations considering creation of a competitive intelligence function.

Nettleship notes that the first step in assembling a CI program is to create a documented organizational policy, which provides both a code of conduct and a methodology for the systematic collection, analysis, and dissemination of corporate intelligence. Documented guidelines, with which all requestors for, and producers of, competitive intelligence in the organization should be familiar, would spell out the process by which the organization requests, develops, and uses CI. These guidelines will also delineate what the organization considers to be acceptable forms of information collection and use. Nettleship adds the guidelines will ensure the integrity of the CI process, preservation of the organization's and its employees' reputations, and a high quality and useful CI product. When devising the organization's policy, common sense (as well as the law) should guide its formulation. As Nettleship suggests: "Think about how you would feel if your actions were made public knowledge—would you still make the same decisions? Think about how you would react if you found out a competitor obtained information about your organization through means you are considering."[4]

In the United States, the legal boundaries of CI are largely defined by the Economic Espionage Act of 1996, insider trading laws (i.e., securities laws), and antitrust legislation relating to the sharing of price and marketing information between companies in the same industry. Penalties for violating these laws can be severe, both for the individual who obtains or shares information illegally, and for companies that benefit from it. Apart from the financial penalties and prison time that can result from breaking these laws, the reputational damage and resulting loss of share price and business volume that a company may suffer from the exposure of a CI operation that either violates the law

---

4. Chuck Nettleship, "Everyday Ethics: The Importance of Documented Guidelines," *Competitive Intelligence Magazine,* Vol. 9, No. 2, March/April 2006, available at http://www.ciphersys.com/Everyday%20Ethics.pdf.

or puts a company in a bad ethical light, may far outweigh any benefit garnered from the CI operation itself.

One must be cognizant as well of the laws of any foreign jurisdiction in which commercial information is being gleaned for the purposes of CI. What may seem like a perfectly acceptable and legal information-gathering practice to a U.S. investigator may be viewed differently under the laws of another country. It is vital that any U.S. investigator, and any local agent he may be using, who is obtaining information in a foreign market know and adhere to the local jurisdiction's laws regarding the acquisition of commercial information.

In many countries, particularly those with more authoritarian regimes, commercial information is often intertwined (at least in the minds of the local authorities) with national security interests. And the notions of what constitutes "trade secrets" as relates to commercial information may be amorphous to the outsider, or even somewhat baffling.

A good illustration of the dangers of obtaining information in such markets is the highly publicized trial in China of four executives of the Anglo-Australian mining firm Rio Tinto, who were charged, tried, and convicted in March 2010 of stealing commercial secrets in China. The Rio Tinto employees received sentences ranging from seven to 14 years in prison. Although the trial was characteristically held under great secrecy, and the Chinese government never disclosed in detail what illegal information the Rio Tinto executives were said to have possessed, the *Wall Street Journal* reported: "[T]he [presiding] judge said the secrets primarily involved how much Chinese steelmakers were willing to pay for iron ore, information executives at other companies considered routine market intelligence."[5]

In discussing the nebulous definition of "commercial secrets" in China, the article also notes, "Chinese courts have been known to convict citizens on secrets charges for mailing newspaper clippings overseas."[6] Information-gathering, particularly in dictatorial countries, is a risky business, and the dangers, particularly for foreigners working in them, should be borne in mind.

---

5. James T. Areddy, "China Defines Corporate Secrets," *Wall Street Journal,* April 27, 2010, available at http://online.wsj.com/article/SB20001424052748703465204575207760568382020.html.
6. Ibid.

THE ROLE OF THE PRIVATE INVESTIGATOR IN CI

Corporations seeking market intelligence that will give them a competitive edge often know what information they need, who might possess it, and where it may be found, but they generally are not investigative professionals. They are, after all, busy performing their core business function, whether it is the design of semiconductors, the manufacture of steel, the formulation of life-saving pharmaceuticals, or a myriad other occupational pursuits. Therefore, they may need to turn to individuals whose business specialty is the gathering of information.

The private investigator, while not necessarily being well-versed in the products or services of companies needing his or her investigative skills, will have the resourcefulness, discretion, persistence, and methodological skills to develop the information needed by the client, regardless of the industry in which the research is to be conducted.

At the outset of a potential assignment, the investigator would be wise to invest a small amount of time researching the field in which the client operates, so that the investigator has a rudimentary understanding of the client's business. This brief education will better enable the investigator to grasp the issue the client is trying to have addressed, give the investigator some familiarity with the business lexicon of the client, and allow the investigator to ask more informed and pertinent questions.

The outside investigator will often need to help a client frame the issue with which the client needs assistance. Frequently, clients will have a general idea of the problem they are facing and the nature of the information they need, but a good investigator will often be able to hone in more precisely on the information that will most benefit the client, and be able to guide the client on what is most realistically obtainable from an investigative standpoint.

There is a tendency among many corporate executives who are not familiar with the investigative trade, to inundate an investigator with information that is extraneous or muddled. This is particularly true when dealing with in-house or outside counsel, possibly because the training of lawyers tends toward additive thinking as opposed to the deductive reasoning of investigators. The outside investigator can be helpful to the client in drilling down to the crux of an issue, and then offering suggestions on practical ways in which specific information can be obtained that will directly address the client's needs.

Typically, after receiving a very thorough briefing from a client on the issue with which he needs assistance, and helping the client frame the issue by developing a clear and concise list of questions to be addressed through an investigation, the investigator will then want to spend several hours devising an investigative strategy. It is generally best to draft a written proposal in which the issues to be addressed by the investigation are clearly stated at the outset. This introductory statement of the assignment's purpose would then be followed by a logically ordered list of concrete investigative steps the investigator proposes to undertake in order to develop the information required. Finally, the proposal would conclude with an estimated budget to carry out the work, and an approximate timeline to complete it.

The proposal gives the client a clear understanding of what the objectives of the investigation would be, the steps that would be carried out to meet those objectives, and the budget and time requirements needed to perform the work. It helps prevent misunderstandings between the client and investigator, and provides a roadmap for a successful assignment.

TYPICAL RESOURCES USED IN A COMPETITIVE INTELLIGENCE INVESTIGATION

The methods and resources employed by an investigator in conducting a CI assignment are almost infinite, and are as unique as the industries that might require the CI specialist's services; however, broadly speaking, information will be obtained from electronic databases, public records, and human sources.

There are literally tens of thousands of public and proprietary databases existent now with information on every conceivable industry. They are far too numerous to discuss in detail here, but they are maintained by government agencies, private information database companies, nonprofit organizations, and academic institutions. Increasingly, they are being made available through the Internet, and many are available at no charge, or for a small fee (through either subscription or on a pay-as-you-go basis).

The general trend toward increased availability of datasets, industry analyses, survey results, and countless other information sources online has made the acquisition of information phenomenally easier today than in years past. In addition to public interest, data made available through nonprofit organizations and state, local, and federal government agencies make litigation indices available for many courts, if not court filings themselves, as well as real estate transaction records, vehicle registration information, professional licensing filings, regulatory agency disciplinary actions, Securities and Exchange Commission filings, patent and trademark filings, and a plethora of other records accessible via the Internet. Proprietary databases such Accurint, Merlin, Factiva, and the like offer neat, concise profile reports drawn from public information on individuals and companies. Indeed, an individual today can make a living purely as a database research specialist.

Many records, such as civil and criminal court records (particularly at the state level), are still largely available only in hard copy form These are what are generally referred to as "public records," as opposed to database information. While still derived from public records, database information is often merely a synopsis of more extensive hard copy public records that are maintained in physical files. Thorough research of an individual or company will require sending individuals to court houses, county recorders' offices, and other brick-and-mortar repositories of information. No database search, at this point anyway, will yield all the information available on a subject in the public domain.

The heart of any CI assignment will be interviews or inquiries with human sources of information (human intelligence, or "humint," in industry parlance). These sources may be investigative journalists, industry analysts, former employees of a company that is the subject of an investigation, senior and/or knowledgeable industry executives, who may have their own reasons for sharing information on a subject company or individual. As noted above, the CI professional will not use illegal or unethical means to induce someone to share information, but there are other reasons that people may be forthcoming with information. As long as the investigator stays within the boundaries of the law and his own, and his clients', code of conduct, no problems should arise.

CI is a creative profession, in that its practitioners must be clever and resourceful in devising their information-gathering strategy. Generally, one would wish to begin the investigation using the most non-alertive steps possible, and work their way in closer to the subject of the investigation. Discretion should always be of paramount concern in carrying out the investigation, and the investigator generally will want to conduct database research first, then public record research, and finally human intelligence measures, which must be crafted carefully, as they pose the greatest risk that the operation will be exposed.

THE CONSEQUENCES OF INSUFFICIENT CI IN A COMPETITIVE MARKET

The failure to maintain an effective CI program can be devastating, and may result in the loss of significant market share, even for companies that had heretofore been very successful. An example of one such company that allowed itself to become complacent in monitoring its competitors, with near disastrous results, was the retail coffee chain Starbucks.

Howard Schultz, Starbucks' chairman and CEO, grew Starbucks from a company with four locations when he took the reins, to a chain of over 16,000 cafés worldwide, over a 20-year period. By introducing European-style coffee beverages to American consumers, Schultz ingeniously recognized and tapped into a market that few others had seen. After building a globally recognized brand, Schultz stepped down in 2000 as the company's CEO, but stayed on in the role of chairman.

In 2007, the company's fortunes began a rapid decline under the stewardship of the company's new CEO, Jim Donald. The company's share price plummeted from a November 2006 high of over $40 per share to just over $17 per share by May 2008. Part of the company's stock drop was due to a November 2007 report of a year-over-year drop in café register sales from 2006 to 2007. The company's declining sales was undoubtedly due in some measure to the economic recession that was then taking hold, but the inattentiveness of the company's CEO to his competitors in the retail coffee market space may have contributed significantly as well. In a February 2007 analyst conference call, then-CEO Donald, when asked about Starbucks' rivals (specifically, McDonald's recently introduced premium coffee), reportedly said: "I don't know the details."[7]

---

7. Todd Sullivan, "Starbucks Begins to 'Consider the Competition,'" January 3, 2008, blog article available at http://seekingalpha.com/article/59377-starbucks-begins-to-consider-the-competition.

Four months later, in a discussion about Starbucks' financial results, Donald was reported to have said, in response to a question about the company's competition, "We don't really consider [the competition]." These admissions were stunning, coming as they did from the CEO of a Fortune 500 company with numerous competitors trying to capture his company's market share.

One would expect an individual in the role of CEO of a major player in a tremendously competitive market like retail coffee shops to view monitoring the products and market shifts of his dominant rivals to be one of his primary responsibilities. Of course, this lapse by Donald may have contributed to his sacking in January 2008, and the return of Howard Schultz as the firm's CEO.

Some industry analysts attributed some of Starbucks' market share decline to the introduction of better coffee drinks by its major competitors, McDonalds and Dunkin' Donuts, in addition to other moves by these rivals, such as design changes to McDonalds stores to replicate the "Starbucks experience." Other moves by McDonalds included the introduction of wireless Internet capability for customers, more comfortable seating, and more muted color schemes in McDonalds' stores. While other factors played a role in Starbucks' problems, such as a weaker economy and people having less disposable income, which naturally favors lower-priced franchises like McDonalds, the failure to closely monitor its competitors was a serious oversight by its former CEO. Schultz subsequently announced the closure of 600 Starbucks outlets. Had Starbucks maintained a robust CI program, some of their rivals' moves may have been foreseen, countermeasures taken, and some of the painful cost-cutting moves averted.

THE OUTLOOK FOR CI

CI is a rapidly growing and increasingly pervasive field, particularly in the fast-changing areas of high tech, telecommunications, and bio-technology. Empirical data on the growth of CI is largely lacking, due to the inherent secrecy with which it is conducted. Anecdotal reports, though, indicate that it is expanding, both as an internal function at many corporations and as an outside service offered to corporations and law firms.

The demand for sophisticated investigators, particularly those with good technological skills, is going to grow. The ability to utilize the most advanced technical means to monitor markets, glean information, and refine it rapidly into actionable intelligence will be a high value commodity. Information will increasingly be made available through electronic means, but the value of old-fashioned humint-gathering techniques cannot be overstated, as the most cutting edge information will always be in the minds of people before it is documented in any form. Companies, particularly those in the most advanced fields, live or die by information, and those individuals with the ability to develop that information will be highly prized indeed.

Chapter 3

POLYGRAPH EXAMINATION

Steven L. Kirby

Of all the investigative techniques and aids available to investigators, polygraph is arguably the most controversial. It has been attacked by some in the legal, medical, and psychological professions as unreliable. The technique has been condemned by politicians, unions, privacy advocates, and civil libertarians as an infringement on individual rights. Yet despite this criticism, the polygraph technique is regularly used by police, the military, federal law enforcement, the government, correctional authorities, and parole and probation officials in countless applications. The reason is simple. Polygraph, when used properly, in the hands of a competent examiner, has and continues to assist in solving numerous cases. For over 80 years, the polygraph has been a valuable aid to a good investigation.

It is critical to understand that polygraph should never be used as a substitute for a thorough investigation. Rather, it should be used as an adjunct in cases when there are conflicting statements (the so-called "he said–she said" cases); lack of strong physical or forensic evidence; or circumstantial evidence, which is denied by the subject; or to eliminate persons when there are numerous suspects.

HISTORY AND INSTRUMENTATION

Throughout history, man has always wanted a method to determine truth from deception. In ancient Egypt, investigators tried to bluff the truth with the "sacred ass" in a tent. Unbeknown to the subject, they would coat the donkey's tail with soot and instruct the accused to enter a darkened tent and grasp the tail of the beast. They would then inform the subject that they were going to ask him a series of questions while he was holding the donkey's tail and if he lied the donkey would bray. Of course, the liar would not grasp the tail. After the interrogation they would look at the suspect's hand and if there was no soot, he would be deemed guilty.

More in tune with the psychophysiology of lie detection, ancient Chinese detectives would have suspects chew uncooked rice while being questioned. Knowing that stress often causes dry mouth; those that could not swallow the rice were considered lying.

In the late 1800s, Ceasare Lombroso utilized a "hydrosphymograph" to measure differences in blood pressure and pulse changes during questioning of suspects. The "hydrosphymograph" was a crude medical device that recorded changes in blood pressure patterns being recorded on a rotating smoked drum. Although unsophisticated, Lombroso claimed successful results in identifying lying subjects.

Twenty years later, William Marston began measuring blood pressure changes as a form of lie detection using essentially the same medical instrument used today by medical personnel to monitor blood pressure. Marston also added the galvanometer, a device that measures resistance to a small electrical pulse from one finger to the other. Around this same time, Vittorio Benussi was experimenting in detecting lies by measuring changes in respiration.

The prototype for the modern polygraph was invented by a student of Marston, John Larson, by creating a machine that simultaneously recorded changes in blood pressure and pulse along with respiration. Six years later, Leonard Keeler added galvanic skin response (GSR). Gradual improvements were made but no spectacular changes until the mid 1970s when many machines were electronically enhanced. By the late 1990s, computerized instruments became the norm, digital, but still recording changes in respiration, blood pressure, and galvanic skin response (GSR).

THE PSYCHOLOGY OF LIE DETECTION

The polygraph does not detect lies, per se, so the term "lie detector" is actually a misnomer. When a person lies about a significant issue, more often than not, there is a consequence to the lie. What the polygraph actually detects and records is stress that occurs when the subject fears the consequences from lying to the critical questions. Those consequences could include jail, loss of job, loss of prestige, etc. Therefore, for the test to be effective, there must be a consequence to the lie; the issue under investigation must be significant to the subject. If the issue is trivial, or if the subject does not fear if his lies are detected, the subject will likely be unresponsive on the test.

The theory of lie detection is simple. When a person is under assault, physical or emotional, the fight or flight reflex takes place. This phenomenon occurs in the sympathetic branch of the autonomic nervous system, which we have no control over. Consider the emotions a driver would feel when he swerves to avoid an accident. In order to react quickly (fight) or avoid (flight), the driver's eyes dilate to help him see better; his heart pumps blood faster; respiration becomes shallow; the capillaries dilate; all designed to react to the immediate threat. The polygraph instrument records similar (although to a lesser degree) reactions when the subject feels he is threatened by his lies. This fear causes defense mechanisms to kick in, among them an increase in blood pressure, a suppression in respiration, and a decrease in resistance in GSR.

During the testing phase of the polygraph examination, while attached to the instrument, the subject is asked a series of comparative questions: questions relating to the issue under investigation (relevant questions); questions designed to evoke a "lie response" (control questions); and questions that are not evaluated (irrelevant questions). Relevant questions are the questions relating to the issue under investigation. Control questions are questions similar to the issue under investigation to which the subject's denial will be an obvious lie or dubious truth. For example, did you ever commit a crime as an adult? If the subject admits crimes, the question becomes, besides what you told me, did you ever commit a crime as an adult? The control questions are developed during the pretest interview and are critical to an effective examination. The skill and experience of the examiner are paramount in ensuring that the control questions are properly developed for maximum effectiveness. The so-called irrelevant questions are those to which the subject's answer is a known truth, i.e., "Are you over 21 years of age?"

While there are several generally accepted question techniques, most are based upon the theory that subject will respond most significantly to the questions that are most threatening. Most tests involve comparing the responses of the issue-related questions, i.e., "Did you shoot John Jones?" to the control questions, i.e., "Did you ever commit a violent act?" At the risk of oversimplification, if the subject consistently reacts more to the relevant questions than the control questions, he is considered deceptive. If he reacts more to the control questions than the relevant questions, he is considered truthful. If there is no discernable difference in the reactions to the control or relevant questions, or if there are erratic and inconsistent responses, then the test should be reported inconclusive.

TYPES OF TEST

There are several situations where polygraph examinations can be of value. Until 1988, many private employers used polygraph as an intricate part of their security program, testing to uncover employee theft and other acts of job-related misconduct as well as using polygraph as a pre-employment screening tool. However, with the passage of the Employee Polygraph Protection Act (1988), for the past twenty years, polygraph in the business world is uncommon. There are some exceptions in the Act, but for the most part, current federal law prohibits employers from requiring, demanding, or (with some exceptions) even asking an employee to submit to a polygraph examination. In the limited exceptions that allow for testing employees, the restrictions are so onerous that for the most part, employment-based testing is a thing of the past.

Polygraph is still common in the public sector. Most police departments and law enforcement agencies, both federal and local, use polygraph as an investigative tool, investigating all types of crimes. Polygraph is also regularly used in investigating matters of national security by the military, CIA, and other intelligence agencies. Similar testing is common with law enforcement agencies and to a lesser degree, private employers who are exempted from the Employer Polygraph Protection Act.

The most common types of tests with law enforcement are specific issue tests. Specific issue tests are polygraph examinations dealing with one issue, usually involving a specific criminal act, such as theft, homicide, arson, sexual abuse matters, child abuse, robbery, and virtually any offense where facts are unsettled.

A second type of test is prescreening, used to help investigate the backgrounds of applicants for sensitive positions such as police departments, intelligence agencies, etc. These agencies use polygraph as a screening tool, trying to uncover past behavior that might reveal substance abuse issues, criminal behavior, falsification of credentials, and other disqualifying conduct.

Intelligence agencies have been known to use somewhat of a hybrid test between a specific issue test and a pre-employment examination, testing informants, assets, and foreign spies to determine if they have been engaging in counterespionage or otherwise being deceptive in their dealings with their handling agent over a specified period of time.

Of late, corrections officials and parole officers are using polygraph to help monitor registered sex offenders. These tests, referred to as maintenance tests, are designed to test the sex offender as to not only whether or not he has reoffended, but to determine if he is violating terms of his parole; for example, possessing pornography, loitering near schools.

THE EXAMINATION IN BRIEF

The typical polygraph examination takes between 90 minutes and 2 hours and is divided into several segments. Most examinations include fact taking from the investigator; question formulation; the pretest interview with the subject of the examination; the actual testing phase; evaluation of records; and in some cases interrogation of deceptive subjects.

Fact Analysis

Learning the underlying facts from the investigator is critical to a successful examination. During this session, the examiner meets with the investigator without the subject being present. It is important that the examiner completely understands the issues to be investigated; the identities of other's possibly involved; any exculpatory or incriminating evidence relating to the subject; any background information about the subject; in short, the entire investigation to date. The more information the examiner has, the more likely a conclusive, accurate examination will occur. Fact taking is so important that in some complex cases, the fact taking session takes place a day or two before the examination, to allow for ample time for the examiner to listen carefully and read any relevant documents. It is also in the fact-taking session that the relevant questions are developed. Once the examiner fully understands the case facts and exactly what the investigator wants to know, it is the job of the examiner to devise the exact wording of the questions and then discuss them with the investigator to insure that the issues are properly covered.

Question Formulation

When formulating questions, it is critical that the questions be concise, unambiguous, and be able to be answered yes or no. Issues that deal with opinion, questions that presuppose guilt, two-part questions, trivial matters, and questions about future intentions are inappropriate for the polygraph. Typically there are three to five relevant questions on an examination. Sometimes investigators come in with a laundry list of questions, relating to alibis, motive, and other secondary issues. The successful polygraph examination focuses on the primary issues. For example, in a murder case, the issue pure and simple is did the suspect kill the victim. Questions as to whether or not the subject had motive to kill the victim, and whether or not he owns a gun, and whether or not his alibi is true are secondary and potentially disruptive to an effective examination. The problem with asking secondary issue questions on the examination is that the subject may be truthful to one issue but not the other. For example, in our murder case, he may not have killed the subject but could still be lying about his alibi because he was actually buying drugs during the time of the murder. The lie to the secondary issue (his alibi) could contaminate the response to the primary issue (the murder), thereby causing the test to be inconclusive, or worse, in error. The polygraph is not designed to answer all the questions, just the important ones.

Sample relevant issue questions for types of tests are as follows:

Specific Issue Questions

Theft: Last Thursday, did you steal $1900 from the safe at Joe's Shoe Store?

Murder: Did you stab John Jones?

Arson: On July 7, did you set fire to the garage behind 123 Main Street?

Child abuse: Last week, did you touch your stepdaughter's vagina?

Vandalism: Last night, did you spray paint any vehicles parked on Main Street?

Intelligence Agency Questions

- In the past year, did you have any unreported contact with foreign nationals?
- Did you receive any money from agents of a foreign government?
- Since your last polygraph test, did you disclose any classified information to any unauthorized person?
- Since your last polygraph test did you receive anything of value from agents of a foreign government?

Prescreening Questions

- In the past five years, did you smoke marijuana?
- In the past three years, did you steal anything of value from an employer?
- Did you intentionally falsify or omit any information on your employment application?
- In the past five years, did you sell any illegal drugs?
- In the past five years, did you buy or sell any stolen property?

Pretest Interview

Once the predicating facts are understood and the questions are established the subject is brought into the examining room. After signing a consent agreement to submit to the examination, the examiner conducts a one-on-one interview with the subject. During the pretest interview, the examiner discusses the case at hand with the subject; listens to the subject's version of events; and questions the subject as to his involvement—or lack thereof. During this time, the examiner also explains the examination process; reviews the test questions with the subjects; and answers any questions the subject may have regarding the examination. The pretest interview phase affords the examiner the opportunity to evaluate the subject's suitability for the test. Some individuals may prove to be unsuitable for the examination. Causes could be physical, psychological, medical, or pharmacological. The pretest interview also allows the examiner to evaluate the subject's behavior symptoms. This analysis is helpful in determining whether or not there are outside factors that might influence the test. Sometimes during the course of the pretest interview, the guilty subjects will reveal information that can be of assistance in either subsequent interrogation or investigation. Finally, during the pretest interview, the examiner develops appropriate control questions and then reviews those questions to the subject, along with the relevant issue questions and the known truth questions.

Testing Phase

Upon conclusion of the pretest interview, the examiner will run a series of tests, each lasting three to four minutes. Most polygraph examinations include at least three of these tests where the questions are asked and responses are recorded. During these tests the relevant issue questions, control questions, and known truth questions are interspersed. The questions should be answered with a simple yes or no with a 15- to 20-second pause between each question. It is during this pause that reactions are recorded and subsequently analyzed.

Chart Interpretation

After the test is completed the examiner reviews the records and makes a determination as to the subject's truthfulness. At the risk of oversimplification, if the subject shows greater and consistent change in respiration, blood pressure, and galvanic skin response to the relevant issue questions than the control questions, he is considered deceptive to the issue under investigation. If he shows greater and consistent reaction to the control questions, rather than the issue questions, he is deemed truthful to the issue under investigation. If there is no discernable difference between his reaction to the control and relevant questions, or if there are erratic and inconsistent responses, the test should be reported as inconclusive. Typically 10 percent of examinations are inconclusive.

Posttest Interview (Interrogation)

Most polygraph examiners are highly trained in interviewing and interrogation. Therefore, when a subject is considered deceptive, usually the examiner will confront the deceptive subject after deception is indicated with the goal of seeking an admission. This also allows the subject to attempt to explain why his test came out with negative results. With some rare exceptions, it is considered unethical for an examiner to commence any type of interrogation prior the examination being completed.

RELIABILITY AND VALIDITY

Some people would argue that polygraph is as much an art as a science. While there is no question that polygraph is based upon sound psychophysiology principals, the examiner's skill and experience has much to do with the success or failure of the examination. During the pretest interview, the examiner must have the skills to prepare the subject mentally and psychologically for the test. Effective control questions must be developed. Finally, the examiner must have the experience and ability to properly interpret the graphs. A calibrated polygraph actually records with 100 percent accuracy what the examinee's body is showing. The skill in detecting deception lies within the examiner's ability to accurately analyze those tracings.

As with most disciplines that require human interpretation, the polygraph, while highly reliable in the hands of a competent examiner, is not perfect. Errors most often occur when the examiner attempts to make a conclusive decision when the charts should be viewed as inconclusive. There are two types of errors. False positives occur when a truthful person is judged to be deceptive. False negatives occur when a lying person is called truthful. Most examiners recognize that it is a more serious error to call a truthful person a liar so therefore the majority of errors are false negatives. Thus, giving the examinee the benefit of the doubt causes some people to think that they "beat the test" when in reality the examiner made a mistake in interpreting the graphs.

It is difficult to arrive at an exact percentage of accuracy since the results of many examinations cannot be verified, particularly in the case of subjects deemed truthful. In many cases, unless the ultimate guilty party confesses, it is difficult, if not impossible, to verify that a person did not do what he was accused of doing. Still, there have been hundreds of studies where reliability and/or validity have been addressed. Generally, studies find a minimum of 85 percent accuracy, 5 percent error rate, and 10 percent inconclusive. When inconclusive reports are excluded, most of these studies show a 95 percent to 97 percent accuracy rate with a 3 percent to 5 percent error rate.

The American Polygraph Association website cites some 80 research projects since 1980, involving 6,380 polygraph examinations or sets of charts from examinations. Researchers conducted 12 studies of the validity of field examinations, following 2,174 field examinations, providing an average accuracy of 98 percent. Researchers conducted 11 studies involving the reliability of independent analyses of 1,609 sets of charts from field examinations confirmed by independent evidence, providing an average accuracy of 92 percent. Researchers conducted 41 studies involving the accuracy of 1,787 laboratory simulations of polygraph examinations, producing an average accuracy of 80 percent.

The problem with reliability and validity studies can be best explained as follows. An examiner tests 100 subjects on a single specific issue examination. Ninety-nine pass the test and are reported truthful. One is reported deceptive, but it turns out that one of the truthful subjects is the guilty party and the person called deceptive was actually truthful. The examiner was still right 98% of the time with only a 2% error rate, but the case was still a disaster. The reality is that each examiner strives to have each test accurate.

LEGAL ASPECTS

Admissibility in Court

As a general rule, polygraph results are not admissible in court. That prohibition was the result of a 1923 decision known as the Frye decision, when the Court held that polygraph had not reached general acceptance in the scientific community. In 1993, the Supreme Court mitigated the Frey decision with the Daubert ruling, which stated that scientific evidence does not have to have general acceptance in the entire scientific community, just the subset that involves that particular science. While Daubert did not directly address polygraph, some in the field feel that eventually the Daubert decision will pave the way for polygraph results to be admitted as evidence. Some circuits have left admissibility up to the trial judge and there are some exceptions in which results are admissible when both parties have agreed to accept the results before the examination is given. This process is known as stipulation. It is important to note that while an examiner can generally not testify to results of the examination, the Supreme Court has held that statements made by the examinee during the course of the exam can be used.

LICENSING

Currently there are 29 states and three counties that have laws requiring some form of licensing or certification for polygraph examiners. Most laws require formal instruction, an internship training period and successful completion of a licensing examination.

PROHIBITIVE LEGISLATION

As previously mentioned, Employee Polygraph Protection Act (EPPA) is the primary prohibition to employment polygraph examinations. EPPA prohibits most, but not all, pre-employment polygraph testing. Testing of employees is permitted to help investigate an employer's "economic loss." There are also exemptions for guards, armored car personnel, and those who handle drugs and narcotics. There are also 20 states and the District of Columbia which have enacted legislation designed to curtail an employer's use of the polygraph. No state prohibits polygraph testing by law enforcement and there is no federal or state outright ban on polygraph. Most state statutes prohibit demanding or requiring a prospective or current employee to take a polygraph examination as a condition of employment or continued employment.

CONCLUSION

Despite its critics, polygraph has proven its value over the past eight decades as an aid to a good investigation. Virtually all law enforcement and intelligence agencies use the technique to identify the guilty and exonerate the innocent. Polygraph can help resolve issues quickly. When used in conjunction with a thorough investigation it can help get to the truth, which should be the goal of all investigations.

Chapter 4

MARINE AND MARITIME MATTERS

NANCY POSS-HATCHL

GENERAL SCOPE

Conducting investigation of maritime and marine matters is much like analyzing cases on land, except that they involve situations occurring on vessels traveling on bodies of water. Matters involving river, lake, bay, and beach accidents, and injuries and crimes from water-skiing, fishing, jet-skiing, surfing, and small craft collisions are handled in local venues such as superior courts. They normally involve local civil and criminal codes rather than federal or international maritime courts and laws. This chapter will pertain only to matters involving maritime situations. Situations on coastal and inland waterways will not be discussed in this chapter. Maritime or marine matters covered here will pertain to cruise ships, commercial freighters, oil tankers, yachts, and other private and commercial vessels in navigable waters or on the high seas. These matters can be cargo theft or property losses, hijacking, passenger or crew injuries from accidents or crimes, collisions, equipment failure, shipwrecks, piracy or mutiny, or other matters occurring at sea. If public vessels or warships are involved, it is as a second party, and would have dual reporting and perhaps separate legal venue.

NAUTICAL RIGHT OF WAY

Generally speaking, in the case of maritime collisions that involve damage to persons or property, the actual vessel with right of way may not be a practical factor. Swimmers have the "ultimate" right of way over all watercraft; next come the rights of rowboats, paddleboards, canoes, kayaks, and vessels powered by oar or paddle; next come the rights of wind-powered vessels, the sailboats, not using engines. Vessels powered by motors or engines have least right of way. Those vessels with least maneuverability, such as steam powered paddle-wheelers, super-tankers, super-freighters, and large cruise ships having the greatest right of way, ranking down to the smallest outboard motor craft with most maneuverability having the least right of way in this class. Large watercraft equipped with side-thrusting jets used to get sidewise motion in docking, have more right of way than the smaller craft, because sidewise jet thrusters are not effective or utilized when the ship is going full speed ahead on the open sea.

Even though a swimmer may have the technical right of way over the QEII, it would be foolhardy and pure madness for a swimmer to swim into the path of the QEII on the open seas, and assume that the QEII would yield right of way to the swimmer even if it could stop on a dime. A good rule on this matter is that the bigger ship normally wins in sea collisions, and usually ends up with less injuries and property damage in case of a collision with a smaller boat.

If two boats of relatively equal size and power are bearing down on each other in the open sea on what would seem to be a collision course, the one approaching from the starboard (right) side of the other has the right of way, and the other should reduce speed and change course away from the other ship's path. In the ideal, if these two ships were in radio communication it would be an even safer way to avoid collision.

GENERAL RULES FOR PREPARATION

Be prepared when doing site investigations that involve going aboard a vessel that is either at anchor or at a mooring. Wear shoes with gripping soles that provide traction on moist decks, gangways, and ladders, and wear appropriate and practical attire. A pair of gripping gloves is also handy.

Take precautions against seasickness in advance. There are a variety of anti-motion sickness medications available at most pharmacies ranging from tablets to acupuncture bracelets. These bracelets, actually wristbands with metal pressure points, are effective only if properly worn. Most of the tablets have side effects of drowsiness. Marezine is a brand that appears to have less drowsy side-effects than other brands of anti sea-sickness remedies.

It is wise to bring some sealed slider zip-lock bags of various sizes to use for waterproof and uncontaminated sample bags for collecting evidence.

It is a good idea to take any necessary photos of loss sites and equipment before interviewing witnesses. In today's technical age, you can use the photos taken with a digital camera as a reference during interviews or to clarify anything needed during interviews. Keep your camera set correctly to the date and time the photo was taken to insure that your case records are accurate.

Being familiar with maritime vocabulary is helpful. If a term is used that the investigator doesn't understand, it is prudent to ask the meaning as well as the derivation of the term, whether it pertains to universal sea linguistics, or to the particular crew involved, which is frequently multinational, and can develop its own idioms.

If the matter involves the loading, storage, or unloading of cargo, it helps to photograph and inspect similar cargo and describe in detail all tasks involved to attempt reconstruction of a particular loss situation. If it involves procedural or vessel regulations, be sure to identify whether these regulations are specific to the particular vessel or recognized to pertain to similar vessels.

If the matter pertains to rules violation, be sure to obtain a copy of the ship's rules or regulations, and any relevant notices or warnings posted on crew or passenger bulletin boards.

Be sure to obtain a copy of the crew list, passenger lists, the itinerary with ports-of-call, and the cargo list with date of acquisition. Also get copies of the ship's log, especially on the date or dates in question. If meals (mess) are an issue, get copies of all menus and trace origins and storage of food supplies, especially of any questionable goods.

Obtain copies of any relevant radio transmissions, weather reports, sick bay or medical notes or records that may be relevant. Also obtain copies of any cargo inventory, any gear safety warnings or recall notices or bulletins, any schematics with operations manual for all equipment involved. Note the manufacturer's data, model numbers, and serial numbers of all equipment involved. If in doubt, it is always better to obtain a copy that you may not need, than to fail to have a copy of something that later becomes critical.

In matters involving military and state property in accidents and crimes, reports are available from corresponding venue records, although they may require Freedom of Information documentation and special subpoenas and paperwork.

MUTINY

The skipper (master) of any vessel on the high seas is the ultimate order-keeper and lawmaker, responsible for all that occurs on the vessel. The word "captain" is a rank or title that may or may not be the skipper or master of a vessel. Mutiny is a crime that must be committed by a crewmember or members, rather than passengers or other noncrew individuals or groups. To go against the skipper's order or control is the special maritime crime of mutiny, which is tried in either the magistrate court at the nearest port or the homeport of the ship, depending on the owner's will and the venue of the next port-of-call after the mutiny has occurred. The crime of mutiny has appropriate punishments up to and including the death penalty, depending on the severity of the crime, the owner's interpretation, and the court where the trial is being held.

In most maritime matters, except in cases where criminal activity is being committed, the decisions and rules of the skipper are the unquestioned law of that vessel. To go against this authority with intent to take over the command of the vessel is a crime of mutiny. Mutiny is strictly a nautical crime that culminates in the crew's taking over the ship by restraining the master of the vessel. In the case of assault and injury or death of a master, mutiny would be a co-crime. It is prosecuted in the port court of the nearest subsequent country to where the crime has occurred at sea, or the country where the ship is registered.

PIRACY

Another purely nautical crime is piracy. This involves intercepting a vessel on the high seas by noncrew with the intent of taking over control and authority, either to steal cargo or hold crew or passengers for ransom, or to sink the vessel. It is inherently a terrorist crime.

During the period before World War I through World War II and the Korean War, only military vessels were supposed to be armed. Attack on an unarmed vessel was a crime found to be against international law. Today, piracy is becoming more and more widespread. And the need for arms on private vessels is becoming more and more essential for survival. There are few security companies that have focused on maritime protection, which opens up a relatively untapped market in the field of armed maritime security.

Especially in certain geographic waters, including the east African coast, especially near Somalia; the Andaman Sea of Southeast Asia; the Persian Gulf and Eastern Mediterranean; the Caribbean Sea near the Panama Canal; the Western Pacific Coast of Central America, Mexico, and southern California; piracy and vessel hijacking is commonplace and the basic need for armed security presence is essential.

Special marine security specialists are needed by commercial freight companies and passenger cruise ships, charter vessels, and private yachts, especially in waters frequented by pirates and terrorists. This may be directly related to the drug trafficking and the spread of international terrorism.

Ships may be scuttled, with all crew and passengers murdered and thrown overboard, and then the vessel is either used for drug trafficking and sunk, or moved to a secret isolated cove and changed in appearance with all identifiable markings removed, and renamed as a vessel with stolen identity. These acts would be included in the crime of piracy.

MARITIME REFERENCES

There have been many recent changes in maritime laws, their interpretation, and regulations. This is due to the increasing international presence of terrorism and piracy, especially since 2000. Although this work is intended for practicing private investigators and security specialists, not attorneys, one concerned with maritime matters should be able to access references needed to clarify an investigation. Maritime investigators do not need to invest in a special reference library. Complete marine and maritime references can be found in unabridged form on the Internet.

Old references may become less important and newer ones may become more important, so the ones described here are only a guide to the type of information available on the Internet.

The most widely used references are the official CFR's (Code of Federal Regulations) for the USA, which are regularly updated. Among these are the 50 Titles, especially the Title 33, Chapter 18 of the U.S. Code which pertains to injured dockworkers, longshoremen, and harbor workers. These codes are found in http://regulations.vlex.com and/or www.legalbooksdepot.com.

U.S. Customs Laws and the full Code of Federal Regulations and other government publications are found in www.customslawyer.net and www.claitors.com.

For the U.K. International Maritime Laws the regulations applicable to Pleasure Vessels, published by the U.K. Maritime and Coastguard Agency at: http://.www.mcga.gov.UK/c4mca/pleasure_craft_informa tion.pack. This has detailed advice on safety equipment, manning, crew agreements, and fire protection measures for pleasure craft and boats used for sport or recreational activities. This guide is available as a PDF file for which Adobe Acrobat reader software is required. The published version 12 was published in 2007. It contains U.K. legislation, regulations, standards, and guidelines and is regularly updated as amendments ensue.

Countries whose Pleasure Vessels may be issued cruising licenses as of October 15, 2008 are listed in the Federal Register U.S. Customs and Border Protection, Department of Homeland Security FRDoc. E8–24523, which is also available on the Internet.

Lloyd's List, which has the leading international maritime news has a website of www.lloydslist.com. U.S. Immigration Services has a website of www.immigrationdirect.com.

Container Ship Schedules from port to port worldwide has a website of www.oceanschedules.com.

The names of vessels that have registration, found with owner and description of vessel documented in the U.S. are found under www.ask .com.

A list that can find ancestors transported across oceans and modern ships' passenger lists, ship wrecks, and marriages at sea is available at "www.cyndislist.com/ships.htm", which can be useful in genealogy and other topics.

The U.K. Ship Registry of Pleasure Craft is found on www.mcga .gov.uk and www.ukshipregister.co.uk/ukr.

The United States Coast Guard Documentation has an ownership and description of registered vessels accessible by either vessel's name or documentation number: www.st.nmfs.noaa.gov/st1/coastguard/vssel byname/htm.

Canadian Maritime Law is found on: www.admiraltylaw.com/.

Australian Maritime Law is found on: www.federalpress.com.au or www.weblaw.edu.au.

If one knows the homeport of a pleasure or commercial vessel, the port authorities would have a full record of that ship, including the site where it is normally kept, the description, and type of engine, age, and ownership.

U.S. privately owned vessels are either federally documented or state registered. The privately owned vessels are either used for pleasure or for commercial purposes, including taking passengers for transport or charter.

Once a vessel is beyond the three or 12 mile limit from the shore, depending on the specific waters involved, it is in international waters. Naturally this excludes rivers, lakes, outer bays, and harbors. Islands at least three miles offshore may be in national and state waters, but three or twelve miles offshore from possessory or national islands are the boundaries where international waters exist. Each depends on the particular island chain involved.

At this limit, scattering ashes and human remains, marriages, and birth records fall under the auspices of the skipper of the vessel and the nationality of the ship's registry. In many cases, there are no records on these events except perhaps in ships' logs, especially for records pertaining to funerals with ashes scattered at sea.

If a crime or injury takes place aboard a vessel in international waters on the high seas, in many cases, it falls under the jurisdiction and laws of the nation where the ship is registered. Many commercial vessels, especially cargo and cruise ships, are registered in a nation that is in an island group in the South Pacific or in small nations of Africa, because the registration costs are less expensive than registration in larger or more well-known countries. When crimes are committed, these registered countries are not prepared to hold admiralty trials and bring prosecution of criminal acts to modern international concepts of justice. Usually, the accused criminal is held in a magistrate court at the nearest port until he can be extradited to the nation where the vessel is registered, unless other circumstances occur. It's not the investigator's place to evaluate these matters. Maritime law is not always fair and just in its outcome.

A source of reference for most U.S.A. maritime matters is Title 33 Chapter 18 of U.S. code, which pertains to injured dockworkers or staff loading or unloading a vessel. These injuries, sustained in the course of employment, are within the jurisdiction of a magistrate or judge in a U.S. Federal Court, not in a state court. The exact site of injury is critical to determining the jurisdiction. The federal benefits given to workers compensation injuries are greater than those awarded in most state jurisdictions. It is not unusual for an injured dockworker to jump onto the ship from a dock, where the injury actually occurred, and claim it happened aboard.

ROLE OF MARITIME INVESTIGATOR

The maritime investigator should remember that they serve as the eyes and ears of the client. They should uphold their professional standards at all times during their investigation of maritime cases. Investigation must be reported in an objective and ethical manner at all times. Never put words in witnesses' mouths or alter or distort facts as they are uncovered. Equipment involved should be inspected and photographed as thoroughly as possible. All details should be described as accurately as possible. All rules for general investigation apply to maritime work to produce a professional and satisfactory work product.

Chapter 5

FORENSIC ACCOUNTING

Forensic accounting services have prominent stature in the civil process as applied to corporate mergers and acquisitions and the sale of business assets. Fraud-related services receive more public notoriety; however, they are less dominant in the accounting marketplace. The primary fields of service for forensic accountants includes: *Business Valuations* where a sale, purchase of liquidation of a business requires valuing the net worth; *Asset Valuation* in *Divorce Settlements* where assets may have been hidden or assets or liabilities have been inflated or devalued; and *Personal Injury* where monetary damage calculations need to be established for settlement purposes. However, *Corporate Fraud, Deception,* or *Intentional Manipulation of Records* will be the focus of this treatise. This chapter shall serve as an introductory overview for the private investigative profession. The objective will be to enlighten investigators in how to integrate limited accounting knowledge and experience into their management oversight of fraud cases. The intended result is to expand their service offerings for additional business opportunities by partnering with a forensic accountant expert.

UNDERSTANDING FORENSIC ACCOUNTING

There is a certain "mystique" in fraudulent situations when referring to forensic accounting services. There are two distinct references and roles between the terms "Forensic" and "Accountant." The word forensic has relevancy within the courts of justice; the word accountant refers to expertise in the field of accountancy. The forensic accountant then becomes an expert in accounting theories and application in legal principles. The Generally Accepted Accounting Principals (GAAP) in accounting, auditing, or tax matters is applied by the forensic accountant in the court system on both civil and criminal issues. To better understand the context from an investigative perspective, the definition of forensic accounting given by Jack Bologna and Robert Lindquist applies: Forensic and investigative accounting is the application of financial skills and an investigative mentality to unresolved issues, conducted within the context of the rules of evidence. As a discipline, it encompasses financial expertise, fraud knowledge, and a strong knowledge and understanding of business reality and the workings of the legal system. Its development has been primarily achieved through on-the-job training, as well as experience with investigating officers and legal counsel.

Robert G. Roche, a retired chief of the Criminal Investigation Division of the IRS, describes a forensic accountant as "someone who can look behind the facade—not accept the records at their face value—someone who has a suspicious mind that the documents he or she is looking at may not be what they purport to be and someone who has the expertise to go out and conduct very detailed interviews of individuals to develop the truth, especially if some are presumed to be lying."

The modern role of forensic accounting has been defined by Wayne Bremser and includes the following scope of support services:

- *Pretrial support:* gathering facts, establishing causation, translating jargon, organizing data, and formulating strategy
- *Trial support* as a consultant
- *Expert witnessing* in court or other hearings
- *Settlement support* for the case resolution

When dealing with civil actions involving contract disputes, the forensic accountant must generally deal with three elements: proximate cause, reasonable certainty, and foreseeability. When working with fraud issues, the forensic accountant addresses four areas:

1. Misrepresentation of material fact,
2. Misrepresentation made knowingly and with intent to defraud,
3. Reliance on the misrepresentation by the victim company, and
4. Damages resulting from such reliance.

TYPICAL CRIMINAL CASES

Forensic accounting cases involving fraud fit into several categories. Normally the forensic accountant is engaged after a fraud is uncovered, typically from the following sources: an audit, an anonymous hotline tip, disgruntled employee or ex-employee, observance of a dramatically changed employee lifestyle. The subject(s) may be company employees or third parties such as vendors, competitors, or someone from the general public. The four primary legal elements of fraud are:

• There is a false representation or willful omission regarding a material fact.
• The perpetrator knew the representation was false.
• The recipient relied on the representation.
• The victim suffered damages or incurred a loss.

The Public Company Accounting Oversight Board (PCAOB) is the private-sector nonprofit corporation created by the Sarbanes-Oxley Act to oversee the auditors of public companies, in the interest of investors. The PCAOB is also charged with promulgating auditing and related attestation and ethics standards for audits and reviews of public companies.

According to the American Institute of Certified Professional Accountants (AICPA) in SAS No. 99/PCAOB, the primary factor that distinguishes fraud from error is whether or not the underlying action is intentional, or unintentional. Executive perpetrators of corporate financial crimes employ any number of deceptive tactics to prevent detection, including these categories as described by the AICPA:

• *Dazzling*–revealing information set forth in footnotes rather than the body; aimed at concealing truth.
• *Masking*–neglecting to record or reveal expenses/liabilities; aimed at concealing truth.

- *Decoying*–emphasizing "blind alleys" that turn out to be legitimate and handled correctly; aimed at concealing the truth.
- *Mimicking*–creating false transactions/transactions without substance; aimed at influencing the victim's process of interpreting information.
- *Repackaging*–making it seem that hard to sell inventory is sellable, reorganizing issues to justify favorable accounting procedures; aimed at influencing victim's process of interpreting information.
- *Double play*–misapplying GAAP's where an item is not material; aimed at influencing victim's process of interpreting information.

There are numerous schemes that describe financial crimes. The most relevant that may require private investigative services include those set forth below:

- **Billing Schemes**–Type of asset misappropriation scheme where the perpetrator misappropriates company funds without ever actually handling cash or checks. There are three principal types of billing schemes: false invoicing from shell companies, false invoicing from nonaccomplice vendors, and personal purchases made with company funds.
- **Bribery**–Includes official bribery, which includes both the corruption of a public official, and commercial bribery, which involves the corruption of a private individual to gain a commercial and business advantage. The elements of official bribery vary by jurisdiction but generally are (1) giving or receiving, (2) a thing of value, (3) to influence, (4) an official act.
- **Bustout Scheme**–A planned bankruptcy which can take many different forms. The basic approach is for an apparently legitimate business to order large quantities of goods on credit, then dispose of those goods through legitimate or illegitimate channels. The perpetrators then close shop, absconding with the proceeds, and leaving the suppliers unpaid. Another involves an acquisition or merger where the buyer depletes inventory, fails to pay invoices, disregards maintenance, etc. driving the business into bankruptcy.
- **Check Tampering**–Type of fraudulent disbursement scheme in which the perpetrator physically prepares the fraudulent check. Usually, the perpetrator takes physical control of a check and

makes it payable to himself through one of several methods. Most check tampering crimes fall into one of four categories: forged makers schemes, intercepted check schemes, concealed check schemes, and authorized makers schemes.

- **Computer Fraud**–Any defalcation or embezzlement accomplished by tampering with computer programs, data files, operations, equipment, or media, and resulting in losses sustained by the organization whose computer system was manipulated. The distinguishing characteristic of computer fraud is that access occurs with the intent to execute a fraudulent scheme.
- **Conflict of Interest**–Occurs when an employee, manager, or executive has an undisclosed economic or personal interest in a transaction that adversely affects that person's employer. As with other corruption frauds, conflict schemes involve the exertion of an employee's influence to the detriment of his company. In bribery schemes, fraudsters are paid to exercise their influence on behalf of a third party. Conflict cases, instead, involve self-dealing by an employee.
- **Corporate Fraud**–Corporate fraud is any fraud perpetrated by, for, or against a business corporation. Corporate frauds can be internally generated (perpetrated by agents, employees, and executives of a corporation, for or against others) and externally generated (by others against the corporation, i.e., suppliers, vendors, customers).
- **Defalcation**–act of embezzling; failure to meet an obligation; misappropriation of trust funds or money held in any fiduciary capacity; failure to properly account for such funds.
- **Financial Statement Fraud**–Fraud committed to falsify financial statements, usually committed by management, and normally involving overstating income or assets or understating liabilities or expenses.
- **Kickbacks**–In the commercial sense, refers to the giving or receiving something of value to influence a business decision without the employer's knowledge and consent.
- **Occupational Fraud and Abuse**–The use of one's occupation for personal enrichment through the deliberate misuse or misapplication of the employing organization's resources or assets. Simply stated, occupational frauds are those in which an employ-

ee, manager, officer, or owner of an organization commits fraud to the detriment of that organization. The three major types of occupational fraud are Corruption, Asset Misappropriation, and Fraudulent Statements (which include financial statement schemes).

In most instances, an investigator may be engaged to develop facts on a very limited aspect of a case. It is important for the investigator, at the outset, to develop a complete understanding of all relevant facts for these reasons: (a) demonstrate to the client the investigator's value and expertise; (b) provide recommendations to expand the scope of services (if deemed appropriate); and (c) become a consulting strategist and an expert witness for the client.

COMMONLY APPLIED FEDERAL CRIMINAL STATUTES

The typical corporate mindset of a fraud is fourfold: to maintain a low corporate profile and rationalize reasons not to pursue recourse; and/or to seek restitution thru civil litigation; and/or to pursue criminal charges; and/or terminate the employee(s). Many factors enter into this decision-making strategy. Are owners or officers involved? Is the loss not of a material amount? What other corporate issues will be problematical if the matter is outwardly pursued? Is the company currently under investigation or scrutiny from government investigative or regulatory agencies? How has the corporation addressed similar incidents in the past? What are the costs to pursue an action? Is restitution likely? Will this matter result in the loss of government or other company contracts? Will there be public relations issues to address? Will the stock price be impacted? The truth is oftentimes buried as a result of a corporate decision to take remedial action.

However, with the Sarbanes-Oxley Act and other similar legislation, companies are obligated to pursue criminal sanctions. The most relevant federal criminal statutes under the U.S. Code are identified below:

18 U.S.C. SECTION 1341–MAIL FRAUD

There are two elements in mail fraud: (1) having devised or intending to devise a scheme to defraud (or to perform specified fraudulent acts), and (2) use of the mail for the purpose of executing, or attempting to execute, the scheme (or specified fraudulent acts). The mailing does not itself need to contain the false and fraudulent representations.

Whoever, having devised or intending to devise any scheme or artifice to defraud, or for obtaining money or property by means of false or fraudulent pretenses, representations, or promises, or to sell, dispose of, loan, exchange, alter, give away, distribute, supply, or furnish or procure for unlawful use any counterfeit or spurious coin, obligation, security, or other article, or anything represented to be or intimated or held out to be such counterfeit or spurious article, for the purpose of executing such scheme or artifice or attempting so to do, places in any post office or authorized depository for mail matter, any matter or thing whatever to be sent or delivered by the Postal Service, or deposits or causes to be deposited any matter or thing whatever to be sent or delivered by any private or commercial interstate carrier, or takes or receives there from, any such matter or thing, or knowingly causes to be delivered by mail or such carrier according to the direction thereon, or at the place at which it is directed to be delivered by the person to whom it is addressed, any such matter or thing, shall be fined under this title or imprisoned not more than 20 years, or both.

18 U.S.C. SECTION 1344–BANK FRAUD

The statutory language is modeled directly after the mail fraud statute. It proscribes the use of a scheme or artifice either to defraud a federally chartered or insured financial institution or to obtain any of the monies, funds, credits, assets, securities, or other property owned by, or under the control of, such an institution. The institutions protected by the statute are those chartered under the laws of the United States or insured by the Federal Deposit Insurance Corporation, the Federal Savings and Loan Insurance Corporation (now defunct), or the National Credit Union Administration. Whoever knowingly executes, or attempts to execute, a scheme or artifice–

(1) to defraud a financial institution; or

(2) to obtain any of the moneys, funds, credits, assets, securities, or other property owned by, or under the custody or control of, a financial institution, by means of false or fraudulent pretenses, representations, or promises; shall be fined not more than $1,000,000 or imprisoned not more than 30 years, or both.

18 U.S.C. SECTION 1343–FRAUD BY WIRE

Whoever, having devised or intending to devise any scheme or artifice to defraud, or for obtaining money or property by means of false or fraudulent pretenses, representations, or promises, transmits or causes to be transmitted by means of wire, radio, or television communication in interstate or foreign commerce, any writings, signs, signals, pictures, or sounds for the purpose of executing such scheme or artifice, shall be fined under this title or imprisoned not more than five years, or both. If the violation affects a financial institution, such person shall be fined not more than $1,000,000 or imprisoned not more than 30 years, or both.

18 U.S.C. SECTION 157–BANKRUPTCY FRAUD

This statute prohibits devising or intending to devise a scheme or artifice to defraud and, for purposes of executing or concealing the scheme either (1) filing a bankruptcy petition; (2) filing a document in a bankruptcy proceeding; or (3) making a false statement, claim, or promise (a) in relationship to a bankruptcy proceeding either before or after the filing of the petition; or (b) in relation to a proceeding falsely asserted to be pending under the Bankruptcy Code. Violators, upon conviction, shall be fined under this title, imprisoned not more than 5 years, or both.

18 U.S.C. SECTIONS 1956 AND 1957–MONEY LAUNDERING CONTROL ACT OF 1986

These statutes make it illegal to conduct certain financial transactions with proceeds generated through specified unlawful activities, such as narcotics trafficking, Medicare fraud and embezzlement, among others.

Section 1956 (a)(1)(A)(ii)–Tax Money Laundering

The tax division of the IRS must approve any and all criminal charges that a United States Attorney intends to bring against a defendant in connection with conduct arising under the internal revenue laws, regardless of which criminal statutes the United States Attorney proposes to use in charging the defendant.

Tax Division authorization is not required when (1) the principal purpose of the financial transaction was to accomplish some other covered purpose, such as carrying on a specified unlawful activity like drug trafficking; (2) the circumstances do not warrant the filing of substantive tax or tax fraud conspiracy charges; and (3) the existence of a secondary tax evasion or false return motivation for the transaction is one that is readily apparent from the nature of the money laundering transaction itself.

Violators of this section shall be sentenced to a fine of not more than $500,000 or twice the value of the property involved in the transaction, whichever is greater, or imprisonment for not more than 20 years, or both. For purposes of this paragraph, a financial transaction shall be considered to be one involving the proceeds of specified unlawful activity if it is part of a set of parallel or dependent transactions, any one of which involves the proceeds of specified unlawful activity, and all of which are part of a single plan or arrangement.

- **Section 1956 (a)(2)** provides that whoever transports, transmits, or transfers, or attempts to transport, transmit, or transfer a monetary instrument or funds from a place in the United States to or through a place outside the United States or to a place in the United States from or through a place outside the United States— with the intent to promote the carrying on of specified unlawful activity; or knowing that the monetary instrument or funds involved in the transportation, transmission, or transfer represent the proceeds of some form of unlawful activity and knowing that such transportation, transmission, or transfer is designed in whole or in part to conceal or disguise the nature, the location, the source, the ownership, or the control of the proceeds of specified unlawful activity; or to avoid a transaction reporting requirement under State or Federal law, shall be sentenced to a fine of not more than $500,000 or twice the value of the monetary instrument or funds involved in the transportation, transmission, or transfer, whichever is greater, or imprisonment for not more than 20 years, or both.

- **Section 1956 (a)(3)** provides that whoever, with the intent to promote the carrying on of specified unlawful activity; to conceal or disguise the nature, location, source, ownership, or control of property believed to be the proceeds of specified unlawful activity; or to avoid a transaction reporting requirement under State or Federal law, conducts or attempts to conduct a financial transaction involving property represented to be the proceeds of specified unlawful activity, or property used to conduct or facilitate specified unlawful activity, shall be fined under this title or imprisoned for not more than 20 years, or both.
- **Section 1956 (b)** provides penalties as follows:
  In general.–Whoever conducts or attempts to conduct a transaction described in subsection (a)(1) or (a)(3), or section 1957, or a transportation, transmission, or transfer described in subsection (a)(2), is liable to the United States for a civil penalty of not more than the greater of the value of the property, funds, or monetary instruments involved in the transaction; or $10,000.

18.U.S.C.Section 1957 provides penalties as follows:

(a) Whoever, in any of the circumstances set forth in subsection (d), knowingly engages or attempts to engage in a monetary transaction in criminally derived property of a value greater than $10,000 and is derived from specified unlawful activity, shall be punished as provided in subsection (b).

Anti-Kickback Act of 1986–The provisions of this act are contained in Title 41 (U.S. Code, §§ 51-58). The act outlaws the giving or receiving of anything of value for the purpose of improperly obtaining or receiving favorable treatment in connection with U.S. government contracts.

Civil Monetary Penalty Law (CMPL)–The Civil Monetary Penalty Law (42 U.S.C.§1320a-7a) was passed to impose administrative sanctions against providers who defraud any federally funded program by filing false claims or other improper billing practices. Any person (including an organization, agency, or other entity, but excluding a beneficiary) that presents or causes to be presented a claim for a medical or other item or service that the person knows or should know the claim is false or fraudulent is subject to a civil monetary penalty.

Computer Fraud and Abuse Act–Title 18 U.S. Code, Section 10301, makes certain computer-related activity a specific federal offense. In brief, Section 1030 punishes any intentional, unauthorized access to a "protected computer" for the purpose of: obtaining restricted data regarding national security; obtaining confidential financial information; using a computer which is intended for use by the U.S. government; committing a fraud; or damaging or destroying information contained in the computer.

False Claims and Statements–Chapter 47 of Title 18, U.S. Code, contains a number of related provisions that punish false or fraudulent statements, orally or in writing, made to various federal agencies and departments. The principal statute is Section 1001 that prohibits such statements generally and overlaps with many of the more specific laws, such as Section 1014, that apply to false statements made on certain loan and credit applications.

Racketeer Influenced and Corrupt Organizations Act (RICO)– Title 18, U.S. Code, §1961, *et. seq.* The statute outlaws the investment of ill-gotten gains in another business enterprise; the acquisition of an interest in an enterprise through certain illegal acts; and the conduct of the affairs of an enterprise through such acts. Criminal penalties include stiff fines, and prison terms as well as the forfeiture of all illegal proceeds or interests. Civil remedies include triple damages, attorney fees, dissolution of the offending enterprise, and other penalties.

CIVIL APPLICATION OF FORENSIC ACCOUNTING

The preceding paragraphs and sections have focused on the criminal aspect of forensic accounting as it pertains to corporate fraud. Let's switch gears and explore the areas of the corporate environment in which forensic accounting services might apply in the civil litigation arena.

As it was mentioned previously in this chapter, companies may find they are either obligated to, or it makes more sense and is more practical to, pursue criminal sanctions than civil remedies when they are faced with addressing and resolving corporate fraud situations. However, in those cases where it is beneficial and logical to pursue civil litigation or civil sanctions, the forensic accountant's knowledge and use of nontraditional financial record sources and methods and his ability to develop his own information affords him the option of obtaining sufficient evidence with which to reach a conclusion and positive resolution to the specific fraud situation. This might not necessarily occur otherwise, especially in those instances where the amount of information available from the client or subject is limited, or when certain information that is available is deemed to not be credible or is tainted in some manner.

Listed below are some examples of practical benefits and investigative values the accounting professional trained in forensic accounting can provide to the fraud investigator:

- **Computation of Lost Earnings**
  - Disability
  - Personal Injury
  - Workers Compensation
- **Examination of Historical Information**
  - Work History
  - Employee or self-employed earnings
  - Earnings/payments from related or previously owned business entities
  - Rental property management
  - Real property ownership
  - Litigation Issues
  - Challenging historical reports
  - Over reporting of income
  - Under reporting of income
- **Lifestyle Pattern**
  - Spending habits
  - Personal/Business Assets
  - Liabilities
- **Comparison of Earnings**
  - Industry Average
  - Similar employment/profession

- **Fraud**
  - Ownership in or affiliations with one or more business entities
  - Conflict of interest
  - Hidden financial assets and liabilities

THE INVESTIGATOR'S ROLE

For private investigators to assume a more active role in corporate fraud, they must demonstrate to management their professional background and experience and convince the client of their ability to:

1. Oversee strategic management of the case.
2. Conduct professional field investigative services such as identifying, locating, and interviewing witnesses for public record research, open source internet research, document analysis, and any other expert services of a specialized nature.
3. Expand the investigative scope to include digital forensic discovery.
4. Analyze audit results or accounting irregularities.
5. Develop evidence and comply with rules of evidence and chain of custody.
6. Maintain case management on a fast track which will allow corporate staff to focus on its core business.
7. Be compliant with local, state, and federal statutes and regulations.
8. Control costs by limiting the need for outside counsel in preparing for criminal proceedings.
9. Develop evidence and format reports so that they meet the elements of the state or federal statute(s) and are likewise useful for the civil litigation process.
10. Use law enforcement relationships to help meet case objectives.
11. Provide expert testimony.

SUMMARY

In summary, it is not necessary for the corporate investigator to also be a forensic accountant. However, the corporate investigator should, at a minimum, have a good working knowledge of forensic accounting concepts, tools, and techniques to make a determination as to when it makes sense to engage the services of a forensic accountant. It is especially important that the corporate investigator be familiar with the accounting terms and situations to quickly identify those red flags that could indicate the occurrence of one or more fraudulent actions having been committed by one or more individuals and one or more business entities. Having this knowledge, then, better enables the investigator to best utilize the resources available to him so as to maximize the efficiency and effectiveness of his investigative projects.

Chapter 6

INVESTIGATING EMPLOYMENT CLAIMS

S. BEVILLE MAY

INTRODUCTION

Employment claims investigations can be a bulwark against costly and protracted lawsuits. When conducted properly, an investigation can result in a claim being dismissed against the defendant without further litigation. An effective and professional investigation can also minimize the client's exposure to hefty damage awards and settlements. Thus, you want an airtight investigation to protect your client from liability and damages.

Investigations of employment claims must be prompt, thorough and detailed, and well supported by the evidence. They must assess credibility and come to reasoned factual conclusions. The tension between conducting a prompt investigation and one that is thorough is ever present, and is a challenge for the investigator.

After the initial phone call, you will undertake the following phases:

- Outlining the investigation
- Gathering/reviewing documents
- Contacting witnesses
- Interviewing witnesses
- Assembling exhibits
- Writing the Investigative Report
- Possibly acting as a fact witness at deposition or trial

Start by assessing the nature of the claims(s). Do they involve sexual harassment or pay inequities? Or is it a matter of age discrimination? Consider, too, whether you will need any expert advice. For instance, if a woman is claiming age discrimination but has embezzled company funds, you may need to enlist the help of a corporate fraud investigator to show the facts supported a nondiscriminatory discharge.

CREATING AN INVESTIGATIVE FILE
AND OUTLINING YOUR INVESTIGATION

Next, create an investigative file with the following folders:

- Correspondence
- Notes
- Documents (segregated by source)
- Witness files (interview outlines, interview notes, and exhibits for each)
- Affidavits based on interviews, or transcripts of witness interviews
- Investigative Report

Outline your investigative approach. Consider what documents and electronic information you want to review. Determine what witnesses you want to interview, and decide on the order of witness interviews. Analyze what are the essential facts or issues you must uncover. Identify the credibility disputes that must be resolved, and create a timeline of key events and relevant dates.

Employment claims investigations tend to be document-intensive. Files typically reviewed include corporate policies and procedures, relevant personnel files, performance appraisals and any disciplinary records, emails, letters, memos, photos and/or videos.

BACKGROUND RESEARCH

Although you are conducting a factual, not a legal, investigation it is helpful to know some of the basic law underlying the complaint. Without such basic legal understanding you may omit some questions that are key to your conclusions. For example, in age cases, you need to ask the complainant's age in order to see if there is actually a bona fide age discrimination claim. In a race discrimination case, you need to have a record of the complainant's race as well as the race of the alleged wrongdoers.

In order to get a summary knowledge of the legal claims, you can go online to government sites such as www.EEOC.gov or the Department of Labor website which have basic primers on various employment law claims. For a more sophisticated understanding of the legal underpinnings, employ a service like www.Lexadigm.com (for a very reasonable fee) to get a basic legal analysis. A working knowledge of the legal claims permits you to know where to delve deeper to flesh out facts relative to those claims.

Discrimination claims can have costly effects on productivity. A 1995 United States Merit Systems Protection Board survey found that sexual harassment, for example, cost the federal government $164 million per year. Loss of productivity in the work group of the victim was highest, weighing in at $96.9 million per year in losses. Knowing this, you might scrutinize assertions by supervisors or others that the victim(s) were not being as productive as they should have been since the fall off in productivity could be a by-product of the discrimination. Conversely, if there appears not to have been any sexual harassment, a loss of productivity could indicate that discipline was warranted and nondiscriminatory.

Discrimination claims also cause physical and psychological illnesses when the conduct complained of is severe. Victims' testimony about headaches, gastrointestinal ills, or insomnia can be indicators that harassment or discrimination may have occurred. Psychological ailments include suicidal ideation, depression, lack of self-esteem, and anxiety. Medications prescribed for any of these ailments are also an indicator that discrimination may have taken place. Naturally, if the medications predate the alleged discrimination, the conditions that are being treated may have pre-existed—and not been caused by—the alleged discrimination. Thus, questions concerning the victim(s)' physical and psychological state are warranted.

WITNESS INTERVIEWS AND THE WITNESS LETTER

An employment investigation will have one or more complainants, one or more alleged wrongdoers, and secondary witnesses such as co-workers, bystanders, or supervisors. The inclination is to interview the complainant first, and this is the traditional approach. Then the wrong-doer is interviewed second. But there are times when it makes more sense to shake up the order of witness interviews.

For example, in a hostile work environment claim, it may make more sense to interview disinterested bystanders to see if they witness-ed the alleged conduct. Or in a comparable pay claim, reviewing pay scales and salaries may be the most fruitful initial approach even before interviewing any witnesses. If one party is claiming harassment and the other is saying a relationship was consensual, it might make more sense to interview coworkers to see if the couple in question seemed romantically involved.

Consider using a witness investigation letter to contact your witness-es in the first instance. Such a letter explains to witnesses what they can expect and sets forth the ground rules for the interview. Most impor-tantly, the letter should stress the confidential nature of the inquiry or investigation and advise witnesses that they should not discuss the in-vestigation with others.

The letter must also contain language explaining to witnesses that they are strictly prohibited from engaging in any type of employment reprisals against anyone participating in the investigation. You should provide three separate avenues to report instances of suspected retali-ation, usually two within the company's Human Resource department and one to an outside source such as yourself.

Ground rules for the investigation that are laid out in the witness let-ter include telling the truth, arriving on time for the interview, not ex-aggerating or understating the facts, and bringing along any relevant documents or other materials. You should also alert witnesses to the fact that you will be tape recording their remarks or having them sten-ographically transcribed if that is the case.

Rather than sending the witness letters by email, consider sending them by overnight mail instead, or have your client's Human Re-source professional deliver hard copies by hand. Why? It is simply too easy to forward an electronic version of a witness letter that will threat-en the confidentiality of the investigation. Admittedly, witnesses can scan and forward electronic copies of hard copies they receive, but they will have to consider that step more deliberately than simply hitting the forward button on their email task bar.

If a witness is reluctant to cooperate, cite the company's handbook, policies, and procedures. Every company should have a handbook with a policy requiring that employees cooperate with a company investigation. You can also appeal to the witness's sense of fairness by telling him that you need his perspective and views to determine the truth about what did or did not happen. If a witness is concerned about retaliation, remind him that company policy prohibits this and let the witness know of the various lines of communication that exist to report any suspected instances of retaliation.

Investigators differ as to what form of information gathering is most effective. Without question, a stenographic transcript compiled verbatim from testimony will yield the most accurate and detailed report of what a witness says. Some investigators feel that having a court reporter, though, is intimidating to witnesses. Others are concerned about cost. Some investigators favor tape recording interviews. Tape recordings, however, have the distinct disadvantage of needing to be transcribed. Others favor taking notes by hand. While this approach cannot capture the witness's every word, it is less likely to intimidate and less costly than hiring a stenographer.

If you don't have the luxury of having a court reporter, be sure to date your notes and note the date on your tape recording. If you have multiple witnesses in one day, put the time of day on your notes and recording as well. The order in which you have interviewed witnesses could later be important for follow-up interviews or if there are charges of retaliation.

QUESTIONING TECHNIQUES

It is the investigator's responsibility to set the tone of the interviews. While individual styles vary, a cross-examination style of questioning is neither desirable nor effective. The goal of a fact-finding investigation is to discover facts, not to lock a witness into a foreordained position. Similarly, an interrogative style as opposed to a conversational tone is likely to close down testimony rather than to elicit more. In short, a professional but informal style is likely to yield the most fruit.

Ask open-ended questions such as who, what, when, where, how, and why. Nonleading questions are key to opening up a witness and getting the maximum amount of information. Opinions, too, are okay. While opinions are not necessarily observations that you would put into your Investigative Report, they can often highlight other areas of inquiry that bear factual investigation.

Two witness difficulties may face an investigator. One is that the witness may ramble. The second is that the witness may be reluctant to speak. Each requires a different investigative approach.

For the rambling witness, first make a note of your question so you can come back to it after the witness has finished rambling. Then, let 'er rip! The witness may just be someone who goes on at length when questioned. Or she may be dissembling or avoiding the question asked. Regardless, let the witness talk without interruption. The chatty witness may well give you clues to other lines of inquiry that you will make a note of in your notes. The dissembling witness will no doubt stumble over her lies as she continues to talk. Either way, remaining silent on your part will elicit key information.

Be sure to return to your initial question after the witness is finished with her discourse. If the witness continues to dodge your line of inquiry, gently rein her in and force her to answer the question.

When faced with a witness who refuses or is too shy to talk, do not despair. First, make sure you are asking open-ended questions which cannot be answered with a monosyllabic 'yes' or 'no.' Questions such as "Tell me about . . . ," "Describe . . . ," "What happened next . . ." are useful. Second, remain silent for as long as it takes after asking your question. People are generally very uncomfortable with long silences and will fill in the silence if you remain quiet. If you feel the witness is refusing to cooperate, remind him that the company policy requires that he cooperate in your investigation and that he can be disciplined if he does not do so.

RETALIATION CLAIMS

Retaliation claims are often present together with discrimination claims. In 2009, the EEOC processed more retaliation claims than any other form of employment discrimination charges. Thus, if a witness has claimed retaliation in addition to discrimination or harassment, those charges must also be examined.

Initially, the line of questioning should cover whether the witness experienced any adverse employment actions such as unwarranted disciplinary actions, undesirable transfers, or threats of termination. Secondly, you must ask the witness if the alleged retaliation occurred close in time to, or was caused by, the witness engaging in a protected activity such as making a charge of discrimination, acting as a witness in the investigation, or the like. Be sure to ask when the allegedly retaliatory activity occurred since actions that are close in time to the protected activity are more likely to be viewed as retaliatory. As with the underlying charges, you must make determinations as to retaliatory facts in your Investigative Report.

DOCUMENTS

Documents are your best friend in this type of investigation as in others. As noted earlier, documents include corporate policies and procedures, personnel files, disciplinary files, performance appraisals, salary information, and the like. "Documents" include e-documents such as email or other electronic information. Generally speaking, you are likely to review email, letters, memos, photos and videos, and other miscellaneous documents that may be provided to you by witnesses when they arrive for their interviews.

Documents are valuable because they provide a contemporaneous record of what happened. They are dated, which permits you to create the essential time line for your inquiry. They also contain the names of the author, recipient and those copied on the email, memo, or letter. Bear in mind that email may have been "blind copied" to another party, and this information would not appear on all copies.

Fear not if electronic information has been deleted or otherwise tampered with, it can still be recovered. You may need the help of an IT specialist in e-discovery, but information can be retrieved.

If your case is document intensive, you may want to consider purchasing a software package that will help you in time mapping and general organization. A number of commercial products are available. You may also want to use an online, web-based document storage and management system. Both these approaches are likely only needed in the most document-heavy types of cases.

Don't write on original documents. Also, try not to confuse nonidentical duplicates as different comments or stray marks on nonidentical documents may provide valuable evidentiary clues. Try to keep clear where a document came from as this also can be probative. When examining a witness about a document, it is helpful to "lay a foundation" by asking the who, what, when, where, how questions. This way you are likely to cover the waterfront with regard to each document.

THE INVESTIGATIVE REPORT

The meat of the matter is your Investigative Report. Begin by listing the witnesses you have interviewed. You may also want to list potential witnesses who have not been interviewed and then state briefly why you did not interview them.

The report should contain facts and only facts, although opinion that is clearly labeled as such can be helpful in limited circumstances. You must also consider–and resolve–credibility disputes. This can be the toughest job you will conduct in finalizing the findings of your investigation, and sometimes your initial credibility determinations will change as you review documents and testimony in the final stages of drafting your report. A report that does not resolve credibility questions is not worth its salt.

Use documents in your Investigative Report. Number relevant documents, label them as exhibits, and refer to them in your investigative findings. Your witness testimony and documents are the infrastructure which supports your ultimate findings. Your report must contain details, details, details!

Do not insert legal opinions or conclusions in your report. That is the job of the lawyers or Human Resource professionals who will review your report. Eschew value judgments as these, too, have no place in a factual report. Finally, while documents can provide key evidence, try not to overwhelm the reader with too many exhibits.

The format of your Investigative Report is a personal decision, but consider making it spiral-bound so the document lies flat while being reviewed. Exhibits should be separately bound so that they can be referred to easily while the Investigative Report is being read.

Create a limited number of Investigative Reports, providing only as many as your client requires for those with a need to know your results. Consider enumerating your reports, such as "copy 1 of 3," "copy 2 of 3," etc. In order to protect yourself from any liability due to the report being disseminated beyond those with a need to know, place a restrictive legend on the front. Something like the following should suffice: "The author disclaims any responsibility for the dissemination of this report beyond those persons who have a need to know of its contents."

Again, in order to make it less likely that the report will be widely disseminated, consider providing the client with only hardcopy versions of the report and sending it via overnight delivery rather than emailing or scanning it. As is the case with a witness letter, the document can, of course, be scanned and forwarded by the recipient, but at least you will have done your best to limit circulation of the report. This is consistent with and responsive to the paramount need to keep investigations as confidential as possible.

CONCLUSION

As noted at the outset of this chapter, investigations must be prompt yet thorough and detailed. They should be well supported by the evidence and should resolve any credibility disputes. Finally, they must come to reasoned factual conclusions if they are to benefit the reader. If your Investigative Report meets these criteria, it will likely hold up to scrutiny in any later administrative or court proceeding. Indeed, you may be instrumental in having the claims against your client dismissed. Your report may also form the basis for further action your client deems appropriate.

Chapter 7

CAPITAL DEFENSE INVESTIGATIONS

KEVIN W. MCCLAIN

As a professional investigator, there may be times you are called upon or appointed to a capital murder investigation. There is no greater commission one can have than to have their fellow man's life literally in his or her hands. This type of investigation is not for the weak at heart. Your investigative efforts can be the difference between a person living or dying. Most of the time, when you are involved in a case of this magnitude, society has already prejudged your client guilty. This type of investigation requires all of the investigative skills you have ever learned and have applied. One of the mantras that should be stressed is to never assume anything; always verify everything. As investigators, we are to be fact-finders, and to be impartial and objective in our findings. We are the seekers of the truth. The attorneys need to know everything: the good, the bad, and the ugly. It is better to know in advance than to be surprised in court. The following methodology has proven to be a very successful approach to these types of investigations.

LET'S GET STARTED

At your first meeting, you will be reviewing the case with the attorney(s) and other members of the defense team. These other members could include a mitigation investigator, crime scene investigator, paralegals, and psychologist, just to name a few. You want to understand

71

exactly how the state is trying to convict your client, how they have charged the case, and the theory of defense at this stage. It is important to understand what the attorneys want you to do, i.e., specific assignments, or a full investigation. You also want to clarify how the attorney wants you to conduct interviews, i.e., verbal, tape-recorded, first person statements, or video recorded. You need to establish routine defense team meetings so everyone will know what the other members are doing and will communicate. The defense team meetings also make everyone accountable and also help to compare notes especially on trying to locate difficult witnesses. It is also essential that all members of the defense team understand that the attorneys are the captains of the ship.

INVESTIGATION

Investigative Case Review and Analysis

The investigator should start the initial investigation by doing a comprehensive review of all discovery materials. This material, simply put, is the information the state has gathered against the defendant that has relevance to the case. It is imperative that you receive the entire discovery that your attorneys have been provided. The amount of material in a capital murder case can be upwards of hundreds of thousands of pages. As the lead investigator, you must read the entire discovery. There have been several wrongful convictions that have been reversed simply based upon a professional investigator taking the time to read all of the material that had been provided. As they say, the devil is in the details. You have to know the facts of the case before you start any type of investigation and hit the streets. Keep in mind that additional discovery will be coming as the case progresses.

People List

You now have the discovery and have been given the assignment to review the entire discovery. You will need to have a legal pad and several different colored highlighters to highlight different issues, facts, and people as you start your review. You may want to highlight each of the people with a certain color and the other issues with different colors. This approach helps in systematically identifying different issues in the material. As you are reviewing the discovery, list every name you come across as you are reading. The name may not seem significant, but it may prove to be invaluable later on. Be very alert to any name you come across even that is briefly mentioned and has no supporting statement. These types of witnesses are the ones the investigator should make every attempt to locate and interview. Just because a person didn't have anything favorable to say to the police doesn't mean there couldn't be something helpful for the defense. As you are identifying the people, you may also want to note what their role is in the case, i.e., neighbor who witnessed, friend of defendant, alibi witness, etc. You also want to list any facts and a brief summary of that fact, i.e., cell phone call was made, they went to Walmart, he was on the computer, etc. Though the fact may not seem relevant on the surface at the time, later on, it may prove to the missing piece of the puzzle. As you are reviewing, you also need an eye for detail and to not assume because a fact is stated a certain way, it is true. You will need to assemble a list of issues that have to be verified. As you are identifying issues, you need to make notes of possible experts you may need, i.e., pathologist, crime scene investigator, DNA expert, psychologist, etc.

Five W's and the H

All professional investigators know that to conduct a thorough investigation, the investigator should be looking for information in a methodical approach that would answer his inquiries by applying who, what, where, when, why, and how. This type of approach as you are reviewing discovery helps develop your task assignments that you will do in the field. A technique you may apply is to list all of the questions you want to ask, i.e., who did it, what happened, where did it happen, when did it happen, why did it happen, how did it happen. After your questions are answered, then document your findings in one of the above categories, which may help you better identify and categorize the areas to prioritize for investigations. One of the most important areas that the state overlooks or doesn't give much weight to is the question of Why. This question is going to be the most important for your defense team, and more importantly, the jurors are going to want that answer before they go to deliberate. If we have done our job, then that question should have been answered for the jurors so there are no assumptions on their part.

Frame-By-Frame Analysis

This methodical approach of reviewing your discovery has uncovered many hidden facts as well as additional information and areas to be interviewed that could not have been ascertained if the conventional method of review was done. Imagine you have a remote or Tivo and you can start, stop, rewind, pause, or take the scene forward frame by frame. By doing this type of approach and looking at every word in every sentence, you will be able to spot the gaps. Just imagine each sentence as a scene from a movie. You want to see what everyone is doing? Why is it happening? Exactly how did it happen? As you are analyzing each frame (or sentence), you are trying to visualize the entire scene. Do the body mechanics support the allegation? For example, is it physically possible for the defendant to be holding both of the victim's arms over her head with his hands as he unbuttons her button-fly jeans at the same time? One of the best books written on this subject is the *Rape Investigations Handbook* edited by Brent Turvey and John Savino published in 2005 by Elsevier Academic Press.

Timelines

One of the areas that is often overlooked but essential to conducting a complete and thorough investigation is the timeline. You need to keep in mind that timelines will change as new information and evidence are developed. As you are you doing your investigative case review and analysis, you should also be listing dates and times. Once you have compiled all of these, you will need to place them in chronological order with a brief summary of the facts relevant to that time. Once you complete this timeline, you will be amazed at some of the gaps you have discovered as well as identifying additional areas to investigate. You then can do a summary of findings based upon your timeline. A program called "Timeline" from the company Casemap is very useful for this.

SUMMARY OF INVESTIGATIVE
CASE REVIEW AND ANALYSIS

At this stage of the case you should now have an extensive people list, fact list, and issues list as well as specific questions you have uncovered based upon your frame-by-frame analysis and construction of your timeline. One of the key areas you need to identify at this time is if your attorney needs to issue any subpoena duces tecum for any time-sensitive materials such as police transmissions, 911 calls, Call Detail Records, surveillance videos of any areas along the route or the police videos from their on-board video systems. These items may make or break a case and it is the investigator's job to bring these items to the attorney's attention as soon as they are discovered during the review. Sometimes this may be something you will want to discuss and recommend at your initial meeting.

After identifying all of the relevant areas you believe need to be investigated, you should submit an investigative outline to the attorneys presenting your strategy, reasons, and activities you wish to proceed with. After the reivew and receiving permission, you then would proceed to the field and meet with the defendant.

DEFENDANT INTERVIEW

You now have completed your initial case review and analysis and have identified the areas to investigate and witnesses to interview, but before you can do that, you must interview the most important person on the defense team, the defendant. Like it or not, he or she holds a lot of information and may not even realize it. At your initial interview and meeting with the defendant, be sure that he or she understands who you are and why you are there. A good approach is to just visit with the defendant and get his or her background. The more that you can become familiar with the defendant's background, environment, family, health, education, etc., the more you can assist in his or her defense. One of the common errors that defendants make is that they gloss over certain facts because they have already told them to their attorneys, possibly the police, family, and other inmates and assume you already know all of the facts. Don't let the defendant make that crucial assumption. One of the ways is to start the interview process not from the logical start to finish manner but possibly what happened right after the defendant was arrested. After that, you may inquire about starting at the event and going backwards to the time he woke up or the last 24 hours. This method of interviewing tends to make a person recall facts and events that he may have forgotten. But having to recount events backwards requires him to recall and replay in a format he is not used to. This type of interview procedure can also be effective on all witnesses. Once you have started the actual interview of the defendant, you will want to acquire personal data about them. You want to know all their physical characteristics, i.e., height, weight, hair, eyes, right- or left-handed, education, medical history, etc. Some attorneys will allow the defendant to review his discovery. If that is the case, ask the defendant what his findings were. Try to ascertain what he doesn't agree with and why. After acquiring that information, have the defendant tell you who all of the players (witnesses) are and their relevance to the case. Try to obtain as much information about them as possible, i.e., habits, hobbies, addresses, vehicles, relatives, etc. Obtaining this information upfront will hopefully save you a lot of time in the field. If there are any witnesses you have identified from your case review, you want to inquire with the defendant about them.

CRIME SCENE EXAMINATION AND INSPECTION

Once you have identified your players list and you have additional witnesses you believe are relevant, you then want to proceed to the crime scene. This is another area that many investigators fail to do, as well as attorneys, and it is a critical mistake. If you think about it, how can you do an effective interview of a crucial witness if you don't know the facts, especially when he describes a building he was in and could see and describe the street and location details like streetlights, etc. Always keep in mind that the crime scene is the location where evidence gets manipulated. For example, the EMTs arrive before the police, administer CPR, and accidentally kick some shell casings or move a towel, etc. It is very important that you do a timeline of the crime scene, i.e., who was coming and going, etc. You want to interview anyone who was at the crime scene as well. When you go to the crime scene try to go at the same time of day that the incident happened.

What do you see? What you smell? What do you hear? Are there other witnesses who could have seen something but weren't interviewed? Canvass the neighborhood; just because someone isn't home at the time you are there doesn't mean they didn't see or hear something. You also may want to revisit the crime scene several more times at the same time of day. When you are there, look for the same vehicles such as a mail truck or a delivery truck that is in the area at the same time of day as the incident. The reason the information didn't show up in any police reports was because by the time the police arrived, they were already out of the area and police probably didn't even realize they may have heard or seen something that was relevant. You need to locate and interview them.

When you are at the crime scene make sure you take along the necessary tools of our trade. You will need business cards, identification card, notepads, plenty of pens, tape measure, rolo-tape, crime scene sketch, camera, video recorder, and tape recorder. It is helpful sometimes to just dictate into a recorder your measurements and observations instead of writing it down especially if you are in a congested area with lots of traffic. If you are on a roadway, you will also want a reflective vest for your safety. If you have a crime scene expert on board, it is to your advantage to have them accompany you to the scene.

Take photographs from the witness's perspectives. Photograph from all angles. A rule of thumb that can be applied is to start your photograph process by taking them from the angles of twelve o'clock, three o'clock, six o'clock, and nine o'clock. After you have completed the initial photographs, start taking pictures from the locations where witnesses indicated they were. Be observant for any obstructions as they pertain to line of sight, notice any streetlights, determine if the scene still accurately looks the same as it did on the date of the incident. Always remember that you can never take enough photographs.

A lot of times when you are in a neighborhood doing your measurements and photographs, people from the neighborhood will approach you. This is a great way to break the ice and introduce yourself. Once you have started a conversation with them, it can lead to their knowledge about the incident or in the alternative, who they recommend for you to talk to.

CRIME LAB EVIDENCE REVIEW

One of the areas that should also been reviewed and charted is all of the evidence the state is alleged to have. The charting should consist of a brief description and the evidence numbers that have been assigned to the evidence. Be careful because the local police department has its own evidence numbering system while the state police has another. In Illinois, they have a system called CALMS (Computer Assisted Laboratory Management System), which in theory means every piece of evidence has a bar code and can be tracked through the Illinois State Police crime labs. The reason you want to chart evidence is to have something to compare to when you review the case file at the crime lab.

Another option that quite often gets overlooked is reviewing the case file at the crime lab. The case file is the file that contains every evidence receipt, chain of custody logs, bench notes, worksheets, phone logs, e-mails, etc. from every law enforcement agency and forensic agency that is involved in the case. The manner in which to do this review is to have the attorney submit a letter to the director of the lab requesting to be allowed to view the case file. It is usually wise to have two persons in this process. One person can review the documents from the file while the other compares it to their list and checks them off as the review progresses. One person can do this, but be prepared to spend some time at the lab. If your team has a crime scene expert on board it would be wise to have him or her participate in the review. A thorough review of the case file can help the defense team determine what relevant evidence they have, what needs testing, what are some of the concerns of the state, what are some of the concerns of the forensic labs that are doing the testing, and what is the theory of the case and mindset of the lead investigator? Most reviews have usually revealed something that has been helpful to the defense. It is highly recommended to review the evidence file.

PHYSICAL EVIDENCE REVIEW

After you have conducted your crime lab evidence review, you will want to go to every law enforcement or forensic agency that has the physical evidence for an onsite inspection and examination. You should be armed with the knowledge of what evidence the state is trying to utilize to prove their case and you will want to pay particular attention to those items. You will probably want to contact the state's attorneys office to set up these reviews, as they may want to be there or send a representative. At these reviews, it is a good idea to have the attorney present to view the evidence but also to answer any custody, evidentiary, or legal issues that may arise. You also would want your crime scene investigator along. Always be respectful when you are in any office of the opposing side. Remember you are a professional and you are in their house so have respect for them and their rules.

You will want to bring along cameras, extra batteries, video recorder, notepads, pens, latex gloves, your evidence logs and charts, the discovery relevant to the physical evidence, rulers, and measuring tape.

You want to document the location where the evidence is stored and determined if it is a secure location. You will want one of the law enforcement personnel to handle the opening, sealing, etc. of all evidence. Before you start, put on latex gloves. As you begin to review evidence, take photographs of the outside of the bags for any and all markings as well as bar codes. Once the evidence is removed, then proceed to take photographs of it at all angles as described previously, i.e., all clock positions. Once you have done that, take photographs from every conceivable angle you can. After you have completed this process, you now have the entire evidence inventory at the defense team's disposal 24/7. It is a good idea to make multiple copies of the photographs and put them in a binder so when you call the attorney about a specific item you have located, you can refer him to the particular number so he can review it at the same time, even if you are having a phone conference with other team members. When you are examining the evidence, you may want to conduct a mini-interview of the custodian of evidence and his relevant knowledge and training as it relates to your case.

BACKGROUND WITNESSES

Always remember that to be forewarned is to be forearmed. We have to know who the players are before we hit the streets. The more information we have before knocking on their door, the more prepared we can be. A comprehensive background check will assist you in developing a profile of this person. Is this witness going to be a trustworthy honest person whom I can believe or is there a history of lying and being in trouble? During your background check, you may discover what may be the motive for the person's statements. One of the first places to visit is the local courthouse. It is the repository of all information. Every case starts and ends there. If you do not know how to do courthouse research, contact someone who does and pay them to escort you through the process. You will need to know how to use the in-house computers that most clerks' offices use. At the courthouse, you will want to look up a person by the full legal name and any variations of it. For example, for the name Wolf, you would also want to look under Wolfe, Wulff, etc. The reason for this is because courthouse personnel, law enforcement personnel, dispatchers, etc. are all human and make mistakes because they assume they know the spelling or they may have heard it wrong. It doesn't take but a few more minutes to look up the variations. Remember you have a person's life in the balance and all of your actions could mean the difference.

You will want to do research on all civil, criminal, and traffic files on your witness. If you find any files that you feel are important, you will want to get certified copies of those. You will also want to search the federal records on your witness as well, including civil, criminal, and bankruptcy. An easy way to do this type of search is to subscribe to Pacer, which is a database of all federal courthouses. If you were to locate a file, then you would have to physically go to that courthouse and get it certified. In the local area where your witness resides, you will want to check any courthouses within 50 miles of their residence. Most people tend to get in trouble or conduct their activities within that radius. You also will want to run the witness's name through an investigative database, i.e., IRBsearch, Tracers, Merlin, or Choicepoint to help identify any other areas around the country where the witness may have resided. If you ascertain other areas around the country, then you would want to have someone go to the local courthouse in that jurisdiction and do the same type of background check. To be as cost effective as possible, you may want to locate someone from the PRRN; these are public record retrievers from all over the country who usually visit courthouses on a daily basis.

VICTIMOLOGY

A comprehensive background check of the victim can reveal information that would not be discovered by conventional methods. Conduct the background check of the victim just like you would do with a background of a witness. In addition, go to the areas where the victim lived and canvass those neighborhoods to try to complete an entire profile of the victim. Who were his or her friends? Where did he or she live? What type of work did he or she do? Who were the last people to see him or her alive? You will probably think of other questions to inquire about. You will need to do a timeline of the victim's last 24 hours and then, based upon that information you develop, it may lead you to additional witnesses and leads to follow-up with.

You should also not forget to look at social networking sites as well as doing a Google search to see what additional information may be on the Internet about the victim. This type of approach will give you additional insights into the victim, possible alternative suspects, and the facts surrounding the incident and what may have led to it.

INTERVIEWING OF WITNESSES

Now you have your intelligence developed about each potential witness, it is time to decide what questions you want to ask. Develop a list of questions that you would like answered by the particular witness you are going to interview. Think about if you had only one opportunity to ask one question, what would it be? Decide the best manner in which to approach each witness, i.e., time, location, manner, dress, tone of voice, type of statement to take, i.e., first-person statement, tape recorded, verbal, video recorded, etc. Try to avoid calling a witness in advance to set up an interview; the element of surprise is one of your best investigative tools.

When you arrive in the neighborhood avoid parking directly in front of the witness's residence. As you approach the residence, be observant of the neighborhood, any animals present, and the residence itself. Note any yard ornaments, bumper stickers, political signs, etc. This type of information can help you as you provide the attorney with your thoughts and impressions of the witness later.

As you proceed to knock on the door, don't bang on it, but knock as if you would when visiting a friend's home. When knocking, always step to the side of the door; you never know what is on the other side. If you are tall, you may consider stepping down onto the steps so you are at eye level with the witness and not towering over them. Once he or she has opened the door, politely introduce and identify yourself, and hand him or her your business card. Ask for permission to talk with him or her. This is very important so later on the witnesses can't make any allegations that you intimidated or threatened them. Usually on a capital case you would want to have a prover. This is usually another investigator; often it may be the mitigation investigator who can attest to the professionalism you displayed. It is also very cost effective to the defendant and the state that has appointed you. Once the witness has agreed to talk, try to find some common ground. You want the witness to be comfortable with you and to be able to communicate in a manner that he or she prefers. When first talking to the witness, don't immediately take out your note pad and start writing. A witness should be allowed to freely talk and not have any distractions. Once he or she has completed speaking, then you can ask questions and clarify any areas. At this time, you may want to take out your notepad and indicate to the witness that you want to make sure you get the information he or she has shared with you down accurately. Then proceed to go back over and repeat to the witness what he or she had said as you are writing down the facts. Depending upon the manner in which you were instructed to do the interview, you may stop at this time not taking any notes, if you report your thoughts back to the attorney in a timely manner. In the event the attorney wishes you to proceed with obtaining a statement, then you would go over everything with the witness prior to taking the statement. At the end of the statement, you would want the witness to acknowledge the statement and that they agree and will attest that it is accurate and correct. There are several good books on methods of interviewing which would be highly recommended if you have any questions about the proper format or methods to obtain a statement.

Some of the pitfalls to avoid include never interviewing a witness in the presence of another. This could give the appearance of tainting a witness or, worse yet, contaminating a witness. You also never want to leave blank witness statements with potential witnesses and then come back later to collect. If you are doing a first-person statement, the investigator needs to prepare the statement. When preparing a statement, always use a witness's words regardless of the grammatical correctness. The statement must be the witness's words and not yours.

REPORT OF INVESTIGATION AND TESTIFYING

After you have completed all of your fieldwork, you will prepare a report with the attorney's permission of all of your findings and submit them to him. When preparing your reports, you will want them to be clear, concise, and with correct spelling. Your reports should be in a format similar to the order of your investigation, i.e.: investigative case review and analysis, frame-by-frame review and summary, timelines and summaries, defendant summary, observations and findings at the crime scene, etc. Once completed, you should proofread before submitting. Remember your report could be read by others and is a direct reflection upon your abilities and professionalism.

After submitting your report, you may be required to appear in court to report your findings. If so, review with the attorney so you understand exactly what you will be testifying about and then prepare by re-reviewing your report. The day of your appearance, be properly dressed in a business suit, no flashy clothes or jewelry, with polished shoes, and be well rested. Keep in mind that the jurors have watched TV and have heard about professional investigators but now they will see one in action. First impressions can be lasting ones; make sure you put your best foot forward. When you are on the witness stand, have good posture, speak clearly, look at the jury when you answer, and answer only the question that is asked. Don't give a narrative. If you don't know the answer, indicate that you don't know. If you don't understand a question, ask the attorney to explain the question. Never get into an argument with anyone. Your job is to report the facts and to be impartial and objective as to your findings.

SUMMARY

Conducting a death penalty investigation will be the most stressful and rewarding work you can ever do as a professional investigator.

You will literally have your client's life in the balance of your hands. You want to turn over every stone and leave nothing to chance or second guess. At the end of the trial, you will be going home. As for your client, his final destination will be largely dependent upon your skills as an investigator and those of your defense team. You will need to familiarize yourself with the American Bar Association rules on proper representation of a capital defense client.

As a very good friend of mine shared with me, you have a ministry of sorts. You are representing someone whom society has turned their backs on and already judged. What greater commissioned calling can one person have than to have their fellow man's life in his or her hands. You represent the weak, poor, and the downtrodden and less fortunate. This is the band of brothers and sisters I hope you will join and fight the good fight and always keep the faith.

Chapter 8

DENIED PARTY SCREENING

BARRY RYAN

There are federal laws that restrict or make it unlawful to conduct business transactions or have vendor relationships with individuals and/or entities that are classified as terrorists, terrorist-funded organizations, or those otherwise posing a threat to the security of the United States of America. Various U.S. agencies and departments have developed lists of names of such unlawful persons and entities. Executive management and boards of directors are now held legally accountable for a company's business transactions and operations, and for compliance with government laws and regulations. There are long- and short-term severe penalties for failure of a business to comply with a continuously evolving set of government standards. This chapter serves to explain unlawful business relationships, identify the applicable statutes and cite the repercussions for violators.

OFFICE OF FOREIGN ASSETS CONTROL (OFAC)

The Office of Foreign Assets Control (OFAC) is a division of the United States Treasury with its origin being traced prior to the War of 1812. Since its inception, this organization has worked to advance the safety and international agenda of the United States by using its enforcement powers to achieve its goals. By issuing embargos and sanctions and fining violators, OFAC attempts to stem the flow of cash to parties deemed hostile by the U.S. and, through this, cripple their endeavors. These government measures apply to individuals, businesses, organizations or entire nations, classifying them as persona non grata in any transaction with U.S. affiliated entities. Typical recipients of this debarment include terror-related persons and entities that are nationals of hostile countries, or those connected to narcotics trafficking.

OFAC is the agency that has taken the primary lead in prosecuting violators. The judgments and fines imposed have clearly demonstrated the responsibility of compliance belongs to the U.S.-affiliated parties transacting business. Although current legislation and regulations do not mandate a proactive screening process, OFAC imposes strict liability and harsh consequences when prosecuting perpetrators, thereby eliminating ignorance as justification for offenses. While OFAC is the agency with the highest profile, there are other agencies with equal enforcement powers within the U.S. Departments of Commerce, Treasury, and State.

LEGAL EVOLUTION

The current structure of OFAC sanctions and enforcement are essentially based upon three federal legal actions. These are: Trading With the Enemy Act (TWEA), International Emergency Economic Powers Act (IEEPA), and Executive Order 13224 (E.O. 13224).

Created originally in 1917, the TWEA (US federal law, 12 USC. § 95a) is the oldest. The TWEA enables the President of the United States to direct and control trade primarily during times of war. At present, Cuba is the only country with complete sanctions under the TWEA. North Korea is still subject to a bevy of trade barriers but had its total sanctioning lifted in June of 2000.

The IEEPA (Statute 1626, US Code Title 50, § 1701–1707) also granted powers to the President, but did not limit its primary scope to times of war. Rather, this legislation allowed the President to proclaim a threat to the nation based either primarily or exclusively outside of U.S. borders. Upon enactment, assets and accounts may be frozen, seized, or confiscated. This Act also provides congress a means to override the presidential declaration. Sanctions stemming from the IEEPA have been used against organizations and individuals, as well as against entire countries. The Supreme Court has traditionally backed the "broad scope" of the Executive branch under the IEEPA (Dames & Moore v. Reagan, 435 US 654) despite the congressional measures intended to limit these powers. In 2007, the IEEPA Enhancement Act (Public Law 110–96) sharply increased penalties for entities caught violating the IEEPA.

It should be noted that this legislation also grants power to the Bureau of Industry and Security. This government agency maintains its own listings of parties that U.S.-affiliated entities must seek explicit permission to export goods or services. These lists are the Export Administration Regulations, the Denied Persons List, and the Unverified List. Though different, these lists bear resemblance to OFAC lists in purpose, enforcement, and power.

Executive Order 13224 was issued in the days immediately following September 11, 2001. Through this act, the President enabled the Department of the Treasury to wield his economic sanctioning power. By vesting the Treasury with this ability, a more complete and forceful execution of the IEEPA was enabled. This investiture primarily, but by no means exclusively, was done for the search and seizure of terror-related assets and, with this, the OFAC became fully capable of creating, maintaining, and enforcing the lists of denied parties and individuals.

These three documents do not represent the entirety of legal documentation that supports the OFAC and its policies, but rather provide a general framework by which the operating system can be roughly gauged and understood.

There is a common misconception that OFAC's power stems from the USA PATRIOT Act (Patriot Act). This may be the case since the Patriot Act, which updated the IEEPA, has been widely publicized. Until recently, the regulations in these three acts have been relatively obscure.

PRIMARY GOVERNMENT LISTS

There are multiple listings of denied parties that are maintained by OFAC. Of these listings, there are two main types: country-based and list-based. The former serves as a blanket ban on conducting business with nationals, organizations, businesses, or government entities relating to the offending state. Currently, the countries that fall under this jurisdiction are: The Balkans, Belarus, Burma, Cote d'Ivoire, Cuba,

Democratic Republic of Congo, Iran, Iraq, Liberia/Former Liberian Regime of Charles Taylor, North Korea, Sudan, Syria, and Zimbabwe.

List-based compilations are composed of individuals, groups, or businesses that are not tied down to a specific geographic area and must, therefore, be listed separately. Entities may be added to these lists for a variety of reasons, including being linked to terrorist causes, affiliation with diamond trading, narcotics trafficking, weapons proliferation, or undermining certain democratic institutions. All of these lists are lumped into a comprehensive single listing called the Specially Designated Nationals (SDN) list.

Both types of listings are dynamic and publicly available. Entities are constantly being added and removed, as deemed appropriate by OFAC. As an example, entries on these lists resemble the following:

"HUSSAIN, Saddam (a.k.a. ABU ALI; a.k.a. AL-TIKRITI, Saddam Hussein; a.k.a. HUSAYN, Saddam; a.k.a. HUSSEIN, Saddam); DOB 28 Apr 1937; POB al-Awja, near Tikrit, Iraq; nationality Iraq; named in UNSCR 1483; President since 1979 (individual) [IRAQ2]"

- There are more than 40 lists naming individuals and entities who are identified as denied parties. Some include:
- U.S. Department of Commerce, Bureau of Industry and Security (BIS), Entity List
- U.S. Department of State Directorate of Defense Trade Controls (DTC), Lists of Administratively and Statutorily Debarred Parties List
- U.S. Treasury Department, Non-Specially Designated Nationals Palestinian Legislative Council (PLC) List
- U.S. Treasury Department, Office of Foreign Assets Control (OFAC), Specially Designated Nationals and Blocked Persons List
- U.S. Department of Commerce, Denied Persons List (DPL)
- U.S. Department of Commerce "Unverified" List, Bureau of Industry and Security (BIS) World Bank List of Ineligible Firms List
- Department of Commerce General Orders (RFC); 15 CFR part 736
- Department of Commerce Denials List (TDO); 15 CFR Part 764 Supplement No. 2
- Weapons of Mass Destruction Proliferators

- Specially Designated Terrorists
- Specially Designated Global Terrorists
- Specially Designated Narcotic Traffickers
- Missile Proliferators (MT); 22 CFR Part 126
- Chemical and Biological Weapons Proliferators (CBW); 22 CFR Part 126
- Designated Terrorists Organization (DTO); 22 CFR Part 126
- Financial Crimes Enforcement Network list (FINCEN)
- GSA Debarred Bidders Lists–Reciprocal, Non-Procurement and Procurement
- GSA Debarred Bidders List–Non-Procurement
- GSA Debarred Bidders List–Procurement
- Canadian Restricted Entities
- World Bank–List of Debarred/Ineligible Firms
- U.S. Food & Drug Administration Debarment List

PENALTIES AND IMPACT

The Department of Treasury has not mandated a proactive approach to screening potential debarred parties. In layman's terms, there is no penalty assessed for a lack of screening, in and of itself. However, when OFAC determines a U.S.-affiliated company has committed a violation in one or more business transactions, ignorance will not be accepted as a justifiable reason for doing business with a denied party. If the offense is deemed civil in nature, then the agency employs a theory of strict liability. Criminal proceedings are different, in that they require a "willful ignorance"; however, case history indicates failure to conduct appropriate background investigations is not justifiable. There is also no minimum monetary figure for a violation under the jurisdiction of OFAC. So, theoretically and while highly unlikely, a convenience store could be prosecuted for simply selling incidentals to a denied party.

The IEEPA is the primary legislation that is used to pursue most offenders. Prior to 2007, civil and criminal offenses incurred a maximum penalty of $50,000 per violation. Since the passage of the IEEPA Enhancement Act, civil offenses now start with the greater of twice the amount transacted or $250,000, and can reach up to $1,075,000 per violation. Criminal violations now carry a penalty of up to $10 million along with up to 20 years imprisonment. The actual sentence levied on violators is dependent on different factors, including intent, compliance programs in place, cooperation, and creating an effective deterrence of future incidents. The Department of the Treasury has established baseline amounts for punitive fines that rely primarily on two factors: nature of disclosure (self-disclosure versus involuntarily disclosure) and nature of offense (egregious versus nonegregious). Below is a simple schematic depicting the baseline punishment amounts.

	Egregious Case	
	NO	**YES**
YES	(1) One-Half of Transaction Value (capped at $125,000 per violation)	(3) One-Half of Statutory Maximum
Voluntary Self-Disclosure		
NO	(2) Applicable Schedule Amount (capped at $250,000 per violation)	(4) Statutory Maximum

Image taken from Federal Register–Vol. 73, No. 174, 51940 Via (http://www.ustreas.gov /offices/enforcement/ofac/policy/enf_guide_09082008.pdf).

In section (2) above, the diagram references scheduled amounts that are a previously established guideline put forth by OFAC and portrayed below.

Amount Transacted:	*Penalty Levied:*
Less than $1,000	$ 1,000
Between $1,000 and $9,999 (Inclusive)	$ 10,000
Between $10,000 and $24,999 (Inclusive)	$ 25,000
Between $25,000 and $49,999 (Inclusive)	$ 50,000
Between $50,000 and $99,999 (Inclusive)	$100,000
Between $100,000 and $169,999 (Inclusive)	$170,000
$170,000 or greater	$250,000

Information transcribed from Federal Register–Vol. 73, No. 174, 51936.

Beyond the monetary penalties ascribed by OFAC, violators will likely have to address public relations damage since offenses are publicly disclosed by the Department of the Treasury. Such a gaffe could easily be seen as "aiding and abetting enemies" of the United States and could adversely affect a company in the marketplace and on the stock exchange.

The true short- and long-term impact of barred party violations is very difficult to gauge. Possible considerations include loss of government contracts, suspension of approved vendor status, increased financial scrutiny from regulatory agencies, higher probability of investigative audits, and possible loss of CT-PAT status. The simple fact is OFAC violations have a negative impact for any business. It is in the corporate best interest to understand the ramifications of denied parties screening and to proactively address the issues before a violation unwittingly occurs and sanctions are imposed.

MAINTAINING COMPLIANCE

The breadth of these sanctions is both their bane and their brawn. Keeping track of these constantly evolving lists and cross-checking them with all parties related to a business can be quite a daunting task; however, we as citizens recognize the necessity and nobility of it.

The most up-to-date versions of these lists can be found on the website of the Department of the Treasury in both spreadsheet and text format for public use. These listings are commonly searchable for exact matches using simple word processing tools, but this method will only yield exact results. For instance, in the previous listing excerpt of Saddam Hussein, a search conducted on "Sadaam Hussein" would not yield "a hit." This means even though a search was executed, if business was conducted with a denied individual, in spite of its due diligence, the business could be subject to OFAC penalties because of the application of strict liability.

Arguably, the best approach a business can take to minimize the risk of OFAC violations is the utilization of a preemptive screening program. Whether this is done in-house or outsourced, the establishment and employment of a proactive research plan will help to limit transactions that are contrary to the current U.S. embargos and sanctions.

Furthermore, these measures would certainly help perform damage control for a company that is already under scrutiny for illegal or other regulatory transgressions. Any violations would be more likely to qualify as "nonegregious" if there is an established and documented screening process in place by the company in question. In addition to significantly decreasing any monetary penalties, such processes would help classify all violations as accidental instead of malicious, a valuable difference with regards to sanctions and public opinion.

SUMMARY

Aside from government sanctions, with narcotics trafficking and international terrorism so globally prevalent, it is prudent to take proactive measures to do business with only law-abiding partners. Mitigating risk to safeguard corporate assets and to assure continuity of the supply chain with law abiding partners is critical in today's global economy. For those investigators having corporate clients, providing or outsourcing "Denied Party Screening" services may represent a new business opportunity.

Chapter 9

DEFENDING THE CRIMINALLY ACCUSED

GEORGE MICHAEL NEWMAN

A crime, an offense against society, a person, or property, occurs. It is report-*ed, when someone witnesses an incident or encounters the result of the crime. In certain cases the discovery initiates as a result of an omission rather than an act, such as when a child does not return home from a trip to the store, versus when a person observes someone force a child into a car, or perhaps discovers a body.*

The discovery of a crime sets into action a response. In most instances, a person is eventually arrested as a result of a crime. A majority will avail themselves of the services of a "criminal defense" attorney to represent their interests as the dominant weight of society and the judicial system is brought to bear upon them.

In a significant percentage of those instances wherein justice prevails on behalf of the innocent, or is contextually applied with regard in appropriate proportion to an offense, the vehicle for resolving the case was the incident investigation conducted by an investigator working with the defendant's attorney.

In reality, the phrase "criminal defense" is a misnomer, insofar as a criminal is one who has been tried and justly convicted. Instead, it is better said that one is working on behalf of the criminally accused. It is also true, however, that in many instances, those laboring on behalf of a previously convicted individual may be retrofitting justice by investigating wrongly assigned guilt.

At every juncture, every facet and development in a defendant case is essentially akin to the grain of sand in the oyster; each irritates sensitivities that respond by attempting to coat the coarseness and intrusive presence with a less offensive exterior. As has been repeatedly proven, particularly subsequent to the advent of DNA testing having become a vehicle with and by which many formerly convicted persons have been factually exonerated, and in no small measure owing to the fact that the "justice system" is, in reality, more often than not driven by politics rather than equitable resolution, innocents are routinely convicted of crimes they did not commit. Regrettably, owing to the adversarial context of forensic proceedings, a reality is that in court, what is the truth may not matter. What is right does not matter contextually. All that matters is what one is able to prove. This process of revelation relies on the dedication of each member of a defendant's team in order to prove the whole of the client's truth before the tribunal of fact. In most instances, the proper evolution of the defense of a criminal case is akin to a vertical spiral, with each participant morphologically uplifting the other.

THE INVESTIGATOR'S ROLE AND REALITY

Attorneys have three speeds: I'll look into it;
we'll get to it; and, oh my God trial's tomorrow!

–Ron Watkins, Sr.

The role of an investigator working on behalf of the criminally accused is among the most unrecognized roles in the justice process. In a majority of instances, the foundation for the success of a case may well rest squarely on the shoulders of those investigators who dedicate themselves to the pursuit of truth and its raw and often conflicting realities. Additionally, if one looks carefully at the backs of competent, dedicated investigators, one sees the footprints of the many lawyers whose work, reputation, and abilities have been elevated and elaborated by the labors and commitment of their investigators.

The investigator's endeavors during the course of a case often interdict and impeach agendas, perceived evidence and individuals, including those in positions of power and authority. In the many instances wherein it is the diligent work of the investigator that snatches a defendant from "the system," enmity is often engendered toward the investigator even if the defendant is obviously factually innocent.

Unlike attorneys, prosecutorial detectives and other segments of the trial arena, defense investigators stand virtually alone and at the mercy of the integrity and level of responsibility of the defense counsel. There are no unions; Bar Associations, special interest or power groups to disallow abusing the investigator; to protect the investigator when he or she is being violated, accused, or assailed; to ensure the investigator is getting paid; or to acknowledge the investigator's contributions to a righteous outcome. This responsibility of the defense counsel too often is abdicated or ignored, and its omission is often at the root of investigative laxity.

Additionally, and in all too many instances, the contribution of and by the investigator is muted by a failure on the part of counsel to appropriately address, and in some cases sufficiently comprehend, the investigator's roles. This applies to addressing the investigator's role and contributions from the moment he or she is hired, during the pendency of the investigation, and at trial. It further applies to understanding and assimilating the broad range of potential abilities offered by the investigator. Lastly, it applies to the failure to comprehend that the destiny of virtually every case is dependent upon the proper application of the investigator and the proper allocation of resources to ensure the investigator can effectively do the job.

THE APPROPRIATE INVESTIGATOR

Seek not to know all of the answers, but to understand all of the question.

—Chinese Proverb

When properly selected, an investigator brings to a defense team a bounty of experience, knowledge, instinct, and insight. From the very beginning, the investigator contributes perspective. He or she is able to help identify and prioritize the needs of a case and assign those needs sequence and potential resolution. In reality, the investigator should be the most valuable asset counsel wields, literally becoming an overseer, as well as a facilitator and problem solver of many facets of the case.

The investigator's direct roles include identifying, gathering, and validating/challenging purported evidence; documenting facts; identifying, locating, interviewing, back-grounding, maintaining relationships with witnesses and, in many cases impeaching the unreliable; "running interference" for counsel; and, acting as a general shepherd of the milling herd of incidentals involved in the progress of a case.

An appropriate first consideration in selecting a case investigator is to ascertain the type of abilities the investigator might bring to the job. Evaluative factors to consider are background, range and length of experience, and training.

Assuming an investigator has been retained for the purpose of playing a primary role, versus a legal intern, or support-staff-like role, he or she should certainly have direct, significant experience in the defense of criminal cases. Experience supports the investigator's ability to comprehend and even sense the dynamics integral to the predicate event.

Having done only prosecutorial cases, even with a wealth of criminal-related experience, does not necessarily prepare one's mindset for the chase involved in a defendant case. A blunt fact is that, routinely, law enforcement agents function from a perspective wherein they have an objective to subjectively pursue, and are thereby caused to abandon global objective reason and logic.

The breadth and depth of the investigator's experience should also support the ability to pursue the witnesses, evidence, and overall dynamics of circumstances in whatever modality they may eventually be found. In some cases, this calls for the investigator to have a facility to function from those levels of society that enfold the depraved and/or otherwise damaged or vicious, through all of the other spectrums of human reality. Each and every type and nature of understanding the investigator brings from his or her personal life history and experiences enables the ability to effectively run the course.

An investigator must be able to be both dedicated and pragmatic, and also should be able to communicate with and empathize with witnesses and clients; but should never get drawn into conjoining or sympathizing with them. Conversely, an investigator to whom their role is "only a job," or who is not dedicated to the pursuit of whole truth, will generally do an ineffective job, particularly when under duress or during protracted cases.

The amount and kind of training an investigator has pursued will often reveal the level of dedication to the craft, and may offer certain unique capabilities or attributes to his or her abilities and to the case. Those who have no training, particularly independent of some prior job they may have had in their past, may be demonstrating by omission a tepid concern for their craft.

Investigators who participate in professional organizations generally may have the resources of the organizations available to them, particularly in today's world of Internet e-mail and list servers. Association with others in the field further provides an ongoing, informal training perspective to an investigator's list of qualifications.

Prior law enforcement brings certain abilities and liabilities. Contacts or in-depth knowledge in certain instances may contribute invaluable opportunities and options. However, investigators who have done all of their previous work as "proprietary" (in-house) investigators, whether government, law firm, or corporate, may not know how to function as independent entities, being dependant on structure and assigned focus. Deeply forged loyalties from prior relationships may both give such investigators opportunities, and restrict their willingness and ability to undertake certain endeavors.

There is also the reality that in all too many cases, prior law enforcement is incapable of doing a true deductive investigation, having fallen into a habit of inducing rather that deducing facts and evidence. This debility may also infect a case in the reverse when applied by those private "investigators" who perceive their task to be trashing "the system" for the sake of ideology, rather than constructing the revelation of individual or specific truth.

If an investigator's background is primarily in the civil end of the investigative spectrum, he or she may have little knowledge or capability with respect to doing street work and the skills of interviewing and interview report writing might be limited; conducting and memorializing a witness interview involves significantly more than recording a statement. Those with this type of experience might, however, have talents which lend themselves to postconviction phases of a case owing to an enhanced ability to do, and articulate, research.

In some capital case circles, there is a theory that it is important to utilize two primary investigators, one in the guilt phase and one for the penalty/mitigation phase. Exigent circumstances always dictate into the equation as to whether or not this is appropriate, but, in general, it is not optimal. A truly competent and experienced investigator should be able to conduct both phases of the case, assuming he or she has the resources and stamina. Further, since both phases intensely interlock, this can reduce overall costs to the case by eliminating redundant review of materials, witness contacts, and attorney/investigator conferences. It also may significantly enhance the cohesion of the investigation. If the case is truly too complex for one investigator, two or more may be retained, but there should be one who is expected to support and represent the case investigation at trial.

There may be those investigators who have a particular, succinct, niche-like enhancement to offer and are hired for a limited purpose or function. They should work with and under the primary investigator; generally, in major cases, one investigator should focalize all investigative efforts, and maintain a cohesive assignment tracking and application narrative. This is not to say that the other investigators and experts are excommunicated from conferring with counsel. This would clearly be counterproductive for a team effort. However, structure is vital to surging forward in a focused manner.

The lead investigators should participate in the selection of experts, should participate in all of the initial meetings with the experts, and should have the freedom and ability to communicate with the experts. The parameters of such communications should, however, be defined with and by counsel so they are understood by all team members.

The professional foundation of the investigator is very important. Many "investigators" operate out of the boundaries of basic licensing requirements and other professional regulations. These requirements vary from venue to venue, but adept prosecutors are applying themselves to learning the nuances and technicalities of investigators' operating regulations and are progressively more successful in indicting an illegitimate investigator's legal status, thereby vilifying him or her, counsel, and unfortunately the client.

It is incumbent upon counsel to ascertain and ensure the retained investigators meet all licensing requirements. If the investigator is unknown to counsel, it may be appropriate to check with the state's licensing bureau to see if the investigator is actually licensed, has ever had a complaint filed against him or her, and to check the local civil and criminal defendant index to see whether he or she has ever been sued or charged with a crime. Being a defendant with regard to a complaint or a lawsuit may not necessarily mean a bad investigator, but it is something to be reviewed with respect to possible impeachment should the investigator be called to testify.

Equipment, logistical capabilities, and other resources available to an investigator are relevant considerations because they will indicate whether or not he or she can assemble and draw upon adequate and appropriate resources to do the work required and sustain the output required over the length of a case.

The ability to stay the course in certain types of cases requires a particular stamina and "heart" few can muster. The requirements involved with investigating active cases allow little leeway for indulgence and demand a significant amount of commitment with sparse forgiveness for failure.

A significant pitfall in many instances is the tendency to hire an investigator with whom the attorney may share a commonality. Women attorneys frequently hire other women to support "sisterhood" and promote equality or parity. While that is a noble and potentially needed endeavor, care should be utilized in determining whether or not it is appropriate to gamble someone's future, or even their life, on that premise. Male attorneys will often hire someone because they are good buddies, golf partners, or have some similar relationship, which is also generally a foible.

Too often, the premise that the investigator should be of the same race as the defendant or important witnesses is used as criteria and is as bad an idea in as many instances as it is good. Suspicion from within a certain community may actually more quickly cause rejection of one of its own working for or in the judicial system.

Very often female investigators are hired in the frequent misconception they have some particular touch or forte with other women or children. Male investigators may be hired because it is presumed they can face dangerous elements easier. Both of these indulgences are, in general, fallacies. The imperative needs to be able to keep an eye on the prize and forego personal biases and issues.

Another pitfall is the "Nowhere Man" investigator, or the "Talking Head," who can iterate in succinct detail how something could, should, or would be done. However, when the onus is on that person to produce, his or her ability to do so may have no depth. For instance, just because a person is noted for having presented on a regular basis at seminars does not mean he or she actually has any practical ability in "the field"; talking heads generally have no corpus.

There is a tendency in human nature to want to put together a "warm and fuzzy," we-all-admire-each-other, "feel-good" team. In most instances this is a recipe for disaster. Either everyone will spend too much time being warm and fuzzy with one another and fail to accomplish anything of depth and merit for the case or the reality of stress and grit will rupture the team, very often at the most inopportune times.

Counsel should remember that they may have a limited depth of life experience beyond their career, particularly in earlier years. Most have gone from parents to college to practice and have committed their life experiences to getting through law school and starting a practice. Even a brilliant counselor, adroit and adept at dueling on issues of law, might well be functionally ignorant in terms of the realities to which the rest of the world subscribes. Choosing an investigator who can function apart from the structured, defined confines of the severely formatted legal system, and who can work with the attorney to translate those realities into courtroom currency, depicts insight.

CONDUCTING WITNESS INTERVIEWS

Facts are not the truth, but may only indicate where the truth may lie.

–Unknown

Often in a set of facts or circumstances, there is potentially an axis upon or within which a perspective may be found with which to reveal or lead to those keys that release foundational, exculpatory, and/or mitigating evidence or information. In many instances, differential analysis of the linkage of circumstances, events, and recollections with a witness will allow them to comprehend and offer facts that they might otherwise have not felt were relevant or that they had inhibitions about revealing.

Perhaps the greatest skill and ability in investigation is the ability to approach, interview, and develop a positive relationship with a victim or witness. Unlike the technical aspects of a case or issue such as compiling medical records, forensic examination of evidence, and similar tasks that, in essence are formulaic or mechanical, the ultimate joust is reflected in connecting with the victim/witness. Having them relate not only their understanding of events, but also to view and relate those events through an expanded perspective, having released their fear of "the defense," greatly enables objective fact finding.

Most human beings wish to express their opinion, to be listened to and *heard*. Most want others to accept, understand, or otherwise embrace their perspective of an occurrence. Most internalize events, experiences, and information from the physical, to the mental, to the emotional, and express in reverse order; from the emotional, to the mental, to the physical.

One might imagine a witness's experience being rather like a stream of water, pouring into a cistern which then empties through a spigot. The stream is equivalent to emotion. The cistern might represent the conscious mind. The water flowing through the spigot is its expression. If the free flow of water is interdicted, dammed by fear, anger, or uncertainty prior to reaching the cistern, the water inside the cistern becomes tepid, dank, and foul. The flow of water from the spigot (clear, free-flowing expression, or recollection) has ceased. Should the dam be removed, fresh water will flow into the cistern, pushing water out the spigot. It is both important and relevant to note that the first water to extrude from the cistern will frequently not be the new, fresh water, but will be instead the fouled water initially pushed out by the fresh. Only then does the clear expression break free and follow.

Thus, in many instances, witnesses should initially be allowed, even encouraged, to express themselves as freely as they wish without interdiction. An experienced investigator will not necessarily try to bluntly get the answers he or she believes may come from the witness or challenge their initial, original narratives. In some instances, the witness may need to excoriate the defendant, the investigator, defense counsel, the system and other edifications of all the defense represents to him or her. What the witness feels he or she may have suffered or experienced, or simply have an opinion about, will be expressed. Doing so may bring a victim or witness to a point of equanimity and balance. Many times this evolves into a prelude of/for more rational discourse. It is often very revealing of the personality and agenda of the witness.

Preparation for an interview should include a rigorous self-examination on the part of the investigator and attorney. Each must understand their relationship to the case and the goals of the interview. It is imperative to comprehend what positive and negative factors each brings to the interview and to the witness's perception. Embarking into an interview with personal biases inflicts an often unredeemable predisposition to the effort, even if those biases tend to be in favor of, rather than against, the witness and his or her attitude and character.

Unless physically impossible, the scene where the incident took place, and any other points or locations where related activity occurred, must be visited by the investigator and defense counsel. Not only does this put everything into perspective and focus, it allows more insightful questioning of witnesses.

An investigator must receive and review all related documents and any other source of information before conducting victim/witness interviews. A chronology of known events should be constructed, and a cogent list of all individuals relative to the case developed. During the course of interviewing a witness, these lists may be referred to; the lists will assist in stimulating questions, confirming answers, and making the interview process more fluid. Defense counsel who, for whatever misguided reason, does not provide all documents in a case to the investigator does a tremendous disservice to his or her client.

Nonpercipient individuals, and even percipient witnesses, obtain a lot of their knowledge and even "recollection" of a circumstance from media presentations, rumor and gossip, and the succession of investigators who interview them. Prior to initiating interviews, all information disseminated to the public through the media should be screened to discern what perceptions and emotional hooks have been broadcast. What witnesses report or recount needs to be filtered as to what influences may be integral to their narratives.

Studying current, related or similar cases, issues and politics might also facilitate the interview process. During the O.J. Simpson, Michael Jackson, and Bernie Madoff cases, everybody had an opinion about the defendant, lawyers on both sides, and the process. In some instances, using this commonality as a mutual talking point may get witnesses to express their perspective on a particular matter. Once they are engaged, the conversation may be eased into the relevant case issues. At other times, it is found to be at the root of hostilities directed toward an investigator approaching people in cases absolutely unrelated to the media case. Realizing this sometimes affords an opportunity to deflect the hostility and still engage the witness by agreeing that "that" was outrageous but "this" is different; explaining the differences is another method of engaging the witness in a dialogue.

The approach to the interview and the witness is an important consideration. Cultural considerations are highly relevant. This does not have to mean cross-racial, cross-ethnic, or similar cultural realities. It might be as simple as a white lawyer and a white investigator going to interview a white "tweeter" (methamphetamine abuser), or a black lawyer and black investigator going to interview a black Rastafarian. Even though the usual perceived differences might be ameliorated, there is probably going to be "cultural" disparity between the parties. The attorney and investigator need to familiarize themselves with the dictates within which the witness exists.

In many instances, it behooves the attorney to have the investigator make the initial contact with the subject. Attorneys generally have the capability and propensity of ruining a witness when interviewing him or her by unconsciously trying to inflict courtroom protocol onto the interview. It is better to allow the investigator to develop a rapport and nurse the witness "up" to the attorney; the attorney should then respect the relationship the investigator has developed with the witness and include the investigator in contacts with the witness.

From the initial contact, it is imperative to attempt to discern the motivation behind the responses of the individual being approached. The true art of interviewing is to both create and allow the environment necessary for the interview to take place in a free-flow form, often oscillating cyclically toward the facts and truth. Remember, any individual has an agenda of his or her own and might be also intimidated for an unending multitude of reasons by involvement in, or contact with, the case or by factors totally unrelated to the case.

In many instances, an ability on the part of the investigator to step out of his or her role as an investigator is a positive attribute. If and when common grounds or bonds are affected with the witness, they may relax and communicate freely.

In actuality, the investigator has a great deal to offer the witness or victim, including an explanation of the overall process they are, or are going to be, going through. Most people in the process will pillage witnesses. The majority of witnesses will appreciate that person who takes the time to explain to them the process associated with the case. The investigator and counsel should remember that these are people and their lives are being impacted and affected, even in those oft-encountered instances wherein that person is distressing or even thoroughly revolting. Prosecutors very often fail to keep victims and witnesses apprised of the status of the case. Keeping in touch with such people can help greatly.

When an individual is approached for an interview, there is in most cases an inhibition or concern about what they are being involved in, or an agenda against some particular facet of what the investigator, defendant, or system may represent. Astute investigators might in many cases quite literally talk their way into an interview by explaining the process from the actual, initial moment of contact. Providing an explanation of what is happening even in the introduction stages of the contact informs the witness of the investigator's intention, allowing him or her to relax about what is happening. Pausing after establishing a reason for being there in the first place invites the person to relax and allows him or her to express his or her opinion, thoughts, or knowledge. Thereafter, he or she has been engaged and a dialogue may ensue.

During the course of the interview, it is extremely probable that there will be many distractions, such as children, spouses, or parents. Flexibility in dealing with these interdictions and interruptions will facilitate a relaxed interview. In some instances, a witness will inflict interruptions into the interview so as to wear down or frustrate the investigator in the hope that he or she will terminate the effort and leave, or become so distracted that he or she does not ask enough or the right questions. As in all things, perseverance has its rewards.

Interviews should always be approached as open-ended as possible, conceptually and literally; a "free-spooling" or freely-talking, witness who has become comfortable, entranced with his or her own narrative, or perhaps angry, often becomes a font of information. Whenever possible, it is most practical to not set a predetermined time to end an interview, such as with another appointment or similar deadline. It is sometimes difficult to resume an interview with the same degree of momentum once it has been interrupted. Additionally, other forces may interdict into the relationship that had been initiated with the witness. Although a majority of people will later remember other details that can then be collected whenever possible, it is often wise to exhaust all that a witness has to offer when such an opportunity presents itself. Nonetheless, in most instances it is fruitful to return to witnesses some time after an initial interview; often facts will percolate in their memory after the initial contact, activated by the conversation with the investigator.

In every instance, it is imperative to leave a bridge to or with a witness. All too many investigators, sometimes with glee, exploit a witness. That tactic is sure to dawn on that individual sooner or later. Thereafter, the bridge is destroyed, the witness is not cooperative, and in many cases becomes hostile, feeling or knowing he or she has been duped. At all times, honesty, honor, and integrity should imbue the investigator's contact with individuals, even in adversarial or confrontational circumstances.

The context of the interview should have sincerity as its wellspring.

The experienced investigator creates the environment of the interview, external circumstances notwithstanding. The investigator's approach, tone, and attitude will frequently enfold the witness who should then be led back to and through the incident, over and over, moving from perspective to perspective. Rather like peeling from the outside in on an onion or artichoke, returning the witness to the incident and addressing it from a different line of questioning (lighting, what he or she had been doing during the incident, how he or she first noticed the perpetrator or victim, what his or her emotions were in the moment, etc.) will in virtually every instance illicit new, different, and/or expanded facts.

An "echo effect" is an effective way of interviewing an individual. Often giving back to the person, perhaps in a slightly different form, the very same information that he or she had just expressed will comfort him or her and will encourage him or her to continue the narrative as well as tell him or her that the interviewer is listening to what he or she has to say. Understanding whether the person is responding to or reacting to questions, recollections, facts or events is also part of the art of interviewing, and allows the interviewer to discriminate with respect to where, then lead the thrust of the interview.

The ability to translate what is being said into what is being expressed and revealed is also an art of interviewing. Discerning what the person is "really" or otherwise saying allows information to be led out into the open.

The wise investigator, even after a witness's utility has been exhausted, will re-contact that person and apprise them of the status or result of the case, thank them, and, perhaps, as appropriate, share with them the more global impact of his or her role in the case. Not only is there some overall esoteric value in treating the individual with such courtesy, but one never knows when the case might have to be revisited. Individuals who have been treated throughout with respect and honor will invariably be there again for the investigator when he or she needs him or her to stand up for truth as he or she knows it.

THE INVESTIGATOR TESTIFYING

First they came for the Jews and I did not speak out—because I was not a Jew. Then they came for the communists and I did not speak out-because I was not a communist. Then they came for the trade unionists and I did not speak out—because I was not a trade unionist. Then they came for me— and there was no one left to speak out for me.

–Pastor Niemoeller
(Victim of the Nazis')

With rare exception, investigators will have not attended law school. Even if they have, this does not necessarily prepare them to testify on behalf of an investigation within which they have become a percipient and pertinent element.

An attorney must prepare the testifying investigator. In too many instances, an investigator has unknowingly opened a door which debilitated the case by accident or innocent ignorance. This is generally the fault of the attorney for not properly laying the groundwork for the investigator's testimony both before and during that testimony.

The attorney and investigator must have some flexible idea of the direction the investigator's testimony is expected to take and the anticipated or potential counters to it. Locking "the plan" into concrete, assuming nothing can change it, is a recipe for disaster. Murphy's Law will apply, and the investigator is then stuck out on a limb that is either breaking or being sawed off.

Counsel further needs to understand that to the average person, the average citizen on a jury, an investigator is often synonymous with someone who looks into people's bedrooms, peers through their keyhole, or in one way or another otherwise invades their privacy. Their perception is gleaned from television, movies, and sensationalized media. Add the ingredient of a general mistrust of those who do "criminal defense," and the odds are frequently stacked against the investigator before he or she ever opens his or her mouth.

The defense attorney frequently exacerbates that suspicion, contempt, or disdain from the beginning by failing to properly and appropriately introduce, qualify, and establish the investigator's credibility to the court. This should be thoroughly established before any evidentiary questioning is approached. For the investigator's testimony and revelations to be effective, the presence, role, and integrity of his or her assignment must be presented in sufficient detail.

The work of the investigator quite literally must be oriented for a court or jury.

All too often a jury may perceive the testimony of an investigator as worthless and manipulative when underdeveloped. As it is often counsel's task to "humanize" their client, it is also their task to "professionalize" their investigator. This is accomplished by displaying for the court the training, stature, and experience of the investigator and applying this foundation in the investigator's testimony to his or her labors and the subsequent results.

One of the necessary discussions pretestimony has to do with rehabilitating an investigator's testimony in those instances wherein a stumble has occurred. There should be discussion about this possibility, and options or alternatives may be considered. Most stumbles can be rectified. Juries are frequently sympathetic with human foibles, but are intolerant of what they perceive to be trickery, deception, or abject inability.

There are those attorneys who put an investigator on the stand and subsequently proceed to place the investigator into a position wherein he or she is required to either be disingenuous or, by revealing a truth, destroy the case. These individuals should not be surprised when the issue erupts to the detriment of all.

THE CAPITAL CASE INVESTIGATION

From the onset, investigation of a death penalty case is a thoroughly different type of dynamic from other types of cases and the effort itself is literally a struggle through concentric layers of expectations, concepts, beliefs, and ideologies during and until the termination of the case or until, and even after, the death of a defendant, should that occur.

Throughout the case, every single person involved who truly commits himself or herself to his or her role faces shortcomings.

Politics play a primary, significant, and permanent role in a case from its inception among warring factions in the community, such as police, coroners, prosecutors, defender counsel, investigators, courts, legislators and politicians, funding entities, innumerable special interest groups such as crime-victim and religious organizations, and unlimited individuals and groups—all with their own agenda.

The uniqueness of a capital case dictates a different level of statutory responsibility, incarceration-related circumstances, trial procedures, investigative challenges, overall perspective, strategy, and effort than any other criminal trial.

Into the mélange of competing and colliding interests, the death of the victim takes on a macabre life of its own.

PERSPECTIVE

A capital case is a very thriving dynamic, with an evolutionary rhythm not unlike that of an actual person. Conceived in the death of one or more individuals, its gestation period is the time between the incident and the identification and arrest of the suspect(s). The arrest initiates the inception of a capital case.

Rather like a physical birth, everybody and everything subsequently related to or with an interest in the event begins to have an impact on its life by act or by omission.

This birthing entity brings with it certain predispositions from its individual, "parental" heritage; i.e., the victim and defendant, and the extended circumstances of the life of each as those circumstances converged. "Relatives" of the infant case begin to exert their influence in terms of wanting influence in its existence, or rejecting it in part or completely. An example of this might be a prosecutor generating publicity for him or her in a blatant act of overcharging a case. Such overcharging will then resonate throughout the case in the form of the prosecution having reached a subjective set of conclusions, and tailoring testimony and evidence to fit a perception.

A great many relatives are appended to a capital case, including not only those entities with interests previously mentioned, but also the media, constitutional and other advocates, and pundits.

Infancy is marked throughout by the influences of parental circumstances and is further influenced by the relationship between the parental and the relative factors. Such relationships may not only change, but may actually develop during the case. The societal constellation into which the case is born also further influences its growth and personality. As the case's features begin to unfold, its acceptance or rejection by society will take on an expanding role relative to what the infant is perceived to be, or represent. A "prettier child," an empathetic defendant, or nonredeeming victim will evoke a different level of emotion, reaction, and response than an "ugly child," such as a tragic victim or heinous, revolting circumstances. Each influence impacts the evolving personality of a case and the bonds others will associate themselves with, throughout.

The early maturation phase of a case occurs perhaps at the initial trial stage. Form begins to assimilate from within, assuming the eventual trial personality by defining its potential physical characteristics.

Throughout this evolution, the capital case investigator fulfills many lead and support roles and is called upon to nurture this most important search for balance in a fashion not unlike a literal sibling guardian. In an ideal situation, the role of the capital case investigator and that of defense counsel complement one another to form a synergistic creation capable of inputting equilibrium into such cases, which by their nature are imbued with, and entwined in, emotion.

SUMMARY

Contributing to balance and equity is the ideal cornerstone and benchmark of all who strive within society's quest for safety and justice. Working within such parameters, and in the brilliance of the U.S. Constitution's Sixth Amendment, the endeavors of the accused defendant's investigator may rightly be described as law enforcement.

Chapter 10

LOCATING MISSING HEIRS

HARVEY E. MORSE

Finding unknown or missing heirs is, in our opinion, the ultimate paper chase and one of the most interesting and intriguing facets of investigation. It encompasses the following:

1. finding or identifying the estate,
2. knowing the laws of that state,
3. locating all of the lawful heirs,
4. convincing them to sign a contract with you,
5. preparing the case for court,
6. assisting to identify the assets,
7. obtaining the certified documents to prove each heir's entitlement,
8. preparing Affidavits and genealogical charts,
9. testifying in court, and
10. patiently waiting while the wheels of justice turn ever so slowly until you are paid.

Payment in this field is usually on a contingent basis. If and when the heirs receive their share, then the heir finder receives as a fee, a percentage of the amount the found heirs receive, ranging from 10 percent to 40 percent, never any higher. Other methods of payment are hourly or per diem. Since many estates involve tracing families back to Europe, China, Africa, or other more exotic countries, additional fees may be assessed for foreign research, which typically requires the use of translation services or people on the ground.

Developing a substantial and vast network of genealogists located worldwide is of prime importance. Their experience and reputation are equally as important as is yours and time is always of the essence. You may ask, "Why"? Although today many private investigators advertise that they locate missing heirs, there are only a handful of true forensic genealogists for which this effort is their prime source of income. As a result, the very nature of the business is competitive beyond belief. For example, although you might not think this, the difference of one hour can determine which of several firms will ultimately be successful. One reason attributed to the urgency is the limited number of foreign professional genealogists, and that they will only work with one U.S.A. company on each individual case, never for two competitors simultaneously. That makes it essential to contact and tie up the best staff in a specific foreign country for a specific case ahead of competition. For example, if a private investigator has an estate and the decedent's family originated in Hungary, for example, whoever associates with the best Hungarian heir finder first has a form of exclusivity, especially if there is only one firm in the needed geographic locale.

You will find that despite your best efforts, there will be heirs that you simply cannot find, heirs who were found and who figured out who died and refused to sign a contract, and heirs who just didn't want the money for a multitude of personal reasons; such as, "I was illegitimate and I don't want anyone to know." Today, as a result of divorce and multiple marriages being more prevalent than 50, 75, or 100 years ago, heirs finders often deal with half-blood versus whole blood issues, and laws that have different provisions for each category of heir, as well as which categories can inherit in the first place. In Florida, if a person dies and has a cousin who would have been entitled to inherit, who has also died, that cousin's child will inherit in place of the parent. Compare that to Massachusetts where all heirs of the same category will inherit equally. If there are four cousins and one deceased with a child in Florida, all those living will participate, while in Massachusetts, only the four living people will inherit.

Remember that there are two types of genealogists: One does exactly what everyone understands, tracing a family tree or "roots" back as far as time and documents permit, and forensic genealogy, which only requires the heir finder to go back in time far enough so living relatives are determined which category of relationship are in compliance with a specific state or country's laws. Private investigators, who locate heirs, are the latter.

In bygone years, genealogical research to find missing heirs was done by letter or telephone. There were no databases to check, no court record retrievers, no computers, and each and every case was a tedious "on-the-ground," in-person, and hands-on investigation in whatever state, country, or location was involved. Today, some genealogical data is available by computer, such as census records, so some searches may be done from the comfort of a desk instead of a long drive, or airplane ride, with no guarantee of success.

A typical case follows: John Doe died intestate (without a Will) in Orlando, Florida, on February the 21st with no known heirs. He came to the United States in 1924 from Russia. Often times not much more information than that is presented. Then the research and investigation begins. In today's world, one would start by asking the lawyer if he can access the Decedent's personal belongings. He looks for address books, memos, notes, and especially family bibles and certified records. Each small piece of data is another piece of the larger puzzle. When did the person get a Social Security number and where was it issued? Obtain a copy of the application and see if it gives the city in which the decedent was born. Retain a cooperative and friendly competitor who covers Russia to tie up the foreign genealogist, and so the search begins.

Unfortunately, there is no one way to describe a specific set of procedures or rules to follow when conducting missing heir research, as each case is different, if for nothing else, based upon the amount of initial information that was either available or given to commence the tracing of a family.

In this example, you have now found the specific city in Russia; you have found whom you believe to be heirs; you have had your contracts and documents translated, you have sent them to your Russian correspondent; and in this case, assume that the heir actually signed everything he was asked, and in an expeditious manner, the first time around and without any fee negotiations or negotiations of the contractual terms and conditions. Next, you must now gather all of the records and documents throughout Russia and the United States and present them to the court in an understandable and logical format, taking into account variations in the spelling of names, cities that no longer exist, countries that no longer exist, and attempt to prove to the court, that in fact you have found the right heirs beyond any question or doubt. The waiting process begins. If there is one thing that you will learn in this business, it is to never count your money before you have it in hand! Moving on, the case is now scheduled to go to court for a Determination of Heirship proceeding, wherein our heir in Russia is supposed to be declared the lawful and only heir to the estate. You have spent thousands of dollars, countless hours, an untold amount of phone calls, but you are smiling because all is well. Suddenly and without expectation, you now receive a call from the Personal Representative or the attorney for the estate. He proceeds to tell you that they never opened a safe deposit box until yesterday, and when they did, they found a valid will disposing of the estate to a well-known charity. That is the end, case closed, no recovery for the heir and worse, no recovery for you, including for the expenses you actually advanced as hard money.

This is one of the biggest risks in the industry of heir finding as it applies to forensic genealogy. There is almost never anything certain when locating heirs or proving an entitlement.

In contrast, let us assume the same scenario but with a will that bequeaths everything to a Mr. John Smith, address unknown, who formerly resided at 123 Main Street in Tacoma, Washington. This is a completely different case now. You need only to locate and prove that one person's former address and, if a relative (it could have been a friend), the matching evidentiary documents.

There is also an interesting licensing issue at hand: Is this a private investigation for which a license is required, or forensic genealogy which is an unlicensed genealogical activity? One could argue that in a case with no names, it is genealogy; however, in a case with a specific named missing person, it is a private investigation. On the other hand, one could equally as well argue that they are both genealogical matters and neither requires licensure. This is especially important as genealogical investigation and research work is conducted in every state and worldwide. You will never know in advance in what jurisdiction you shall be conducting your research. The state of Florida handled this very nicely: The licensing statute for private investigations specifically exempts people whose primary business is locating missing heirs. Once again, to always err on the side of safety, our recommendation is that all personnel within each hold a private investigative license and all cases originate from your home state where you are licensed.

Cases have run the gamut: Brothers and sisters who lie by denying that that they have no other siblings, contemplating a larger share. Then there are husbands and wives who each have wills leaving their estates to the other, and one dies but the survivor believes they already have a valid will yet in truth, although the Will is valid, the disposition is now in question. What if there are spouses who die in a simultaneous accident or crash? Who was the survivor and whose heirs inherit? What are the provisions if there is a will and what if the laws of Intestacy dominate when there is no will? This is especially important if this was the second marriage for each, and each had surviving children by a prior marriage. The heirship fight is now on.

Locating missing heirs to estates is not for the faint of heart, due to the many challenges and unknowns that lie ahead, including the possibility that there are truly no heirs who can inherit based upon the law. So what happens if heirs cannot be found or if there are none who can legally inherit? The states have found an answer. The remaining assets are deposited into the treasury of each applicable state, usually into its education fund, earning interest for the state. The process is called "Escheat." Claimants have a statutorily limited time frame to attempt to recover the money, typically 20 years. After that, claims are barred, and title to the money (real estate, stocks, and bonds will be liquidated), reverts permanently to the state forever and is unrecoverable. Should you have an heir who wants to make claim within the statutory period, just look at what you are facing: The State with unlimited resources and a multitude of lawyers on staff desirous of retaining the money versus you and your client. Rest assured it will be in an expensive legal battle if there is any gray area at all. The same is also somewhat true for unclaimed insurance policies.

Obviously, you have seen the advertisements on TV and the web to visit each state's unclaimed property section. This used to be a good place for heirfinders to look for cases. Then, some states limited the fees that can be charged to 10%, and have established waiting periods before one can even assert a claim by a third party.

Hopefully, you now have a little better insight into the field of locating missing and unknown heirs. Yes, it can be lucrative, but be prepared to continue to pay your light bills, employees, and expenses, as the probate process rolls along. Usually you will not see any distribution for a year or even longer, especially if it is a foreign case. To exist, you need to fill a pipeline with cases and hope they spit out with some degree of frequency.

"How does one find the cases to work on in the first place?", you may ask. One method is to compensate employees who go to courts on a regular basis to personally examine newly filed estate matters; then there are freelancers who have agreed to receive a commission for cases first brought by the heirfinder's attention; referrals from lawyers, banks, and the judicial system as well as guardians, personal representatives; and newspaper obituaries, news stories, police agencies, medical examiners, and administrators. Some firms also pay a finders fee to whomever first makes them aware of a case in which they are eventually successful, but at the conclusion of the matter, providing there are no legal conflicts. We suggest you get the word out by doing public speaking at many different types of organizations, clubs, and associations; as well as by advertising in legal periodicals and by attending many types of Bar, Estate Planning and Tax seminars and conventions.

Chapter 11

THE CRAFT OF BUSINESS INTELLIGENCE: AN AMERICAN VIEW

FRED W. RUSTMANN, JR.

Business is war. And in war, it is a matter of survival of the fittest. In order to survive in today's cutthroat business environment, we must be properly armed. And one of the most important arrows in the executive's quiver is accurate knowledge of competitors and their business environment. In other words, detailed knowledge of the enemy and the terrain of the battlefield.

Every major country on earth recognizes the importance of intelligence and employs an intelligence agency to collect it for them. Over 2,500 years ago, the Chinese General Sun Tzu wrote: *If you know the enemy and know yourself, you need not fear the result of a hundred battles. If you know yourself but not the enemy, for every victory gained you will also suffer a defeat. If you know neither the enemy nor yourself, you will succumb in every battle.* Frederick the Great also expressed his opinion on the importance of intelligence when he said: *It is pardonable to be defeated, but never surprised.* In today's highly competitive business world it is becoming more and more important to know your competition—know your enemy—and, particularly in the international arena, to know your battlefield. There are minefields out there, and it is imperative to be able to identify and avoid them. You can still lose, even when armed with superior forces, if the terrain is against you. Possessing accurate intelligence is like having a flashlight in the dark. It won't remove any of the obstacles in your path, but it will illuminate them so you will not stumble.

Realizing the importance of good, solid intelligence is the first step toward being prepared. The second step is employing experts to collect that intelligence. Some companies (W.R. Grace, AT&T, for example) have special competitive intelligence units within their organization structure. Others hire professional consultants from outside of the organization to handle their intelligence collection requirements or augment their efforts. Either way, the craft of intelligence gathering and analysis is sufficiently arcane that it should be left to the experts. CIA case officers, for example, spend about a year attending formal intelligence training courses before being released to employ their skills abroad. Part of what they learn is how to collect information discreetly through the use of clandestine tradecraft methods, how to evaluate the sources of that information, and how to report that information accurately, objectively, and dispassionately. The FBI and some police departments also run intelligence collection courses for their officers. The main difference between the CIA training and the FBI/police training is that the latter places more emphasis on techniques that utilize the power of the badge, while the CIA employs a more covert approach, relying more heavily on the use of cover and deniability to assure a greater degree of discretion in its collection efforts.

Companies employing in-house resources often have difficulty in obtaining objective information because of problems with training, resources, and vested interests. Company personnel are usually not trained in intelligence collection techniques, the companies usually do not have the requisite resources (computer databases, personal contacts, etc.) to collect the information they need, and, finally, employees with a stake in the company's output will almost certainly lack the objectivity to report information accurately, without bias. The tendency is to paint pictures that support company policy or please superiors. This is precisely why professional intelligence consultants from outside the organization should be called in to handle the most sensitive intelligence gathering missions.

Generally, business intelligence can be broken down into three main categories:

Risk Analysis. This is general background information that a company needs to know to operate securely and effectively in an unfamiliar environment (usually international) where economic, political, criminal, insurgent, labor, or other forces could adversely affect a company's operations. This is usually multisource, analytical-type information. It is designed to prepare a company for all eventualities, and to allow it to operate with "no surprises."

Targeted Collection. This is specific information the company can use to increase its productivity or market share. Market analysis; due diligence; background investigations on potential partners, employees, and others; and competitor intelligence all fall into this category.

Counterintelligence. When proprietary information on a company's process, patent, copyright, product, etc. is leaked, pirated, copied, or outright stolen by a competitor, there is a compelling need to plug the leak and prosecute the offending parties. The purpose of counterintelligence is to collect information that will identify the spies within the company and the organization behind them and to provide enough evidence to obtain convictions or press suits in a court of law. It is interesting to note that the White House estimates the U.S. economy loses $100 billion a year due to the theft of proprietary information.

Within the U.S. government, intelligence collection requirements are generated by the White House, the Pentagon, and State, Justice, and other departments. In the business world, they are generated by company CEO's and other senior managers. These individuals usually know exactly what information they ought to have to insure the trouble-free, efficient running of their businesses. They may also know where to look for unique business information that would give them the competitive edge they desire; they just do not know how to go about collecting it.

Intelligence collection is a systematic process that requires excellent analytical skills and employing proven methods that assure, to the extent possible, the accuracy of the information obtained. The process begins with the requirement. What is the question? Exactly what does the CEO want to know? This is an important step in the process. It forces the CEO to analyze the problem and refine it from "I want to know everything there is to know about my competitor" to "What is my competitor's strategy to obtain the XYZ contract in Jakarta?" or "What plans does my competitor have to enter the widget market in Latin America?" Once the requirement is defined, the next step is to do a target analysis. In other words, to examine the competitor organization with an eye toward identifying where within the organization would the information be normally held (marketing department, research and development staff, legal department, etc.)? Once this is established, the scope is narrowed further down to the individuals within the target department. They are investigated and assessed to determine who would be the most knowledgeable and accessible source. Finally, when the target individual is selected, an operation is designed to extract the information from him or her. This usually requires the use of covert collection techniques including elicitation, debriefing, the use of a suitable cover for the inquiries, and other overt methods including database searches, interviews of other knowledgeable sources, and the like.

Thus, the intelligence process, whether in government or industry, involves four major steps:

1. defining the requirement;
2. collecting information on the requirement from all available overt sources (databases, library research, etc.);
3. analyzing the overtly available information and organizing it into a cogent preliminary report on the subject; and
4. identifying the gaps in the information and filling them through the use of more targeted covert collection techniques, and writing the final, comprehensive report.

This is the most efficient and efficacious approach to intelligence gathering and analysis. It is the technique used by the CIA and other government intelligence agencies, and it is the proper way for industry to collect business intelligence.

But all of this begs the question: If the collection of business intelligence is sufficiently arcane as to be left to the experts, and if the government is expert in the field, why then won't the government collect it for U.S. industry? After all, other countries, friends and foes alike, have been aggressively involved in intelligence gathering activities targeted against U.S. industry for many years. Some of these activities have even crossed the line into illegal, state-sponsored, industrial espionage. (The main difference between industrial espionage and competitive intelligence gathering is that the former uses illegal collection methods like electronic monitoring, trespass, theft, etc., while the latter does not.)

In fact, there has been considerable debate, for instance, within the government, and the CIA in particular, on this very issue. It began in earnest in 1990 when the Soviet Union collapsed and it was thought that the CIA could be retooled away from Soviet collection activities to helping the failing U.S. economy with needed business intelligence. Debate continues to this day. Unfortunately, however, there is very little chance that the U.S. government (particularly the CIA and NSA) will ever get involved in the routine collection of business intelligence for U.S. industry. The problem is that the very nature of clandestinely acquired information makes it classified–not for dissemination to the general public–because sensitive sources and collection methods must be protected. So if the decision were made to collect business information and disseminate it to companies outside the intelligence community, to whom would the information be entrusted? Certainly not to all of the companies. But then which ones? And to whom within each company? Only the CEOs? Could they be trusted not to disseminate the information down to the rank and file? Probably not. There is also a strong argument against the idea of diverting scarce government intelligence gathering resources away from the national defense to the private sector, and the ethical conundrum of asking CIA case officers to spy for IBM rather than the White House.

This is not to say that the CIA and other law enforcement agencies will not fight to prevent illegal industrial espionage in this country, or that they would fail to alert major companies if they learned, *inter alia,* that some very unfair business practices (payment of bribes, etc.) were hurting U.S. companies' chances to compete fairly in a particular country. It only means that the government will not develop and fund programs to collect business intelligence for U.S. companies. Thus, if a U.S. company wants to collect information that will help it level the playing field and perhaps give it a competitive edge over a foreign company, it must use its own resources.

Sadly, the proliferation of charlatans, crooks, and scam artists has become a fact of life in the 1990s. Outside U.S. borders, this danger is even more profound. Executives in countries lacking the laws, regulations, safeguards, and reporting requirements in place in the U.S. know that their American counterparts all too often rely solely on limited information and luck when dealing with foreigners. Consequently, they are far more inclined to engage in misrepresentation and deception in their business dealings with Americans.

Managers who choose not to do their homework before they embark on a course of action are doomed to failure. Successful people always do their homework. Years ago, when I was teaching the craft of intelligence to new CIA officers down on "The Farm," I discussed the concept of thorough preparation as the single most important key to success in the intelligence business. I explained that although all good operations officers certainly have the ability to wing it when necessary, the best officers never go into a situation with that intention. They try to prepare for every possible eventuality in advance, and then only have to improvise when a real unexpected curve is thrown at them. That is good advice for any business.

To quote Sun Tzu once again, "To remain in ignorance of the enemy's condition simply because one grudges the outlay of a hundred ounces of silver . . . is the height of inhumanity." Perhaps it would be more accurate if the word *stupidity* were substituted for *inhumanity*. The military advice that Sun Tzu espoused so long ago applies equally to today's business. Know your own and your competitor's capabilities, and know your battlefield. Armed with this knowledge, you cannot lose—the worst thing that can happen is that you decide not to engage.

Chapter 12

ON PROVIDING PERSONAL PROTECTION

STEFAN SALMONSON

The early definition of "harm" probably referred to assassination attempts and personal assault(s); however, today's personal protection agent must also consider kidnap/ransom, loss of personal/protected information, electronic eavesdropping, public embarrassment, and/or a multitude of twenty-first century risks that must be avoided, reduced, and/or mitigated. Executives, senior management, spouses, children, and even pets have become unwilling pawns in the (now) global security arena. As such, the new **protectors** (Personal Protection Specialists) must be up to the task. This brief article will examine several critical areas of consideration for both protective agents and their employers. They are by no means the definitive method(s) for protection, rather a starting point for discussing and utilizing accepted **proactive methods** based on hard lessons learned.

QUALIFICATIONS/TRAINING

The hundreds of protective agents, I have had the pleasure to work with, all had a common trait . . . their eyes reflected their intelligence. Representatives from government agencies often speak of this observation and how difficult it is to erase for successful covert missions. None of the agents were "hot dogs," "grandstanders," or "lone wolves"; rather they were very respectful, courteous, extremely competent professionals who transmitted a message to the client(s) that they were being protected 360 degrees. How does one arrive at that level of competence? Core values, diversity, talent(s), training, and experience seem to be the best place to start. I am fortunate to work with an eight-person (male/female) team. They were not only chosen because they knew their skill set(s) better than anyone, they are also the most ethical individuals I have ever met. Ethics, I have found, trumps almost every other skill set. If I can't trust you to do the right (ethical) thing, I probably can't trust you in other situations . . . most of them potentially fatal.

"I don't hire cops." That was the response to my first EP position inquiry. I have proudly spent many years as a deputy sheriff, firearms instructor, SWAT instructor, and investigator only to learn that my law enforcement experience was not a qualifying factor! When asked, why I was disqualified, the spokesperson for an international personal protection firm announced, "we can't take you out in public and you are always reactive, NOT proactive." Over the course of the next few weeks, I proved to them that I was in fact very proactive and that I could be seen in public; however, the message was clear. Appearance, demeanor, and staying ahead of the curve were definitely the rule! I later observed employees being sent home for picking a portable radio up by the antenna. That might seem drastic until you can't commo because your radio malfunctions due to a damaged antenna.

Graduating from an established/recognized EP program(s) (Examples: Executive Protection Institute, ESI) is also helpful. Consider it "basic training" for agents. It will not guarantee you a job, but you will (probably) use same/similar techniques as do other agents. Experience will hone those techniques into valuable skills.

I have found that there is one (1) constant as an EP agent. That constant is **change!**

ETIQUETTE

Even though many details are run "low key" and informal, there remains the possibility that your principal will attend a formal dinner/reception. If agents are not familiar with the formal protocol (process) or the specifics of the formal event, if can be a very uncomfortable evening for everyone. Discrete protective agents will need to be seated in close proximity to the principal. Needless to say, the wine glass should be turned over as a signal to the waiting staff to pass you by. Perimeter agents need to "blend in" with others, appear to mingle, and yet remain vigil for threats or embarrassing moments. A word of caution. A day in the sun can significantly dehydrate an adult. Imbalanced electrolytes may cause your principal to suddenly collapse . . . in their food. Enough said.

Additional dining considerations would include any/all known allergies of the principal(s). Risk mitigation would include knowledge of local hospitals, their medical specialties, and the availability of an "epinephrine pen." Corporate executive support personnel and nannies (for children) will have prior knowledge of food and/or other allergies.

LICENSING/INSURANCE/PASSPORTS

As always, "who is liable" is a key phrase that must be addressed. "Due diligence" negligence is very expensive. Is your detail operating in a State where licensing is mandatory? (Note: Assuming you are providing services for hire.) Many state attorneys general may charge you criminally for unlicensed activities. Take time to research State laws and subcontractor (employment) options.

Don't just buy the most cost-effective business insurance you can find. Take the time to locate a professional specialty insurance agent who can explain the specifics of the policy and your associated liabilities. Many of our corporate clients require that they be co-listed on our policy. Surprisingly, that simple request disqualified many of our (former) competitors.

I also suggest purchasing an additional personal umbrella policy. A multimillion dollar policy is typically a few hundred dollars annually. If needed, it is money well spent.

A current passport with greater than six (6) months remaining before expiration is mandatory.

If escorting a parent/guardian and child to a foreign country, be sure to verify travel rules when only one of the two parents/guardians are traveling with their child.

THREAT ASSESSMENT(S)

An initial client request for service(s) will usually include a **perceived threat**. Often someone "in house" has determined that there is a clear and present danger; hence, the request for the service(s). We also generate a threat/risk assessment based on the information supplied (Example: Order For Protection violation against a victim employee), recent criminal history of the subject/suspect, InfraGard information, OSAC (Over Seas Advisory Council), local Law Enforcement reports/input, and/or our own protocols (Example: High Risk Employment Termination). We have found that safety and human resources professionals are excellent client contacts, are considered senior management, and have access to critical information.

Locate and partner with seasoned mental health professionals who have extensive experience working with PTSD and "return to duty" issues. Their efforts and associated documentation are critical, especially when dealing with **workplace violence** security concerns. Their input may turn out to be a critical piece of the threat assessment puzzle.

Having a basic understanding of diversity is also highly recommended. Comments, gestures, and/or showing the bottom of a foot may offend the client. I was required to read *Kiss, Bow or Shake Hands* (Morrison, Conaway, Borden) early in my EP career and I still recommend the book as a reference guide today. The book does not replace high quality diversity training; however, it will give your diversity awareness a jump start.

ADVANCE WORK

The key to any successful detail is quality advance work. The more experience the advance agent possesses, the more efficiently the detail will run. In short . . . the agent will provide you with the answers before the questions are asked. The information they (advance agents) compile should include maps, GoogleEarth and MapQuest printouts, flight schedules and possible delays, vehicle traffic patterns and road construction, hotel and restaurant reviews, medical facilities and their associated specialties, points of interests requested by the client(s), and additional risks that were identified during the course of the advance work. For last-minute and up-to-date road construction and related route delay(s) intel, the package delivery professionals, in their colored vans, are an excellent resource. Remember, they are on a tight schedule but always seem happy to help another professional. If there is a better route, they will know it!

FORMATIONS

Diamond, modified diamond, and single agent are all recognized protection formations. Your principal, surroundings, level of risk, and activity will dictate the formation at any given time. Experienced teams will rely on hand signals, body movements, and (it would appear) each other's thoughts to provide a choreography of protection formations. The more experienced the team, the smoother the flow of the protection. When asked how close a principal wanted his security detail, the principal replied, "I want them close enough to protect me and yet far enough away that I don't have to introduce them."

Be extremely vigilant in England and British or former British possessions. U.S. principals and agents tend to look the wrong way when stepping from the curb into the active roadway. You will only make the mistake once!

PROTECTION OPTIONS

The subject of personal protection is often associated with firearms or other weapons; however, a lesser "use of force" may be the only option needed. "Presence" is usually the lowest level of force with "deadly force" at the extreme end of the scale. Juries will have ample time to decide if the agent made the right choice in a split-second decision. If licensed to use weapons, train often and accurately with a strong knowledge of the "use of force" continuum and its relevance.

Learn to use your "presence" and well-choreographed movements as a deterrent against a random street attack or if under surveillance, that your detail would be a "hardened target."

Agents should be practiced in multiple forms of defensive and offensive tactics. The form(s) should be subtle and yet immediately effective. The exception is to "sound off" regarding imminent danger(s), detected weapon(s), and/or an evacuation based on an (AOP) attack on the principal (see Formations).

Firearms, for CQB (Close Quarter Battle), should have maximum stopping power and limited penetration. With the exception of shoulder-fired weapons, pistols (hand fired) should have maximum effectiveness (translates to stopping power) and limited penetration. Ammunition manufacturers produce "expanding" rounds that transfer all of their energy into the target and not through it. Innocent bystanders (collateral damage), not to mention other agents, are put at risk every time the trigger is pulled. Choose your type (revolver or semiautomatic) of firearm, brand, caliber, spare ammunition, and holster well. Consider purchasing specialty vests (casual) and other clothing that conceal a firearm. Other equipment should include an LED flashlight, small med kit, lock picks and key extractor(s), camera (use phone, if high quality), and spare cell phone and radio batteries.

Courses in IED (Improvised Explosive Device) recognition, VBIED (Vehicle Borne Improvised Explosive Device) methods, suicide vest/ clothing, and general bomb awareness should be mandatory for all agents.

TRANSPORTATION/VEHICLES

I have found that motorcades are often the most difficult and dangerous portion of any detail. In this case, the threat is not external, rather it is internal. Several 4,000–6,000 pound vehicles all traveling the same direction should not pose a significant safety problem; however, experience has shown otherwise! Turning, parking, capturing lanes, loading and unloading all have specific risks involved. Add seating and/or arrival protocols and the fiasco gets even worse! Locate the most experienced local driver(s) who have motorcade (or similar) experience. If none are available, teach them to:

- Drive and do nothing else! As a flight instructor, I am constantly reminding student pilots to "fly the airplane." Everything else is initially secondary.
- Inform them that you and your arrival/departure agents will operate the doors. Yes, they will still get a tip.

- Stay in the car when it is parked. Their (drivers) presence is a security multiplier. Nonglare, transparent tape placed across door, trunk, moon roof and hood gaps make good intrusion detection indicators if secure parking is not available. Extendable pocket mirrors work well for "clearing" wheel wells and the undercarriage of the vehicle.
- Don't smoke, chew tobacco, or "snap" gum. Odors and annoyances are plentiful enough.
- Wear appropriate attire and keep it clean.
- Keep the vehicle clean, full of fuel (planning!), and in good repair.
- Be cautious of interpersonal, cell phone, and radio language. someone is always listening!

Needless to say, locating and maintaining a list of professional drivers in each of your destinations is of paramount importance.

COMMUNICATIONS/ELECTRONIC SECURITY

Cellular phones (with and without push to talk) have been a wonderful addition to the EP agent's communication options. Instantaneous communications over a distance still requires portable radios, repeaters, and the associated base stations, if a command post is applicable. Many teams now rent/lease satellite phones, radio repeaters, secure radios, and specialty microphones. Technology and the associated communication equipment are changing rapidly. We have located a reliable, secure source for our radios.

Operating the newest (relative term) equipment and having repair/replacement available upon request and at a reasonable cost makes for a safer more efficient detail.

The advent of the "smart phone" has ushered in a new wave of security-related threats. Software (Example: MobileSpy, FlexiSpy) is available for as little as $50.00, which will allow the subject/suspect to activate the GPS mode in your phone allowing them to track you continuously. Other software options will allow them to use your own phone as a discrete transmitter and listen to your conversations. Many senior managers now secure their smart phones in their offices before they enter the boardroom or they remove the battery. Excellent information, regarding guarding against this illegal software is available from legitimate TSCM (Technical Surveillance Counter Measures) providers. Be sure that you have the newest software available for your smart phone. Current software may provide limited protection against the phone being "hacked." GSM "bugs" are also now readily available to everyone.

Many members of my detail are now licensed HAM radio operators. New "no code" rules have made the classes and exam much less painful. Powerful FM transceivers, portable radios (short range) and "land line" phones may be our only options in the event of a complete wireless phone/E-mail system shut down or failure.

Sixty-plus percent of corporate security managers have indicated they are concerned with the personal information and risks associated with "social networking sites." Corporate IT/IS personnel can advise as to information currently being posted regarding schedules, planned activities, and destinations. Be sure to review the accounts of the principal's children as well. There is nothing like thousands (potentially millions) of people knowing what you are doing, when, and where!

Verify the credentials of copy repair personnel. We suggest that anyone allowed on-site, without an escort, has completed a thorough background check. Remember that every copy (itinerary, routes, personal information, scheduling) you have made on your copier remains in/on the copier hard drive. The hard drive should be "wiped" and/or erased prior to the unit being removed from your facility.

AGENT ATTIRE

Comfortable clothing and shoes will become a primary concern(s) as an EP agent. Polished shoes (if applicable) are expected; however, overdressing can also be a concern. Never out-dress your client. Nannies, a personal assistant, or a direct conversation with the principal will provide general guidance as to the apparel question(s). A wise agent always has a pressed white shirt/blouse readily available. Remember to have all ties modified by sewing "Velcro" style fasteners hidden under the collar in back. The knot remains permanent. Slip the ends of the tie around the neck and attach the two (2) ends with the fastener. Anyone attempting to use the tie as a garrote will simply pull it off the agent.

WORKPLACE VIOLENCE

Approximately half of the protection details originated in the last few years have been initiated because of workplace violence episodes. Having a proven high-risk employment termination protocol, the ability to respond 24/7 is paramount. HR professionals appreciate having competent, full-service security professional(s) in their speed dial. We also offer security assessments, background investigations, and safety/security-related training. These additional services compliment our total personal protection service.

PRESENTATIONS/MARKETING

We offer security-related presentations and training to several thousand participants each year. The materials must be current, accurate, easily implemented, and offered with the same level of professionalism that is reflected in your protective services. We also send (typically) monthly E-mails (no attachments, unless requested) to specific groups (Example: HR) that contain(s) a short security-related article or information that is timely and pertinent to them, their industry, or their company. Too many protective agents have been "right sized" or eliminated in this recession because there have been no documented attack(s) on the principal(s) and yet the team has been busy 24/7 providing high quality preventive services. The problem is that no one, in the corporate decision-making process, knew of all the prevention efforts being implemented and that your principal, unlike so many others, was not attacked, ransomed, publicly embarrassed, physically injured, and/or emotionally assaulted.

Chapter 13

PRODUCT DIVERSION

REGINALD J. MONTGOMERY

INTRODUCTION

Product diversion, by definition, refers to products sold by the manufacturer, which are distributed into markets other than originally intended by contract, law, or regulation. This enables third parties to undercut the intended price of the product to the public and reap huge profits. This international scheme hinges on an industry practice in which manufacturers set up different prices for the same product. It is a way to break into new markets and expand name recognition outside the United States. Because of tax incentives and other cost savings, American businesses can sell their products to overseas distributors at dramatically lower prices than those paid by distributors based in the United States. When products are diverted, those goods are illegally rerouted by a third party back to American markets.

The hierarchy of the pricing of products is generally familiar to most Americans. It is apparent in everyday life. One store will have a pair of designer jeans for $65.00. That same pair of jeans can be purchased at a discount store for $30.00 and at a flea market for $15.00. Sometimes this reflects nothing more than a legal pricing of merchandise that has been bought from the manufacturer at a wholesale price and sold at various discounts depending on the necessary overhead.

However, there are several tiers of wholesale. That same product might be purchased as a promotional or institutional item at a special rate, lower than the wholesale price available to the regular retail market. This allows special rates to large purchasers of merchandise who are promoting a particular product.

DIVERSION IS NOT THEFT

Most investigators have had exposure to theft of product and tend to confuse the two situations. When is it diversion and when is it theft? The answer is simple. Theft is the unauthorized taking and diversion is the unauthorized distribution achieved by misrepresentation. An example of theft can be seen in an investigation conducted several years ago.

A large manufacturer of designer leather handbags was known for its exclusive and costly product. The company did not sell to discounters. They maintained the quality and exclusivity of their bags because of this limited, but highly priced market. Someone happened to purchase a bag with the designer label from a street vender. To all appearances it was an identical bag. In fact, when compared with a sample from Bloomingdales' showroom floor, it was exactly the same. Upon this discovery, the manufacturer initiated an investigation. It involved the placing of an undercover operative inside the workroom of a company that was subcontracted to assemble and finish the handbags. The operative discovered that the theft was actually an internal problem being perpetrated by one of the senior management personnel in collusion with a subcontractor. Records indicated that only three bags could be cut from a piece of leather. The remainder was written off as scrap. In reality, if the patterns were laid out carefully, an extra two bags could be cut from each piece of leather. This allowed thousands of additional bags to be made, right in the subcontractor's own workroom. The overage was shipped to wholesalers who undercut the product and sold it through venders on city street corners. In fact, it was the same bag and of the same quality. This is theft.

HOW DIVERSION OCCURS

Diversion will most likely occur in the areas of:

- Export sales
- Promotional offers

- Regional promotions
- Samples, trial and travel packs
- Hotel amenities
- Charitable donations
- U.S. (and foreign) government sales
- Destruction of excess merchandise

A classic example is an investigation that was successfully conducted on a dental supply company. For purposes of anonymity and client confidentiality, it shall be referred to here as PC Dental Supply. This is a company that sells products to dentists and institutions where dental work is performed. In May, PC Dental negotiated a special promotional package with ABC Hygiene Company to distribute small bottles (3 oz.) of ABC's most popular mouthwash. The promotion stated that for every $500 in mouthwash sales, the institution would be given a free case of mouthwash to be provided to patients at the time of their yearly checkup. Everything looked legitimate until the records began to indicate that PC Dental had purchased in excess of 100,000 cases of mouthwash in a four-month period. That's over a million small bottles. The original contract allowed ABC's representatives (in this instance, the investigators) to review the records of PC Dental.

This is a key factor in the ability of an investigator to prove effective for his client. When products are purchased according to these specific discount schedules, there is a contract negotiated between the manufacturer and the purchaser. This contract gives the specific right for the manufacturer, or his representative, to review all records related to the purchase and distribution of the discounted product.

The investigators were, therefore, able to review and compare shipping, receiving, and payment records. A large portion of the mouthwash order had allegedly been shipped to a hospital distributor in California. With the help of a local investigator, the distributor's receiving clerk and warehousemen were interviewed. They swore that they never saw, received, or unloaded this product. There were no records of buying the product and no one had ever heard of PC Dental. Ultimately, admissions were obtained from the parties involved in the diversion. Armed with the documents provided by the diverter in the paper trail, information was uncovered proving that the intended party never received the merchandise.

The culprits "rolled over" when interviewed and their statements were verified by polygraph. The product was actually sold to a wholesaler in Brooklyn and then to a large distributor in Maryland. The Brooklyn wholesaler originated and financed the scheme.

This was a diversion case. It was a contractual matter because PC Dental misrepresented the stated and intended use of the product from its contractual agreement, and it was also a fraud. In addition, because it involved more than one party, it was a conspiracy to commit fraud. Because PC Dental was located in New Jersey, the institution in California, the wholesaler in Brooklyn, and the distributor, who ultimately received the product, in Maryland, it became an interstate situation, and thus a RICO charge. The corporate client was interested only in recouping the money they had lost because of product underselling. By invoking the contractual agreement, which allowed for treble damages and the payment of the difference between the very low wholesale price and the actual retail price to the consumer, they were able to recover their lost profit. A negotiated settlement was agreed upon. This case exemplifies the difference in theft and diversion. It also is indicative of the various consequences of diversion in the legal world.

DIVERSION VERSUS OTHER FORMS OF PRODUCT ABUSE

It can be said that diversion is unauthorized distribution achieved by misrepresentation. Diversion is a result of established contractual relationships between the manufacturer and the distributor. When that product is purchased at one price but diverted for a separate and unintended use, it falls within the scope of the product diversion case. Since the concept of diversion is so specific and generally not understood by the public, it is often confused with several other areas of product abuse:

Counterfeiting is the making of an item to look like the original. Generally, it is of lesser quality.

Pirating is the theft of product, such as the bootlegging of HBO or pay-per-view cable programs that are normally sold (such as boxing matches and soccer matches that sell exclusively through television venders).

Trademark infringement involves the use of a name or label, which closely approximates that of the original, authorized manufacturer. We have all seen Cucci, instead of Gucci and initialed designer clothing

Gray market also deals with the sale of American branded products which are manufactured for less in foreign countries and sold in the United States for lower than retail prices. It is not uncommon for items such as shampoo, which is made in Mexico (where the peso is grossly devalued), to be purchased from that source and brought into the U.S. to be sold in Spanish-speaking neighborhoods. The item is purchased for less, sold for less, and has the added value of being labeled in Spanish. These nondiversion forms of product abuse need to be understood, so that the investigator learning about the intricacies of diversion will not confuse them.

THE FOUR AREAS OF DIVERSION

Concentration in the remainder of this chapter will be on four specific areas where product intended for one market is diverted to another: (1) charity, (2) closeout or counterfeit dating, (3) market diversion, and (4) dated product.

Charity

Charity diversions are not only unethical but illegal as well. A prime example of this type of diversion can be seen in the area of comestibles. Food packages are coded uniquely by manufacturers, and each item has a "shelf life" (a date after which the product should not be sold; frequently product safety is an issue, but also used to insure product flow and turnover). When its shelf life has expired, the product is not necessarily unfit for consumption (in fact, it is generally good for a year or more after that date—except, of course, for milk and dairy products). Therefore, when a product has come within a month or so of its shelf life, the retail store (supermarket) will remove it from the shelves. The store receives credit for this unused product from the manufacturer, so there is no loss to them. In the name of goodwill, these products are often shipped to local food banks where they can be purchased at minimal prices by homeless shelters and state subsidized nursery facilities.

The author was once retained in a case where an individual was purchasing great amounts of grocery products from the food bank, alleging to be supplying a daycare center. In fact, what he was doing was storing the product in two rooms of the center (limiting the space for the children) and selling the product on weekends at local flea markets for his own profit. This is a classic case of diversion.

Closeout or Counterfeit Dating

Closeout or counterfeit dating involves these same "shelf life" dates. Often items are packaged in cases and the expiration date for use is stamped all over the outside of the carton. There are highly sophisticated syndicates that specialize in "repackaging" product and stamping new, later expiration dates on the outside. Therefore, they are selling outdated products which appear to be timely. When the closeout dates are replaced by new dates on original packaging by innovative diverters, this is the diversion of product from its intended use. In most cases, this product would be destined for destruction.

Market Diversion

Market diversion is common. It can be observed simply by walking through the ever growing weekend flea market or observing product sold by street venders.

A recent case involved the exposure of a large diverter who was purchasing merchandise by the truckload at institutional promotional prices and selling that same product through regular retail stores. The item was cough syrup. The stated, contractual use of this product was to place a packet of cough syrup in college kits to be given to new students as promotional merchandise. (Similar "kits" are given to hospital patients and generally include a miniature toothbrush, toothpaste, hand cream, and talcum powder.) Because of the stated use, the buyer/diverter was given a large discount off of the normal wholesale cost for these items. The buyer/diverter ordered 40 tractor-trailer loads of this cough syrup. Simple arithmetic would dictate that there was enough cough syrup for every man, woman, and child in the United States to stem a sore throat for a year! The quantity raised corporate eyebrows and an investigation ensued. Surveillance and investigation revealed that the cough syrup was being repackaged and sold directly to retail channels, tripling the normal profit for the buyer/diverter.

Dated Product

Dated product, as previously explained, does not necessarily become unusable after the expiration date has lapsed. One has but to walk through a flea market to note a large variety of items generally seen on supermarket shelves for sale at extraordinarily low prices. A closer inspection of items such as pharmaceutical products (Tylenol®, aspirin, Neosporin® cream, etc.) will reveal that the bottles have dates that have expired. The products were most likely taken off the shelves with intent to be either returned to the manufacturer or sent to another venue by the manufacturer for sale at a lesser price. Their presence in flea markets is indicative of some sort of fraud to the consumer that also lessens the value of the product to the manufacturer.

While the traditional methods of surveillance (undercover operatives, taking witness statements, and interviews) are often useful, the diverter maintains the real evidence himself–the paper trail of his own records. Comparing original contracts and "use" statements (in which the intended use of the product is clearly spelled out) of the diverter against those of the manufacturer is the starting point. Next, the bills of sale from the manufacturer generally provide the dates and quantities purchased and the responsible parties. Shipping orders and bills of lading should be examined and compared to warehouse receipts from receiving clerks. Checks paid for transportation of merchandise are also compared. Invoices reflecting to whom merchandise is sold and method of shipment are scrutinized. It becomes a numbers game and the numbers sometimes just don't match up.

LOSSES CAUSED BY PRODUCT DIVERSION

• First, there is a monetary loss to the Government through the payment of export incentives on goods destined for foreign countries. For example, in the Indictment returned yesterday, Nestle relied on false shipping documents allegedly provided by Kotbey to purchase refined sugar through a U.S. Agriculture Department (USDA) program that allows U.S. manufacturers to purchase sugar below U.S. market prices.

• Second, essential regulatory procedures are compromised. For example, medical devices and prescription drugs sold for export, but distributed in the United States, cause regulatory problems for the

Food and Drug Administration (FDA). Because the FDA requires U.S. pharmaceutical companies to maintain accurate records of drug distributions to aid recall in the event of defective, adulterated, or tampered products, it is particularly concerned about the public health implications of schemes involving diverted prescription drugs.

Although the pharmaceutical products involved in this case are not known to have been mishandled, the diversion of these products violates the strict FDA record keeping requirements regarding sales of prescription drugs, which brings into question the ability of pharmaceutical manufacturers to recall specific lots of drugs, and subjects the drug products to undocumented and potentially unsafe storage and distribution methods.

INDICATORS OF DIVERSION

Word of mouth. Frequently salespersons or even consumers provide information about merchandise being sold for cheaper prices.

The numbers. Figures indicate that sales are down, yet there is an increasing volume of the company product available in a given demographic area.

Complaints. Customers call with the irritating news that they have competitors within their sales area undercutting their price structure.

Physical evidence. Stores, which are not known to carry the product line, are seen to stock and advertise the merchandise at ridiculously low prices. New markets are opened which did not carry the product line previously.

Ineffective marketing. Promotional sales do not result in increased profits.

Profits decline. Merchandise is "on the street" in volume, but the bottom line is not indicative of its sale.

THE ROLE OF THE INVESTIGATOR

Identify the Diversion

This is generally the role of the company. Once the indicators have been observed, management should start pooling its resources to determine the extent of the problem. However, the investigator can become involved at this early stage to organize the proper investigation and obtain information from various sources known to management. Look for unusual shipping requests, excessively large volumes of merchandise going to geographic locations that could not handle the market glut, and so forth. Examining the company's own sales records is perhaps the most logical and effective starting place.

TRACKING SUSPICIOUS SALES

Internal security can secretly mark product in a particular manner which will allow them to determine if merchandise allegedly destined for overseas finds its way to store shelves in the United States. Import databases maintained for cargo vessels, airplane exports, etc. are a source of information, which can be used to verify that materials earmarked for foreign markets are actually shipped to those locations.

USING INFORMANTS

Inside information is perhaps the most reliable source of data. Persons within the industry (drivers, warehousemen, etc.) are often cooperative as informants. In lieu of these aides, investigators can place infiltrators or undercover operatives within suspected warehouses to observe activity firsthand.

Informants can be developed as part of a negotiated settlement that could have resulted in their prosecution. The investigator is instrumental in identifying these individuals and soliciting their cooperation.

INVESTIGATING THROUGH THE SALES FORCE

Diversion cannot happen without the cooperation of someone within the corporation's own sales force, either by conscious collusion or inattention to obviously suspicious circumstances. When a company (such as PC Dental) places an order that is highly unusual, exceeds the normally placed order by hundreds or thousands of dollars, and commits itself to spending money it could not possibly afford to invest, then there is something amiss. The investigator can pull a D&B on the firm, check its assets, and determine its normal functioning ability. These are indicators of a possible diversion scheme in the works. If this is done prior to completing the sale, the potential for fraud is reduced or eliminated.

COUNTERMEASURES

Positive Action

Strong company policy, ironclad contractual agreements, and stiff penalties for dealing with diverters are all preventive steps. Written policy regarding dealing with diverters should be issued. Prohibitions against changing established price categories for purchasers should be enforced, unless justification can be offered. Contracts which prohibit purchasers from ever dealing with the company again and financial penalties for misuse of the product will hinder the potential diverter. Removing the commission from the salesperson who authorizes the sale to a diverter should quickly put an end to collusion.

Regular Checkups

Just like going to the doctor, large purchasers of merchandise should receive regular checkups. A periodic review of records, shipping documents, bills of lading, and the like can and should be performed. The investigator is perhaps the best person to act as the auditor in such a circumstance. Armed with knowledge of the potential for fraud, he can determine if purchase orders, bills of lading, transportation invoices, and accounts receivable checks are indicative of dealing with diverters.

Examples

There is a reality to be recognized and understood. The profits gained by product diversion are astronomical. The possibilities are only limited by the imagination of the diverter. In order to combat the problem, the penalties must be great. The investigation must be conclusive and undeniable. The evidence is in the paper trail, and it must be uncovered by methodical attention to detail. Inconsistencies must be uncovered, discrepancies noted, unusual activity recognized and the possibility for fraud thoroughly investigated.

There has been a resurgence of interest in product diversion by manufacturers and legitimate distributors because of the growing number of diverters. The United States Department of Justice, U.S. Attorney's Office has been bearing down on the diverters. Charges ranging from wire fraud to defrauding the United States Customs Service have been levied against a wide variety of persons involved in the trade of diversion.

The following are excerpts from a classic case, which might prove useful to investigators pursuing this line of endeavor. This is, at the very least, interesting reading for any investigator whose trade revolves around the uncovering of criminal activity. Conspiracy, wire fraud, mail fraud, false statements on a matter within the jurisdiction of a federal agency, the interstate transportation of goods taken by fraud, and the issuing of false bills of lading constitute a large number of the charges you will read about in the following citations.

PREVENTION

Diversion is a totally preventable abuse of product distribution. A well-versed product diversion investigator accompanied by a motivated management team could bring diversion activity to a standstill. Strong corporate policy accompanied by strict controls and harsh contractual penalties would be the first step.

Prophylactic measures can be conducted to avoid the possibility of diversion. Tracking can be done of all large wholesale cash purchases. This is especially important where wholesalers are requesting tier discount pricing for such specialties as closeouts, charity, or international sales.

Product coding (lot numbers, including dating, intended distributor, factory designation, and special packaging) should all be employed as part of the manufacturing process. Contracts should be backed by performance bonds to ensure that distributors maintain the intended lines of distribution. Product and price integrity could be maintained if the proper programs and contracts were put in place. Enforcement of controls and policy must be maintained in order to provide notice to diverters that distribution abuse will not be tolerated. These measures, and their maintenance, are only cost effective for Class A companies.

While the East Coast seems to be the home of an abundance of diverters, diversion can and does occur almost everywhere. The investigative work is exacting and the hours of thrashing through documents seem endless. However, there is nothing quite like the satisfaction which comes from successfully putting the pieces together.

Aggressive corporate policy and security departments that have committed the proper resources, own use agreements, strong distribution contracts, and experienced diversion investigators have recovered millions and millions of dollars of lost profits for many companies. This specialized investigative arena is the home of some of the country's most capable investigators.

Chapter 14

INTERNET PROFILING

Michele Stuart

Internet Profiling is the ability of using open source resources located on the World Wide Web. There are many who feel trying to keep up with the constant change can be somewhat exhausting. Where do I start? How do I limit the information returned? How do I search the subject I am looking for? Have you ever asked those questions, or heard someone else ask them? Learning some simple tips can help you with your research.

Public records are a great source of information that not many use anymore. These records maintain a goldmine of information. Public records, such as corporate; ucc(s); property, civil, and criminal records; inmates; sex offenders; births, deaths, and marriages are now easily accessible at many levels. However, with the constant barrage of privacy advocates and the threat of identity theft, the federal government and independent states are trying to close or restrict access to these records. Thus, our ability to ascertain these records is becoming more limited year after year. For now, learn how to find them and how to use them.

Many of these records can now be accessed via the internet. A simple search within Google, such as "corporation commission," will bring up links for almost all states; however, there are also sites that have categorized hundreds if not thousands of links for you. Using these sites will help you streamline your time by providing them for you in one location. Examples of some of these sites are: www.public recordcenter.com; www.blackbookonline.com; www.brbpub.com.

For instance, using www.publicrecordcenter.com, and clicking on the state of your research, will then provide you with links for every county, city, or municipality that may have online searching available. A great place to locate one's address (and assets) is the County Tax Assessor's Office. In Arizona, our Assessor's page is located at www .maricopa.gov and has an abundance of search capabilities. Not only can you locate current ownership of an address, ownership of rental properties, recorded deed information, financial statements, and lien information, it also allows you to search for civil, criminal, and justice records. The information ascertained from these records can be beneficial in the sense that you may establish a new address, sometimes a telephone number, spouse names, children's names, business affiliations, financial history, and possibly securing a date of birth.

When using the tax assessor's records, it is always important to also search for "recorded information." Although the person or business that you are researching may not have any current property ownership, this search will show the transfer of ownership of the property. This can assist in identifying any new business entities (or personal relationships) that may be affiliated to the subject and/or business. During litigation, many times, research will find that property was being transferred into other entities by their owners to hide their assets. Searching recorded documents will provide you with the necessary information needed to show fraudulent transfers of these assets.

Using open sources can be used in researching assets or conducting corporate intelligence research. There are numerous areas covered by public records that can assist with this research. For example, corporate records and Uniform Commercial Codes located at the Secretary of States office (or Corporation Commission) can provide officer and director information, address information, stockholder information, company history, and annual reports. The information you will be able to access depends on whether the company is publicly held or privately owned.

Publicly owned companies have to follow federal guidelines disclosing information such as, but not limited to, their locations, history information, names of affiliated persons (officers/directors etc.), and most importantly, financial records. A good source of business information can be searched at the Edgar database located at the Securities and Exchange Commission website at: http://www.sec.gov/edgar/search

edgar/webusers.htm.

Moving away from public records and into the world of open sources, when researching a subject, remember to change up your search criteria. You may start with a longer search phrase, then narrow it down with limited words to try to establish a more specific return of results. Learning how to properly conduct searches is very important to obtaining the best results. Google provides a link explaining the "cheats" to use within their search engine at http://www.googleguide .com/advanced_operators_reference.html.

For example, if you are searching for information on Michele Stuart, you want to make sure that you search it as "michele stuart" as you are asking for only Michele Stuart to be located, not every Michele and every Stuart. Also remember to search the name backwards "stuart michele," as many directories (such as associations) lists their members by last name first. Additionally, remember to manipulate your search as names can be misspelled. The common spelling for Michele is normally Michelle. However, don't forget to run by nicknames as Michele can be Shelly, Mich, Mickey; Robert can be Bob or Bobby; William can be Will, Bill, or Billy.

Every day we use search engines and directories on the internet to help us find information on a person, business, and product or just to have a question that needs to be answered. While going to these sites, do you have any idea if it is a search engine or a directory? To understand the difference, we need to know how they work. Search engines, such as Google, search databases of information using "robots" or "spiders." These robots/spiders will map out the links between sites located on the web. On the other hand, directories, such as Yahoo, are sites that have been categorized by humans and placed into directories. They provide a "broader" picture of the web; however, they may not be as receptive to Boolean searching. Remember, if you only have a general idea of what you are trying to research, directory searching is very useful.

Databases are a good starting point; however, the web opens up a whole portal to the personal side of a person. We can use these free online sources to assist us in locating the target, relative or associate information, and business affiliations.

Remember to always try to take the information you find and cross-reference it with additional sources, as not everything found on the

Internet is to be considered the truth! Again, learning how information is stored on the web leads us to understanding where to search. First search will be via Google, Yahoo, or Alta Vista (or any other of your favorite search sites). Then there is a whole other layer to the web called the "deep web" or more commonly known as the "invisible web." This area of the World Wide Web is where the more personal information can be found. It has been reported that this "invisible" layer of the web is **500** times larger than the surface web. This surface area is what is normally searched by the basic "Google" searches.

One of the largest sources of information available to us now is social networking sites. As of May 2010, Facebook listed over 400 million users with an average of 130 friends each (http://www.face book.com/press/info.php?statistics). MySpace has been estimated to have approximately 122 million users. The amount of information ascertained from these sites can be incredible.

Again, learning how to locate associated profiles is important. When profiling individuals, we can use numerous identifiers as search options. Now, the most important and useful information used for researching is the subject's name, email address, or username. The following sites, used for pulling up a lot of social networking information, are unique as they don't only focus on a search engine results but pull information from several deep web sources. They will pull data from search results, images, email searches, documents, address/telephone information, and social networking sites (www.pipl.com, www.123people.com, www.cvgadget.com, www.peekyou.com and one of the best comprehensive searches for social networking affiliations is www.spokeo.com).

Again, with the mass amount of information available on the internet, our lives personally and professionally have changed. Professionally, it also provides us the ability to conduct a more thorough profile on our subjects. Profiling takes time and patience, but the results can be amazing.

Chapter 15

THREAT ASSESSMENTS
AND INTERVENTIONS

DANA PICORE

A person can pose a grave threat without articulating it.
Some people who make threats ultimately pose threats;
some people who pose threats never make threats.

–National Institute of Justice

When navigating the world of workplace violence, you are indeed navigating a world of uncertainty. Human beings, by the very nature of their heads and hearts, are full of volatility. However, as a security professional, my job has been to win against nature and predict the unpredictable.

Threat assessment and management is an integral part of keeping the mystery out of violence and anticipating aggressive behavior among employees once a threat has been made—verbal or otherwise. However, unfortunately, it is an area that can often feel like a mystery itself. While the layers to threat assessment are countless, there is fundamental information that everyone should know to be better able to protect their safety and the safety of others. And although it is important to note that the pages that follow do not and should not serve as a step-by-step guide to assessing a potential threat, it is my hope that they do offer guidance when working with a trained threat assessment expert.

Let's begin with the story of Travis:

Travis joined his co-workers outside for a cigarette. It had been a stressful day at the office, and all of them were eager for a little break. Halfway through, Travis spoke up. "I'm so tired of my boss not listening to me," he complained. "Maybe if I brought in a gun one day and waved it around things would be different? Maybe then he'd finally take me seriously?" A long silence followed. No one had an answer for Travis, and after a few awkward minutes, they put out their cigarettes and returned to work together.

Another employee standing nearby had overheard Travis, and a feeling of unease settled in her gut. She reported what she had heard to Tom, the manager on duty, who himself became very concerned. He hadn't known Travis for very long—guessing it had probably been about four months since he was hired by the recruitment center.

Tom knew he needed to act immediately but had no idea what steps to take next. There was no Security Director on site, and he had never received formal training on a situation like this. He remembered a friend had once mentioned that they knew someone who conducted behavioral profiling, a threat assessment expert who could evaluate how much of a danger Travis really posed.

As Americans, we have grown fearful of terrorists. Yet while the tragedy of 9/11 has directed much of our fear toward terrorists from abroad, it is important to remember that homegrown terrorists still pose an everyday threat to our safety in the community. Ironically, despite being worlds apart, the desire for violence held by both types of extremists shares many similarities. Both want it to be grand. Both want it to be televised. Both want to kill as many people as possible. Ultimately, all of us want a voice and, more importantly, we want that voice to be heard. For some, acts of violence are the strongest voice of all.

However, in a world of fear, I choose to believe more in the power of hope. Although it may be easy to view the world as a Pandora's Box of evils, it is important to remember that Pandora was able to close the lid just in time to keep intact man's greatest gift: Hope. And just as hope lived in ancient Greece, so too should it live in our lives. In fact, it is the very word that separates us from the terrorists we fear. As we reflect on a difficult day in the mirror at night, hope lets us know things will get better. For those with violence on their minds, hopelessness stares back like a mountain of flames.

When Tom reached the threat assessment expert, she made it clear that that there was no black-and-white checklist that would immediately tell them whether Travis would become violent. She did, however, have in place a Ten-Point Threat Assessment Model that could determine whether Travis held certain traits that would make him more prone to violence. She likened the ten points to chess moves that would help them see into the future. Above all, she explained that the Threat Assessment Model would try to diffuse the current situation so that Travis hopefully would not even consider violence as an option.

WHAT IS A THREAT ASSESSMENT?

A threat assessment defines the security risks an organization faces from its employees, customers, and/or visitors. A team approach is used to gather information, with the threat assessment expert working hand in hand with professionals from the organization's human resource, corporate security, and legal departments. When investigating an employee threat, the team will use many methods to understand as fully as possible the true intent of the individual, including supervisor and peer interviews, background searches, personnel files, and other documented data. Interventions are then carefully chosen, recognizing that each option has the potential to escalate or deescalate the threat.

There is no question that threat assessment is indeed an art. We, as experts in the field, must know how to assess violence with a balanced hand, using both science and instinct to understand the behaviors and emotions of the subject. As such, our first move may not always be to deploy big bodyguards. Instead, less invasive interventions may be more effective, much like how the body responds better to arthroscopic surgery than a large incision. Threat assessment is about being open, creative, and clever when choosing and implementing tactics—never myopic. Sometimes slowing down to wait and see can be far more beneficial than thrusting forward in full gear.

To assess their subject successfully, the threat assessment expert must also be able to get in tune with the energy of that individual. They must feel their subjects' fears and desires deep inside of their own bodies, capitalizing on these feelings to plan their next move. For example, in the case of Travis, there are many tried and true warning signs that would automatically spell caution if they turned up in an assessment—feelings of hopelessness, a problem with alcoholism, and other such negative behaviors. However, if Travis does not seem despondent, does not drink, and is otherwise free of the more common indicators of violence, it is up to the expert to instead ride the ebb and flow of the subject's energy to determine what risk exists. In the end, it is important to remember that there is no guarantee that a threat assessment and its subsequent interventions will stop violence from occurring. However, taking action is far superior to turning a blind eye.

After careful thought, Tom decided to retain the threat assessment expert to help him conduct a behavioral profile of Travis. Using the Ten-Point Threat Assessment Model as their guide, they worked together to gain a better understanding of how likely Travis was to follow up on his threat by examining how closely he held each of ten key traits.

WHAT IS THE TEN-POINT THREAT ASSESSMENT MODEL?

To determine the propensity for violence in an individual, the ten-point assessment model examines the following:

1. History of Violence

While violence often begets violence, it is imperative to understand the full picture. A criminal background check on Travis quickly turned up an incident of domestic battery in his past against a former girl-friend. However, as his conviction took place in 1990, the charge had long since passed the seven-year window during which an employer can legally use the offense as grounds for refusing to hire an individual. Indeed, my experience in the field has found that a criminal's propensity for violence does tend to decrease with each year that goes by without incident. Moreover, as Travis does not have a domestic partner at his job site, there is little likelihood that domestic violence will spill over into the workplace. Assessing solely the above information, there is not enough evidence to suggest that Travis will indeed act out. Further evaluation using the Ten-Point Assessment Model is needed.

2. Mental Illness

Although mental illness does not mean that a person will necessarily become violent, there are several psychiatric disorders that increase one's likelihood toward violence.

However, determining whether a subject is mentally ill in the first place can be quite difficult. In the case of Travis, a one-on-one interview allowed the investigator to gently inquire about his past psychiatric history. (Personal interviews, though, are not recommended for all individuals.) Through the discussion, it was learned that Travis had been in the military but had been discharged early after he was diagnosed with a personality disorder. While Travis was not able to specify which disorder it was, an extensive nationwide study found that those with all forms of mental illness–ranging from phobias to schizophrenia–reported rates of violence two to six times higher than those with no psychiatric diagnoses. Interestingly enough, the study did not focus on those residing within hospital or jail settings but rather reflected feedback received from everyday men and women living among the general population.

3. Relationship and Employment Instability

Strong social networks at home and at work have the potential to guard individuals from violent behavior. And at first glance, Travis did indeed seem to have a few solid relationships. He lived with his wife. They, together, were raising two children. Moreover, after several thorough interviews with Travis's neighbors and acquaintances, no domestic violence was suspected at home.

On the other hand, there was still some suspicion that–despite his appearances as a family man–Travis lived a life of isolation. For example, given Travis's personality disorder, it is likely quite difficult for him to hold high-functioning relationships. The investigation also uncovered that Travis had a tendency to switch employers every six months. That being said, negative relations like these have been shown to contribute to such forms of mental illness as depression and anxiety, causing chemical changes in the brain that affect our ability to regulate emotions–including those that lead to violence.

4. Substance Abuse/Dependency

Although substance abuse is strongly correlated to violence, the investigator was unable to obtain any evidence that Travis used drugs or alcohol. However, in those subjects in whom substance abuse is present, there is great cause for apprehension.

It is commonly known that psychostimulants, such as cocaine and amphetamines, can increase a person's propensity for violence. However, research has also long shown alcohol to play a leading role in homicide. The first of such studies–conducted by Marvin Wolfgang in Philadephia more than five decades ago–found that, in two-thirds of all homicide cases, the victim, the offender, or both had consumed alcohol prior to the killing. As alcohol lowers the levels of serotonin in the brain, people become angrier, more aggressive, more depressed and more prone to suicide. Not surprisingly, alcoholics with a history of aggression and depression tend to have the lowest levels of serotonin among all other alcoholic groups.

5. Weapons Use

Weapons use in a subject is always of grave concern. While we know that Travis received formal training in the military on how to use a gun, we do not know whether he still owns one. Moreover, asking Travis directly will very rarely elicit a truthful response. However, given the ease at which guns are now accessible, it is critical to use other means of investigation to determine if there are currently weapons in his possession, if he has recently purchased a weapon, and how proficient he remains in the use of weaponry. If it is found that Travis does have gun access, it is suggested that the firearm be moved to a secure location at the home of a friend of family member or, even better yet, that he is persuaded into turning the weapon over to his local police department.

Note: I, the author, am a gun owner who believes in the Second Amendment Right to Bear Arms. However, it is important that gun rights advocates be responsible and recognize that this entitlement should not extend to those men and women with questionable psychological backgrounds that place them at high risk for homicide and suicide. If you own a gun, I encourage you to think about purchasing the Corbin Sesamee lock. This device allows the firearm owner to program in a personally-selected safety that keeps use of the gun restricted to only those who know the code. In addition, I highly suggest that you keep your firearm securely stowed in a safe to help keep it from winding up in criminal hands.

6. Hopelessness

As discussed earlier, violent behavior can often be intimately linked to feelings of hopelessness. Hopeless people are tortured souls, tormented by an inner dialogue of degrading and derisive commentary. Accordingly, people often express hopelessness in the statements they make. Thus, in assessing Travis, it is important to investigate whether anyone has overheard him make comments similar to those listed below.

- Things will never get better.
- There is no point in trying anymore.
- I just want to give up.
- What do I have to look forward to?
- There is no hope for me.

Not surprisingly, my experience has found that most people who are hopeless also suffer from depression. While untreated depression is the number one cause of suicide according to National Alliance on Mental Illness, there should also be concern that a depressed individual may be dangerous to others as well.

7. Identifies with Perpetrators and Acts of Violence

Individuals prone to acts of violence tend to identify closely with those famous for violence. In the case of Travis, there were no findings that suggested he held an affinity for such well-known murderers as Adolph Hitler, the Unabomber or Osama Bin Laden.

However, it was discovered that Travis did love violent video games, considering himself an avid gamer. This is of concern since research has shown that the interactive nature of video games with violent content tends to increase aggression even more than violent movies or television shows. Furthermore, young men with a history of aggression were even more vulnerable to the negative effects of these games, with stronger consequences for those who began playing younger in life. For example, college students who reported playing violent video games in junior high and high school were found to engage in more aggressive behaviors.

8. Impulsivity

When investigating Travis, it is critical to also assess his or her tendencies toward impulsivity. Can he remain calm under pressure? Does he overact to criticism and disappointment? As research has demonstrated a link between impulsive behavior and violence, the answers to such questions cannot be overlooked.

Over the last 20 years, in fact, a body of scientific evidence has repeatedly demonstrated that low levels of serotonin in the brain (stemming from alcohol abuse and other causes can lead to deficiencies in an individual's ability to control his or her impulses. This lack of impulse control, in turn, can lead to outbursts of severe aggression and rage. A 2003 article published by the National Legal Aid and Defender Association reported that capital murder cases often struggle with making sense of why one child raised in an abusive family will become a killer and another will not. All roads lead back to brain chemistry.

On a sweeter note, in the 1960s, Standford University psychology researcher Michael Mischel conducted a study examining the long-term effects of impulsive behavior among young children. Using marshmallows as bait, each of the four-year-old subjects were given two choices: They could either receive one marshmallow immediately or if they could wait 15 to 20 minutes, they could receive two marshmallows later. After following the children for 14 years until they graduated high school, the study concluded that those who were able to wait and keep their impulses under control developed into more socially-adjusted individuals.

9. The Immediate Means and the Confidence to Believe that One Can Deliver the Violence

Most establishments have in place safety components meant to deter attack. And while it is understood that anyone who really wants to do damage can bypass these components, most people choose not to. At the facility where Travis works, unarmed guards stand at the front gate, access cards are required to gain entrance, and closed-circuit televisions keep watch over the grounds. The key here is assessing whether Travis has a plan to overcome these security measures.

As Buford Furrow set out to Los Angeles in 1999 to embark on a hate-driven killing spree, security measures held by some of the city's most popular cultural institutions helped to save lives. Armed with five assault rifles, two pistols, 6,000 rounds of ammunition, and a bullet-proof vest, Furrow drove from Washington to California determined to kill as many Jewish people as possible. While his attack of the North Valley Jewish Community Center left five individuals wounded, including three children, he had initially considered storming three other prominent Jewish institutions–the Skirball Cultural Center, the American Jewish University, and the Simon Wiesenthal Center's Museum of Tolerance–but decided that the security at these places would pose too much of a problem.

Note: Having lived down the street from the North Valley Jewish Community Center, I knew several neighbors whose children attended their school. Undoubtedly, this incident brought to the community a new awareness that none of us are free from violence. However, it also confirmed that we each hold an obligation to decrease violence by remaining vigilant and never dismissing someone's propensity for violent behavior.

10. Neurological Disorders and Aggression

Sometimes it is possible that a neurological disorder lies behind the threats and aggressive behaviors seen in an individual. In order to properly diagnose this in Travis, a behavior neuropsychologist is needed.

WHAT INTERVENTIONS SUPPORT THE TEN-POINT ASSESSMENT MODEL?

Many interventions can be used following a threat assessment to manage risk and keep the likelihood of violence to a minimum. Examples are as follows:

Surveillance: Surveillance can be an excellent intervention. It can help provide critical information on Travis's living habits, such as whether he drinks, uses drugs, or visits the gun range. However, it must also be used sparingly to ensure that he does not become aware of the fact that he is being watched. It is particularly important to note that should Travis express paranoid tendencies, there is a much higher risk that the methods of surveillance will be discovered.

There have been some schools of thought that have suggested that it might be beneficial to let a subject know that they are under surveillance. In this manner, if the subject does become violent, there will at least be in place the proper security measures necessary to rapidly apprehend him or her. However, extreme caution should be exercised.

Executive Protection: If it is found that Travis's threat poses a real possibility of workplace violence, executive protection agents may be deployed to protect those employees at risk. It is imperative that the agents assigned know how to work in a corporate environment and know their place in the chess game at hand. They are not there to advise the client personally but rather to take directive from the threat assessment expert so as to maximize the safety of those they are protecting. Ideally, agents should blend in among personnel—unless otherwise instructed—so as not to create mass terror.

Meeting Face to Face with the Subject: There are many pros and cons to this intervention. If meeting with Travis personally, it will nearly always be best to meet offsite. Moreover, should Travis be suspended for investigation, it is imperative that he is not brought back to the workplace for any reason until it is known that the risk he poses is low.

Meeting by Telephone with the Subject: While this intervention may be controversial, it is my expert opinion that it can offer many benefits as an assessment tool, especially when working under tight time constraints. While it is suggested that such telephone conversation catch Travis while he is outside of work, should there be no other option, it is important that proper safety precautions are in place to help keep the situation under control—such as the presence of executive protection agents.

During the conversation, do not be afraid to ask such direct questions as:

- Are you suicidal?
- Do you plan on physically injuring anyone?

- Do you own a gun?
- Can you convince me why I should believe what you are saying?

Fitness for Duty Examination: A fitness for duty examination is a formal assessment that would evaluate whether Travis is able to perform his job safely and effectively. It is essential that the professional performing the evaluation is trained in threat assessment. There have been too many cases of subjects being evaluated as fit to work when they are in fact still quite dangerous.

There are several actuarial and clinical tools that can be used to assess violence in a fitness for duty examination, with debates in place over which are more effective. Actuarial methods, for example, can predict the likelihood of violent behavior in a subject by analyzing such variables as the individual's age, marital status and criminal record. Clinical methods, on the other hand, rely on the assessor's personal evaluation of the subject in order to make predictions–a much more intuitive and subjective approach. As such, the majority of experts in the field tend to favor those tools that are actuarial in nature–although a certain amount of clinical experience is indeed needed to properly assess actuarial data.

When assessing the propensity for violence in a subject with a criminal history, common actuarial tools include the Violence Risk Appraisal Guide and, its companion, the Sex Offender Risk Appraisal Guide. These guides look at a dozen or more personal characteristics to determine the probability that a past offender will commit a new, violent offense within a specified period of time. Although the admissibility of these guides has been challenged in court, no court has yet to uphold such a challenge and dismiss testimony.

HCR-20: The HCR-20 is another evaluation tool used by mental health professionals to determine the best treatment and management strategies for mentally ill individuals who have the potential to become violent. Results from the evaluation could be used to predict Travis's future inclination toward violence. However, it should again be cautioned that only professionals trained in conducting individual assessments and the study of violence should administer such a test–enlisting the support of a mental health professional as needed. Moreover, like any other intervention, the HCR-20 is not intended to be a stand-alone tool.

Anger Management Counseling: The effectiveness of anger management counseling depends on the experience of the counselor and the intervention methods used. In fact, certain anger management interventions have actually been shown to increase anger and do little to help the subject learn to control his or her impulses.

The failure of anger management counseling is especially disturbing in the case of Bryan Uyesugi. Uyesugi was a former Xerox service technician in Hawaii who was convicted of killing seven of his coworkers in 1999–the worst mass murder in the state's history. During his employment, Uyesugi displayed signs of escalating anger toward the other members of his team. He eventually began making threats against their lives. In 1993, he was ordered to undergo psychiatric evaluation and anger management courses after being arrested for kicking in and damaging an elevator door. Still, coworkers testified that as early as 1995, Uyesugi was openly threatening to carry out a mass shooting at Xerox should he ever be fired.

Severance Package: There are many instances where it might be a good idea to have the organization's human resource department offer the subject a severance package, especially so that he or she can maintain access to mental health services. In the case of Travis, the goal should be to make his transition out of the organization as easy as possible.

Restraining Orders: The need for a restraining order should be carefully assessed before being implemented. In a best case scenario, a restraining order may effectively keep away someone who is rational and who has no history of violence. Yet in reality, if this was the type of subject being dealt with, there would most likely be little reason to seek a restraining order in the first place. Instead, there is evidence that has shown that restraining orders are largely ineffective. According to a 1998 nationwide study on stalking, 69 percent of women and 81 percent of men who had taken out a restraining order against their stalker reported having that order violated. Furthermore, restraining orders must list all the addresses from which the subject in question must stay away–sharing potentially private information (such as a home address) that can leave the victim of a threat even more vulnerable. That being said, there are still times when a restraining order may be beneficial.

Stay-Away Letter: Stay-Away Letters provide a less invasive alternative to restraining orders. When a terminated subject returns to the workplace despite being given instructions to the contrary, a Stay-Away Letter can be sent following the incident that encourages the former employee to respect the organization's request going forward. To have the most impact, the letter should appeal to the employee with a level of respect that both creates boundaries and recognizes the subject's need for dialogue. Sample language could include: "I would like to hear your concerns surrounding your release from work and encourage you to please call me so that we can discuss the matter privately."

Police Report: While a police report will usually be necessary, it is important to consider timing. Much like a restraining order, there is a chance that filing a report could escalate Travis's propensity for violence and leave him empowered to do more harm. It is, thus, important to carefully assess each case on an individual basis before such action is taken.

CONCLUSION

In the end, if Travis were to have taken the next step and engaged in workplace violence, the threat assessment would have ultimately found his attack to have stemmed from a place of deep hopelessness, a place where violence is justified as the only course of action left against his misfortunes and against those he perceives as his enemy. And, for that reason, in Travis's mind, someone else must always pay.

Such rationale is clearly demonstrated in the suicide note left by Mark Barton, a day trader from Georgia who went on a killing spree in 1999 that ended with the deaths of his wife and two kids, as well as nine others. He wrote, "I have come to hate this life in this system of things. I have come to have no hope. . . . I don't plan to live very much longer, just long enough to kill . . . the people that greedily sought my destruction." Accordingly, it is imperative that we, as a community, do not wait until the guns are drawn or the suicide notes are written to assess someone's behavior. If Travis did indeed act out, the threat he made on his cigarette break would not have been the only warning sign. We must keep learning how to stop evil by never ending our quest to understand and predict violence. As such, this chapter is by no means intended to guide the reader through the entire threat assessment and management process. Rather, it is a general overview that I hope will raise awareness on ways we can better identify and contain danger in the workplace, so we can finally stop the cliché, "He was such a nice guy."

Indeed, it is true that our violent world has caused many to turn their backs against hope. However, as these pages have illustrated, it is also true that if each of us stands proactive against violence, there is much that can be done together to deter it from occurring in the first place.

Chapter 16

COMPUTER FORENSICS

KEVIN J. RIPA

Considering that Private Investigations is widely regarded as the second oldest profession, it is amazing that it is found in virtually every emerging new facet of business. Computer forensics is just such an area. Although it has been around loosely since computers started becoming more widely used, it is only within the last five to seven years that it has begun to take on structure, with companies dedicated solely to its practice. As a result, it can be quite a "buyers beware" environment.

The first hurdle is recognizing when computer forensics is necessary. CF is not something that should be called in at the eleventh hour. It is something that should be a consideration from the very onset of any investigation. Consider this statistic. Variously 91 percent of all information generated today is done in the electronic medium and 86–90 percent of that never leaves the electronic form. It is clear to see that if computers are not being considered in an investigation, a great deal is being left out.

One of the first considerations of the application of CF need not go any further than the Human Resources department. This includes the two-man shop where the owner is the HR department. A forensic image (the second step in a CF examination) should be taken of an employee hard drive immediately after dismissal. It should be an integral part of any walk-out policy. Fully 85 percent of employees currently spend some part of their day utilizing the computer for nonemployment-related tasks. Things like checking personal email accounts, using e-

Bay, Facebook, MySpace, online gambling, cyber chatting, and even viewing pornography are commonly performed on company time. An entire chapter could be written on just the security implications of this!

If a forensic image has been obtained of the departing employee's computer hard drive, it makes it much easier to follow a trail than if the employer is presented with a wrongful dismissal lawsuit six months after the fact. At that point, the computer has already been recycled and put into use by a new employee, making it much more difficult to extract potential evidence. This is merely one example.

CASE INTAKE

The most important part of any investigation and certainly of a CF investigation is the case intake. This will usually start with a meeting between the client and the CF examiner. It is integral to the investigation that all parties have a clear understanding of the objectives and expectations, what is possible, and what is not. To some, CF seems almost magical in its ability to reconstruct computer history and recover what was thought to be deleted long ago. Depending on the scope of the investigation, a common task is compiling a set of search terms to be used against the computer to extract relevant information. The creation of the search terms should be a collaborative effort between the client and the examiner, simply because the client alone may not understand how data resides on a computer. A common example in corporate investigations is wanting the term "contract" searched for, to locate evidence of an employee stealing proprietary data, or planning on working for the competition, etc. A seasoned examiner knows that searching for this term by itself with no context will obtain hundreds, if not thousands, of nonrelevant "hits." One of the reasons is that the word "contract" exists numerous times within the End User Licensing Agreements of every piece of software installed on every computer. Another common mistake is searching for a term that shows up inside larger words. For example, a recent search term provided by a client was the acronym "OTTED." Without proper context, and without a skilled investigator to run complex coding instruction for exclusions and exceptions, this search term would result in "hits" in words such as jOTTED, rOTTED, allOTTED, spOTTED, etc. This would create an overwhelming number of search hits, causing the investigation to take much longer than necessary.

Another common mistake is requesting all the emails from the computer. This is not a difficult task if the client only wants emails that still exist in the regular places on the computer, but if the client wants every email, deleted or not, this becomes a herculean task, simply because when the client asks for "all emails," they are thinking from the perspective of relevant emails. They don't realize that their request for "all emails" can't tell the difference between the one relevant email a day, and the 30 spam emails a day. The issue is far more technical than this book will allow, but this should serve as an indication of how carefully search terms, ideas, and parameters must be considered.

FORENSIC ACQUISITION

The forensic acquisition is extremely important to the resultant outcome of the investigation. If not done properly, all evidence extracted may very well be rendered inadmissible in court proceedings. As in any other type of investigation, continuity and proper documentation must be performed. This includes the standard photography of the scene and of the equipment, as well as proper documentation of the evidence being collected.

In many cases, investigations have been greatly hampered by companies believing their IT department could perform these collection and analysis functions. This could not be farther from the truth. Besides the resultant conflict of issue problems, IT people, although very skilled in their area of computers, are not forensic collection or analysis specialists. The worst part is that they don't know what it is that they don't know. Think about that for a second. They believe they are doing the best they can, and they absolutely mean well, but they don't know the forensics field any better than the forensics field would know the IT structure of the company.

Once properly documented, the issue now becomes how to proceed with the acquisition. This is not a straightforward procedure. There are a number of variables. Is the computer on or off? If off, then the job is much easier, and the specialist can skip straight to the acquisition. If the computer is on, the old school mentality is that it needs to be turned off immediately. While this was the standard three to five years ago, it certainly is no longer. Technology has advanced to the point where we now know that the content of the RAM or Random Access Memory of the computer is a vital part of the evidence collection process. The RAM contains evidence that exists nowhere else on the computer. For example, many types of hard drive security including whole disk encryption, Windows BitLocker technology, and others hold the unlock key in the RAM. If the analyst can capture this, they have the keys to the hard drive. If the computer is off, or they do not collect this before turning it off, there is virtually zero chance of accessing the data on the hard drive without getting the key from the user. As well, chat logs and other data exist only in the memory, and are forever lost once the computer is shut down. Unlike a hard drive, when the computer is shut down, the content of the RAM is lost.

Other crucial data that can be captured only while the computer is on include things such as what programs are running at that particular time, what network connections and open shares are active at the time, and also, what compromises such as malicious software are running. Again, it is imperative to handle the computer properly, and not rush to turn it off. Only a skilled and qualified forensic specialist will have the specialized knowledge, hardware, and software to perform the capture of this memory.

After all evidence is collected from the running state, the various drives of the computer must be checked for rogue software. Floppy disks and CD or DVDs can be in the system that will cause the hard drive to initiate a complete overwrite of all data if it is not shut down in the sequence that a rogue employee or other person has set it up to be. For that reason, these drives need to be checked for media, and if found, it must be removed before initiating any shut down sequence.

Now that the point of shut down has been reached, a decision must be made on how to shut it down. This is usually a trade off between functionality and potential destruction of data. Simply turning the computer off using the normal shutdown method can destroy a great deal of evidence in the process. Pulling the plug, while maintaining the most amount of evidence, could also corrupt many files that are in use at the time, potentially damaging the network. Typically, the rule of thumb, all other things taken into consideration, is that any Windows servers, Unix flavors, or Mac systems should be shut down using the normal procedures. Any other types of Windows machines should have the plug pulled.

At this point, the acquisition can now start. The hard drive is removed and either imaged in a device designed specifically for this task, or it is hooked up to a computer through a write blocking device to perform the same task. The write blocking device ensures that no changes or alterations have occurred during the acquisition process. This process creates a bit-by-bit copy of the hard drive for later analysis at the forensics lab.

FORENSIC ANALYSIS

This is the bread and butter of the entire computer investigation process. Trying to save money by hiring cheaper analysts will almost assuredly lead to failure at this stage of the investigation. In this field, as with most others, you get what you pay for. Unfortunately, in this type of investigation, the client will never know what was missed by an unskilled analyst. Searches on provided terms were discussed earlier, but this is a very small part of a full analysis. A great deal of data is now being missed in investigations by questionably qualified examiners because many files are not being properly mounted in preparation for the search. In today's computer, simply running a search term to find instances of it in potential contracts or emails will fail to provide any results because things like ZIP files, Office 2007 files, PDFs, and Outlook files are compressed in a proprietary fashion that "removes" the plain text content. Therefore, the search term could very well be in a Microsoft Word 2007 document, and would never be found if the data wasn't first prepared properly for the search.

The question is often asked of any analyst, "What can you find for me?" This is a very difficult question to answer. Quite often the sky is the limit, and the analyst will turn the question around to ask for specific details of what the client suspects, or may be looking for. Generally speaking, if it is still on the computer, it can be found. In terms of data resident on the hard drive, as long as it has not been overwritten by new data, it can be recovered. To better understand this concept, it helps to understand how data resides on a hard drive, and what happens when it is deleted.

When deletion of a file occurs, the file doesn't actually disappear. It still occupies space on the hard drive, in what are called clusters. Given that hard drives have millions of clusters, the computer needs a way to find a specific one. The way it does this in the case of the Windows operating system is through the use of a **Master File Table** or MFT for short. This MFT is basically a table of contents that points to individual clusters. If a user creates a file, it will be saved to a space covering one or more clusters, depending on its size. For example, let us say it saved the document to cluster number 3,000,000. An entry will now be made in the MFT so the next time a user double clicks on the icon to open the document, the computer will be told by the MFT where to go find it. If it is then deleted, the document will still exist on cluster 3,000,000, but the entry in the MFT is what actually gets removed. Once the MFT has had the document reference removed, the computer no longer knows where to go and look for it. As well, the computer is told that it is perfectly OK to place a new document on cluster 3,000,000. BUT, until it actually does, the old data is still there. A skilled analyst is able to access the Unallocated Space and find the document based on various parameters. He or she can also use that expertise to actually restore the once deleted file to useable status again.

Beyond finding deleted data, CF can determine a number of activities that have occurred on a hard drive. Below is a list of just a few of the almost limitless possibilities:

- Determine all USB devices ever connected to the computer and when;
- Determine if data was burned to CD/DVD or other media;
- What programs have actually been used on a computer, and how often;
- What user was logged on during a specific time;
- Websites visited, and whether they were typed in or just clicked to;
- Lists showing what files were accessed on removable media;
- Lists showing the last number of various files opened, such as last word documents opened, last videos watched, last music listened to, etc.

As more time passes, computer data will become a routine stopping place in the search for relevant information on any given subject. The business person who is prepared for this sooner rather than later will always have the competitive advantage. An executive need not understand the technology. He or she only needs to be willing to ask the specialist if something can be done to help.

Chapter 17

WORKERS' COMPENSATION INVESTIGATIONS

Lynda J. Bergh

Workers' Compensation insurance, as one might expect from the name, covers injuries sustained by workers on the job. Workers' Compensation or AOE/COE investigations are utilized to determine the facts regarding where, when, how, and why the injury occurred. Most importantly, these investigations involve gathering information and evidence to ascertain and document whether the injury was in fact work-related and occurred in the course and scope of employment. There are times the alleged injury resulted from the actions of a third party, or was sustained somewhere other than at work.

When an employee claims to have suffered a work-related injury, or when an injury occurs in view of others at work, the employer is required to complete an injury report, take or send the injured worker for medical treatment if needed, and submit a claim to their Workers' Compensation insurance carrier. The next step often involves the initiation of an AOE/COE (Arising Out of Employment/Course of Employment) investigation. These assignments are usually received from the insurance carrier; however, they are sometimes initiated by the employer. Claims that appear suspicious from the onset, or may involve a third party, are often assigned by the insurance carrier's Special Investigations Unit and require a bit more in-depth investigation. If more than one person is injured in the same incident, accident, or natural disaster, all involved would be eligible for treatment and benefits, depending on the extent of their individual injuries.

The investigation should be initiated by the investigator as quickly as possible upon receipt of the assignment. This is especially important when obtaining witness statements. The investigator wants to obtain information from the claimant and witnesses before they have a chance to forget details or possibly have their recollection influenced by another party's input.

Prior to scheduling appointments to obtain the claimant, employer, and witness statements, the investigator should review the injury report and all available Workers' Compensation documents. Some find it helpful to create a list of questions, while others prefer to handle interviews in a more conversational manner. Interviews should be conducted in person whenever possible, and statements should be recorded to ensure clarity and accuracy. Also, once a witness has provided a formal statement, either written or recorded, he or she is less likely to change his or her story at a later date.

It is suggested that the injured party be interviewed first in order to obtain a detailed description of the incident directly from the source. Specifics that need to be covered during the securing of the claimant's statement include the date, time, and location of the incident in question, a detailed description of what happened, any unusual circumstances that occurred on the date of the injury, witness names, and details regarding any medical treatment received. It is also important to have the claimant state when, to whom, and how the alleged injury was reported. During this first meeting with the claimant, an authorization to release information (waiver) should be signed for purposes of obtaining employment and medical records during the investigation. If the claimant is represented by counsel, you may not be permitted to interview or obtain a statement from him or her.

During the initial meeting with the claimant, should evidence come to light regarding a nonreported injury or symptom, details should be obtained to determine whether or not the condition or symptom is related to the original injury, has resulted from medication or treatment related to the original injury, or arose due to a different incident or accident. If the new symptoms are attributed to medication side effects, they would also be compensable.

Information that needs to be obtained from the claimant's supervisor(s) and human resources personnel includes the basic details of the claimant's employment. That would consist of, but not be limited to, their work location and environment; position, duties, and responsibilities; special equipment used; work schedule; current employment status; wage details; and any other significant issues related to their employment.

Supervisor, coworker, and witness statements are very important. Depending on the type of injury, all may be able to provide useful information.

There are many types of Workers' Compensation injuries that are reported. It might have been a slip and fall or perhaps a physical injury while using equipment, such as a severe laceration, that was witnessed by several others. Each and every witness should be interviewed regarding what he or she saw. Immediate coworkers, even those who did not witness the incident, should also be interviewed as they may possess valuable information regarding the injured worker's activity prior to, or following, the accident. Perhaps the claimant told a friend at work he planned to slip and fall, or that he had previously injured himself and was going to blame it on his employment in order to get medical treatment. If possible, neighbors could also be interviewed as they might possess information regarding prior nonindustrial injuries.

This is especially important when the injured worker has continued working. Oftentimes the person has been examined or evaluated by a doctor and sent back to work with restrictions or limitations regarding their activity.

The worker could be alleging an injury due to repetitive movements such as heavy lifting, stooping, bending, squatting, and lengthy hours spent on a computer, etc. Immediate coworkers and supervisors would most likely possess useful information in these cases. Human Resources should also be able to provide a written job description that spells out in detail just what the claimant's job duties and responsibilities entail. Specifics should be obtained regarding the percentage of the work day during which the claimant engages in particular activities, i.e., heavy lifting 50 percent, squatting 10 percent, etc. The distance carried, weight of the items lifted, and height lifted to are also significant.

There have been Workers' Compensation claims filed as the result of exposure to chemicals and solvents. In those instances, in addition to the customary information, the investigator should obtain Material Safety Data Sheets regarding the products and verify that the proper safety precautions and equipment were available to the claimant and being used properly.

Other Workers' Compensation claims include allegations of psychological trauma or stress. Although these conditions may cause physical symptoms such as headaches, back pain, difficulty eating or weight loss, there can also be symptoms that cannot be seen such as depression, insomnia, anxiety, or an inability to concentrate. In these cases, the claimant's coworkers and supervisors should be contacted, along with others he or she may have contact with in the workplace. There have been stress-related claims filed due to a worker being upset after receiving a negative performance evaluation or disciplinary action. Human Resources records can shed a lot of light on incidents that might have led to a previously high functioning and upbeat employee suddenly becoming sullen, uncooperative, or depressed.

Another important factor in psychological or stress claims is the claimant's personal life. There have been many cases filed where the claimant's home life is a mess. He or she may be going through a divorce; may have learned his or her spouse was having an affair; lost a child or other loved one; had a miscarriage; have an unruly teenager; or may have lost, spent, or gambled and lost a large sum of money. There are many, many events that take place in one's personal life that can lead to symptoms of stress and/or depression. It is always possible that the home-based stress can negatively affect the individual's performance at work. All of this can create a cycle that needs to be identified for purposes of clarifying the validity of the claimant's allegations.

Sometimes Workers' Compensation investigations involve the death of an employee. For example, construction workers sometimes fall from rooftops, iron workers fall from scaffolding, or an individual driving as part of their duties could be involved in a traffic accident. In those cases, in addition to obtaining the usual and customary information, the investigator must also identify and contact qualified dependents as they may be eligible to receive benefits as a result of the loss. Qualified dependents can include illegitimate children, developmentally disabled adult children, or any relative previously supported by the decedent.

When an alleged injury involves equipment in use at the workplace, it is important to identify or eliminate possible third-party involvement. If a third party is involved in any way, then subrogation may be an issue. When looking for subrogation issues, especially related to equipment, it is imperative that the equipment in question be inspected thoroughly. All maintenance and repair records on the equipment should be obtained. If an OSHA report has been completed, it should be reviewed. It is wise to take photographs of the work area and equipment involved. All of this is done to identify any alterations to the equipment, or the possibility of malfunction.

It is not unheard of for employers, or sometimes even employees, to remove safety guards or emergency shut-off buttons from equipment so they can increase productivity. It is also common for employees to remove safety equipment or gear so they can work unimpeded. Needless to say, this puts both the employees and the employer in jeopardy.

Subrogation investigations require the investigator to identify all of the involved parties or entities, identify insurance carriers for those entities, and possibly obtain statements from individuals affiliated with the third party, i.e., equipment manufacturer.

If an employee drives as part of his or her job duties, of course, attention should be paid to their driving record prior to allowing them to drive. If a worker is involved in a traffic collision driving a company vehicle, or a personal vehicle, the investigator needs to determine just what activity the individual was taking part in. Was she going to get a manicure during lunch? Was he stopping by the hardware store for supplies on his way home? Has he or she been consuming alcoholic beverages or taking medication? Each state has a "coming and going" rule which outlines just what activity is permitted and just when an individual is considered to be "on the clock" while driving their personal vehicle. Many private investigators work from their homes and drive their own vehicles. In most cases, they are considered to be working as soon as they leave their home en route to an assignment, and until they arrive back at their home (depending on their stops along the way).

When traveling out of town overnight or sent to a particular location for business, the "bunkhouse rule" applies. This means that, if the employee is injured in any way or for any reason while traveling to or staying at a particular location on business, he or she is covered by Workers' Compensation insurance. As an example, this would include falling while drunk, being the victim of a robbery, or even being killed in an accident.

Workers' Compensation insurance companies also sometimes assign Sub-rosa investigations, especially to ascertain the nature and extent of the injury, or when fraud is suspected. For instance, an employee who has claimed a back injury has been telling coworkers about the remodeling work he is doing at his home, or about lifting heavy items at home. Perhaps he or she is very active in sports, or has small children. He or she could just be malingering to stay home longer, even though the injury has healed.

Surveillance video can be immensely helpful in defending fraudulent claims. The investigator may be able to catch the injured worker as he or she carries large boxes, works on a vehicle, plays football with the kids, or takes part in any activity that the treating physician has advised him or her to avoid. It is also not uncommon for allegedly injured workers to take a second job or open a business of their own. Incredibly, the claimant's own attorney often does not know he or she is exaggerating his or her condition or taking part in activity he or she claims inability to perform.

Many claims are dismissed or settled based on surveillance video and/or a combination of surveillance video and information obtained from various witnesses.

An extremely important part of Workers' Compensation investigations is providing the client with documentation of what has taken place. An organized and detailed fact-based report should be presented to the client in a timely manner. The report should summarize what took place during the investigation; details regarding the claimant, employer, job duties, and responsibilities; wages; medical information; facts about the accident or exposure; supervisor and witness statement summaries; subrogation issues; any unusual factors discovered related to the claim; any outstanding activity to be completed in the future; and recommendations from the investigator.

Workers' Compensation claims can be frustrating at times, but also very interesting and sometimes challenging. When someone is truly injured while working, he or she is entitled to medical treatment and compensation. These investigations can assist him or her in receiving benefits. In the event of fraud, these investigations help the insurance carrier identify that fraud and, at times, lead to the perpetrator being charged criminally and possibly serving time in prison. Sometimes the employer is the one in the wrong because they are taking short-cuts to increase productivity. In that event, these investigations help protect the employees.

Chapter 18

INSURANCE INVESTIGATIONS

LYNDA J. BERGH

Insurance fraud involves someone intentionally deceiving another about an insurance matter to receive money or other benefits not rightfully his or hers. With the prevalence of insurance fraud, the need for effective insurance investigations has grown.

The insurance industry estimates that, as of early 2010, fraud accounts for 10 percent of property/casualty losses, or about $30 billion a year. Insurance fraud is committed at various times and by different parties. It can involve applicants who are dishonest on their applications, policyholders who pad their claims, and professionals who provide unnecessary services to claimants.

According to the National Insurance Crime Bureau (NICB) the largest number of suspicious insurance claims in 2009 involved staged accidents. Additional common scams include duplicate billing, hail damage, auto glass fraud, mortgage fraud, commercial slip and fall, fire and arson, inflated repairs, suspicious hit and run (parked vehicle), and unperformed repairs. All types of insurance are affected by fraud including, but not limited to, automotive, homeowner, property, business, life, casualty, and health.

Investigating insurance fraud requires knowledge of insurance laws, the ability to recognize "red flags" related to insurance fraud, attention to detail, and a lot of common sense. It is also important to stay up to date on legal changes and trends in insurance fraud. Several significant red flags are included below, each of which should lead to more in-depth investigation that could reveal insurance fraud.

One of the most common auto insurance fraud scams involves staged auto accidents. These accidents are set up in various ways, including what is commonly referred to as a "swoop and squat" and a "drive down." In the first instance, a suspect vehicle suddenly swoops in front of the target and slams on the brakes, causing a rear-end collision. The suspect car often has passengers who pretend to have painful back or neck injuries, even though the collision was at low speed. Other times, the suspect is alone in the vehicle, yet later claims there were passengers with him, all of whom sustained serious injuries. In a drive down, the target vehicle is typically trying to merge into traffic when the suspect driver slows down and waves them over, only to then crash into the target vehicle. This can also occur in parking lots with the suspect waving the target out of a parking space, then plowing into them. In each case, the suspect driver denies having waved the target driver over. Another common auto insurance fraud involves an alleged witness at the collision site later contacting the target driver and encouraging him or her to have repairs performed at a specific auto-body shop, seek treatment from a certain doctor, or visit a lawyer he knows who can help with a personal injury lawsuit.

When investigating auto accidents, the investigator should look for all of the circumstances listed above. The drivers in all involved vehicles should be interviewed separately, especially family members or passengers in the same vehicle. Special attention should be given to the involved drivers' actions just prior to the collision, visible damage to the vehicles involved, parties in each involved vehicle, any evidence of injuries, and the actions of the drivers and witnesses following the collision.

The background of the suspect driver should be checked, including driving history, criminal records, and, especially, civil records. It is possible the individual has a history of filing lawsuits related to traffic accidents. A review of the complaints in those files could be very revealing when it comes to the manner in which the accidents occurred.

Another common automobile insurance fraud scam involves the abandonment or arson of an insured vehicle. This often occurs when the registered owner falls behind in payments. He or she will abandon the vehicle somewhere, often with the keys inside, sink it in a lake or river, or hire someone to steal the vehicle. The owner then files a stolen vehicle report in hopes of collecting an insurance pay-out. This area should be covered in detail during the investigation of any auto theft or disappearance, with emphasis on the payment history on the vehicle and the financial status of the alleged victim.

Homeowner's, property, and business insurance provide coverage for various instances including, but not limited to, fire, burglary, theft, and natural disasters. Homeowner's insurance also covers damage resulting from equipment failure, such as a leaking water heater or pipes. When investigating these types of claims, attention should be paid to the actions of the insured, as well as documentation he or she provides.

For instance, when investigating any type of property loss or damage due to fire, flood, burglary, earthquake, and/or storm, the insured's initial reaction is significant. If he or she is very calm and shows little concern about the situation, especially when informed a fire appears to have been arson, or if the absence of the family at the time of the fire or burglary is out of character, that should raise suspicion. If witnesses, neighbors or family members noticed items being removed from the home or business shortly prior to the loss that would definitely raise suspicion.

In the event of possible arson, the fire report should be obtained and reviewed. When going over the report with the insured, explanations regarding any changes in schedule, a lack of remains of items normally found in the home or business (such as equipment, furniture, business records, etc.), prior structural damage, multiple mortgages on the property, financial difficulties, or a decline in business should be probed. If the insured is in the process of a divorce, has gambling debts or legal expenses related to another matter, or if the commercial contents were outdated or unusable, the circumstances should be looked into.

When investigating any property loss, if the insured is overly aggressive in the desire for a quick settlement, knowledgeable of the claims settlement process, handles all documentation in person rather than by mail, submits questionable documentation or is unable to provide original documentation, the matter should be investigated further. If the insured is recently separated or divorced, or just happened to contact his agent to verify coverage shortly prior to the incident, that too would be of concern. With a business or burglary loss, if the insured provides receipts for inexpensive items, but not for items of significant value, or provides receipts with no sales tax figures, it would be of concern. If the forced entry appears to have occurred from the inside-out, or there is no sign of forced entry, that would raise concern.

With business losses, a forensic examination of the books would be the best place to start. With both business and homeowner's coverage for property damage, evidence should be obtained of what the business location or dwelling looked like, and what was inside it prior to the loss occurring. It is not uncommon for individuals to pad costs for repairs following even minor property damage incidents such as small leaks or minor smoke damage.

When investigating casualty and disability insurance claims, special emphasis should be placed on just how the accident occurred. This would include interviewing the insured and all witnesses; reviewing any accident reports completed by police, fire, or emergency medical providers; medical records; inspection of the loss site; and documenting what took place. As with any type of insurance coverage, the investigation will determine when, where, how, and why the injury occurred, and who or what caused it. The investigation may also include surveillance to determine the insured's activity, nature and extent of injury or disability, and employment status. Oftentimes surveillance video is used to either deny a claim or come to a settlement if the insured is proven to be more able than claimed.

With disability insurance, the policy often requires the insured to provide proof that he or she is 100 percent disabled. If the individual is self-employed, and especially if he or she works from the home, it is very difficult to prove employment activities. One way to do this, at least to some extent, would be by conducting surveillance, especially if the insured is followed making trips to the post office, office supply store, visiting clients, etc.

Long-term care insurance is also easily abused by individuals who claim they are unable to work, yet are doing so from their home. Again, surveillance and activity checks would be the most promising actions to take to determine just what the individual is up to. In long-term care instances, often the insured has visiting medical assistants or nursing care. It is not uncommon for them to claim 24-hour care when, in reality, the caregiver is only present eight to ten hours a day. At times, the caregiver is the one committing fraud by not properly caring for the insured, who may be left in pajamas all day long, go unfed, or not be given medication when he or she should. This can typically be confirmed via surveillance and discreet activity checks. If necessary, records can also be subpoenaed from the caregiver's employer. Of course, direct contact with the insured and/or family members would be the best way to determine his or her condition.

Medical insurance fraud can consist of several types of scams, including doctors and dentists padding their bills or billing for tests and treatments that were never given, providing and billing for unnecessary treatment, selling fake medical or dental insurance coverage, or treating patients even though they are unlicensed. Medical and dental insurance fraud perpetrators often provide substandard care and treatment which can result in further treatment being needed or even death.

Mobile diagnostic laboratories can also be involved in fraudulent activity. There have been documented cases where they have given needless or fake tests or physical exams to consumers, then billed health insurers for expensive procedures.

There have also been cases when individuals have been diagnosed with a serious illness, then went out and purchased medical insurance without admitting they were ill.

When investigating medical and dental fraud, a background investigation should be conducted on the medical practitioner to determine whether or not he or she is licensed and if there is any record of complaints, suspensions, or disciplinary actions. This information is easily obtained through each state's Medical Board.

Insurance companies have access to complete medical histories and have begun to track treatments more closely. When excessive or suspicious treatment patterns are noted, they may initiate an investigation on their own, or hire an outside investigator.

Life insurance policies nearly always include a statement to the effect that benefits will not be paid in the event of suicide. Nonetheless, each year there are multiple attempts made by individuals to fake their own death. The biggest red flag in these cases is that the body cannot be found. When that occurs, an in-depth and often challenging investigation ensues. The best sources for possible information in these cases are family friends and neighbors. There are times the subject manages to disappear for a lengthy period of time and his or her family is able to receive death benefits. Should the person be found at a later date, the family will be required to repay the monies received.

When a death is known or proven to have occurred, investigation would involve determining the facts and circumstances that led to the death, identifying qualified dependents, contacting witnesses (including law enforcement, fire, and emergency medical responders), reviewing the coroner's report, canvassing the incident location, and reviewing all available evidence.

A more common scam related to life insurance involves individuals providing fraudulent information in order to qualify for coverage. Most reputable insurance companies perform in-depth background investigations on potential customers. Probably more concern should be placed on life insurance companies that are willing to sell a policy to just about anyone, or without a medical examination. They are more likely to commit fraud by taking premiums but not really writing policies. To avoid that situation, individuals seeking life insurance should have the potential insurer checked out.

When investigating any type of insurance claim, the basic process is similar. Upon receipt of the assignment and a discussion with the insurer regarding possible areas of concern, the investigator should interview the insured first to obtain a detailed description of the incident or situation directly from the source. That should include specifics regarding what took place, where and how it occurred, witness names, any medical treatment, supporting documentation, and any unusual circumstances. A recorded statement should be obtained to ensure clarity and accuracy. If confidential records will be needed to continue the investigation, an authorization for release of information waiver should be obtained.

The next step would be to conduct witness interviews, possibly canvass the area where the accident or incident occurred to locate additional witnesses, perform background research on the involved parties, and review any available reports from law enforcement, fire, or emergency medical responders.

As the investigation continues, the insurance company or client should be provided detailed, fact-based written reports documenting what has taken place and the information obtained. The report should summarize the steps taken during the investigation, details regarding the incident in question, evidence obtained, and any unusual or suspicious factors.

Insurance investigations can be quick and easy or extremely challenging. Either way they are always rewarding. Legal updates related to insurance scams and laws are a must have, and can easily be found on the Internet, especially through the Insurance Information Institute (www.iii.org) and the National Insurance Crime Bureau (www.ncib .org).

Chapter 19

USING ELECTRONIC RESOURCES IN DUE DILIGENCE INVESTIGATIONS

BARBARA W. THOMPSON

Something wonderful is happening on the World Wide Web. More and more information is becoming available, for free or very inexpensively, via the Internet. Many official document repositories are digitizing their documents and offering the images to the investigator via the Internet. This is wonderful for two reasons. First, the investigator no longer needs to go to or send someone into the courthouse or agency to retrieve documents. Second, the investigator no longer needs to worry about whether the large information aggregators retrieved the information correctly, interpreted it correctly, presented it correctly, and have kept it up to date.

Are you asking yourself, "Why am I reading a chapter about using electronic research in investigations? I know how to use Google, and I have a subscription to two of the major information aggregator databases. What more is there to know?"

The answer is easy: lots. While searching has become much easier and more purposeful due to the constant improvement of search engines, the trick still is finding exactly what you're looking for among the multitude of sources that are available to you, and knowing what it means in terms of the investigation.

What this chapter won't do:

This chapter won't drag you through another explanation of "due diligence." Other chapters in this book do that brilliantly. This chapter won't prepare you for a Ph.D. in computer science. You don't really need to know how computers work in order to use them. And it won't give you a list of 4,000 nifty websites that you'll never remember and that probably will be gone by the time you need to use them.

What this chapter will do:

It will provide some basic sources and search strategies that you can use to find due diligence background information electronically, but more than that, it will attempt to help you understand what you are (and are not) finding when you use these electronic resources. In other words, how good is the information? Is it really what it says it is? What can I use it for?

This chapter will provide you with the general concepts that will help you to gather both the materials you (and your client) need to formulate an opinion or take the action that a reasonable and prudent person would in the same situation. We'll take a look at the basic concepts for successful use of electronic resources in due diligence investigations.

This chapter assumes that the reader has at least a basic understanding of "public records" and basic research strategies.

Concept I: *The sources and resources you need to find will vary with the nature of the investigation, but they all need to come from one place: the original source.*

Have you ever been in a situation in which you obtained some information from an information aggregator, written it up in your investigative report, only to have the client come back and tell you that you were wrong . . . and then show you the source document that proves you were wrong? If you have, I'm certain you don't ever want it to happen again. So, don't let it.

THE DATA AGGREGATORS

Information derived from the data aggregators is a starting point only. Say that last sentence to yourself as many times as you need to get it fixed in your head. *Never* assume that the information provided by an information aggregator is accurate. It usually is reliable, but you must keep in mind that the data compilers really have no control over the accuracy of the information they purchase from the primary sources.

All the database subscriber agreements require their users agree that the information provided is "as is" and that the database company disclaims all liability for inaccurate information. Since the subscribers agree to this limitation of liability when they sign up, they have no recourse if the information they pay for is incorrect.

But being able to point a finger at the aggregator will not solve the research reliability problem. By reporting inaccurate information which was available in correct form from the primary source, you are ruining your reputation as an investigator and possibly losing a client. Suppose the client decides not to enter into a transaction with the subject you are investigating based on the incorrect information you provided? Or worse, suppose your client does enter into that transaction, which soon becomes toxic because of the incorrect information you provided or the correct information you missed? Ouch.

THE CURRENCY PROBLEM

Keep in mind that the database companies generally are for-profit entities and the goal is to sell as many subscriptions and generate as much usage as they can. Sometimes, in their zeal to get you to sign the subscription, the sales reps may describe the information in its best possible light, leaving out some facts that are critical for your analysis of the information.

For example, the sales rep may say, "The information is updated monthly." Technically that's true. The aggregator may do an upload of new data every 30 days. But what the rep may not mention (or not even know) is that the data the company purchases from the primary source was recorded six months ago or more. So, the information you're buying isn't 30 days fresh, its six months (or more) stale. If you need to know whether the subject of your investigation sold his yacht in the last three months, you may not find it in the aggregator's database. You will learn from the database that the subject had a yacht (the starting point), but you will still need to verify it with the Coast Guard (the primary source). Or consider tax assessor information. The data aggregator may provide the assessment from 2008, when the current assessment from 2010 has already been made public.

THE INTERFACE ISSUE

Most information aggregators have designed different interfaces. The interface is the display that allows the user to interact with the system. Aside from requiring you to learn how to navigate different systems, the interface may determine exactly what information from the primary source the database can provide to you and what it can't. The database designers must make a decision as to which fields they will populate with which pieces of information taken from the original document.

For example, consider a database that provides mortgage information. Every database will probably provide the name of the mortgagee and mortgagor, the date of the mortgage, the property that is the subject of the loan, and the amount of the loan. Some may provide the address of the lender and the borrower. But not all of them will provide both the postal address and the legal description of the collateralized property. This becomes frustrating when the researcher is trying to figure out which parcel(s) in a development a specific property owner has used as collateral for the loan, and which parcels may have been subdivided and resold. Further, it may be impossible to connect the mortgage with the tax assessment without an accurate postal address. Many data aggregators do not provide a field to indicate whether the loan is primary or secondary.

The point is that different data aggregators may provide different information about the same source document, depending on how the interfaces are designed. The only way to really know what the source document says is to read it in its original form.

THEY CAN RUN, BUT THEY CAN'T HIDE

On the other hand, consider the "they can run, but they can't hide" phenomenon. The comprehensive database, by acting as a type of search engine, becomes an indispensable resource when trying to connect disparate pieces of information to a single individual.

For example, consider corporate records. Suppose you need to find information about a specific subject whom you believe may be a business owner or officer. Many Secretary of State Abstracts will not include the names of the officers, which may make it impossible to determine whether the subject is an officer of a business. The data aggregator links multiple sources of information, so that if one primary source does not contain the information you need, another will. The name of the officer may occur in a different context in relation to the name of the business. The secretary of a corporation may have signed a Uniform Commercial Code financing statement. If you search only corporate records using the officer's name, the database may not be able to fetch the corporate filing, since the subject's name is not available from the abstract. But, if you request a comprehensive search using the subject's name, the database may catch his or her name from a UCC filing and compile that in the comprehensive report against the subject's name. The UCC filing will reference the company name and indicate the position of the subject as a signer. Voila! You've made your connection.

Please note that this author believes that information aggregators are the best things since pants with pockets. Pre I.A. (information aggregators), investigators had to hope they found every jurisdiction in which a business was registered in order to search for civil litigation or judgments, real property or vehicles, municipal contracts, and the myriad other elements of a proper due diligence investigation. Those were scary times, indeed. Post I.A., the investigator can have a little more confidence that he or she has found the location of most of the rocks to look under. The point of this section is to emphasize that the investigator must not rely only on the information aggregator. It's like preparing a soufflé. First you gather the ingredients, and then the real job of creating the soufflé starts. Purchasing the database report is analogous to gathering the ingredients. It's essential, but it's not the end.

Are you motivated to take the extra step to verify EVERYTHING you learn in an information aggregator's report with the original source material? If so, then the next section will help you get started.

Concept II: *An increasing number of primary sources are making images of their documents available for free or inexpensively via the Internet.*

Government agencies are getting into the electronic age (finally!). Many of them have had database specialists come in and set up systems so that the information the agency stores is more readily available to the agency itself, and consequently, to the public. Sometimes the primary sources make only abstracts of the source information available electronically, and sometimes they provide the images of the documents. When images are available, it saves the investigator (and the client) lots of time and money. So how do you find these digitized primary sources? Use one of the online or paperbound free public record source guides. In my company, we refer to these as "bibles."

SEARCHSYSTEMS.NET

This is a neat little (well, not so little anymore) compendium of as many original document sources as the website administrators can lay their hands on. The gurus behind SearchSystems have recently updated the website to offer more ways to find and access the information at the source. For example, you can look for primary sources by state, by county and state, by type of document, or by zip code (what a good idea that is!). There's a very small yearly sign-up fee, but it's well worth the "all you can eat" nature of the information provided. Note that SearchSystems may point the user to a public record website that requires registration or a fee to search in the primary source database. The SearchSystems lists provide a description of the public record provided at a particular site and whether a fee is required to access the information. SearchSystems will also go to courthouses to collect documents for you. This is a "premium" service for which they charge.

Search Tip: *From SearchSystems, you can get a list of all the public records available in a specific state, county, city, or zip code. If you scan this list, you may learn that a certain type of public record that you hadn't thought about before is available.*

BRBPUB.COM OR PUBLICRECORDSOURCES.COM

The idea behind the BRB website is the same as that of Search Systems. It provides the user with lists of all (or most of) the public records available electronically. The BRB website is free, and also allows the user to sort the public record sources by type of record and location. As with Search Systems, the BRB list may point the user to a website or source for which there may be a charge. The lists also provide a description of the public record provided at a particular site and whether a fee is required to access the information.

BRB provides another very useful tool. BRB has developed the Public Record Retriever Network (PRRN), which allows local document retrievers to advertise through the BRB website. You can access the PRRN directly from the BRB website, filter by state and county, and find a list of all the record retrievers in proximity to the courthouse or agency that houses the documents you are looking for.

The PRRN has established industry standards for the records retrievers it allows to become members. These standards mandate legal compliance, confidentiality, and minimum competencies. The public record retrievers are periodically audited to ensure compliance with the standards. The PRRN also has established a Code of Professional Conduct. The user can be fairly confident that the public record retrievers it locates at the BRB website are capable and accountable. From this author's experience in using the PRRN throughout the United States, the members are indeed competent and reliable. In 17 years of conducting due diligence research, I've only been disappointed once, and that retriever declined to accept payment for his services. Some of the public record retrievers are licensed private investigators, but many are not.

The public record retrievers have made a career out of searching for and obtaining the documents you require. Of course, private investigators also are skilled in searching and retrieving public record. Since the public record retrievers are already in the courthouses where the information is housed, they typically do not charge for travel expenses. Since the public record retriever is so frequently in the courthouse or agency, he or she may have established a relationship with the clerk or custodian of the records, which may assist in getting documents faster than someone who is unknown to the clerk or administrator. Public record retrievers may service more clients in one visit than a private investigator who may need to make a special trip on a case-by-case basis. As a result, the public record retrievers tend to be less expensive and faster than private investigators, while still producing a satisfactory result. This is a general statement and certainly does not apply to all private investigators.

For those of us old enough to remember books published on paper you can touch, BRB Publications, Inc. publishes *The Sourcebook to Public Record Information,* which is a comprehensive guide to local, county, state, and federal public records sources. This book can be purchased directly from BRB, or from other suppliers such as the PI Magazine Bookstore. The Sourcebook provides not only lists of public records, but also addresses, telephone numbers, and web locations of the sources, and a description of which types of records the primary source will release, how to search, typical turnaround time, and other information necessary for deriving information from the source.

Search Tip: *While the title of this chapter refers to electronic resources, sometimes the best and fastest way to obtain information is to telephone the clerk of courts or the administrator of the agency, and just ask him or her to send the document to you. This author frequently is pleasantly surprised at how easy it is to obtain primary source documents—especially from rural locations where it is difficult to find a retriever on the ground.*

Time is money for private investigators. This author frequently uses books written by public record experts to find sources for information rather than search the World Wide Web. It seems to be faster sometimes than waiting for screens to paint and swimming through the advertisements at the websites. Also, by choosing certain authors, the reader can be certain to find quality information. There are literally millions of pages that have been written about how and where to find public records sources. You can find such books by visiting the BRB website, or the PI Store. Other sources for sources can be found at publicrecordcenter.com, and pretrieve.com. If you do a Google search for "public record sources," you'll be overrun with hits. Beware of those websites that promise free information but after the tease, charge a fee to actually retrieve it.

Concept III: *Relevant information is no longer found only with public record sources. Use social networking sites, but use them with care.*

The term "social networking site" is used quite a bit these days. There's Facebook, My Space, Friendster, and Linked In. And then there are lesser known social networking sites like Bebo, Hi5, and Orkut. This author has heard many respected investigators tout how they "cracked a case" by finding some bit of information on a social networking site. This author has had some success as well, but by no means all the time. Social networking sites are not a panacea for information you can't find in a courthouse.

If the use of social networking sites (SNS, both singular and plural) is chosen as an investigative strategy, the due diligence researcher needs to define exactly what kind of information he or she is looking for and then determine the best social networking site in which that information may be found. Most SNS were established so that people can create networks of online friends and engage in group membership to stay in touch, reconnect with old friends, or create friendships. Users can share their interests with other like-minded members by joining groups and forums

The SNS industry has grown beyond the initial uses and is now used to advertise businesses and serve as a job-hunting forum. Many people put their professional biographies on SNS in order to attract like-minded people in the industry and potential employers. Many employers use SNS as recruitment tools. This author has found both business executives' biographies and the work histories of target employees. Remember, however, that the information placed on the SNS is self-reported. The author of the information will publish only what he or she wants to. The middle manager who was fired from two positions probably won't list those positions at his SNS. On the other hand, the middle manager might report that he was a senior vice president. You just never know.

In terms of due diligence investigations, it is this author's experience that the "playful" sites like My Space usually have little relevance, although there are exceptions. An SNS like hi5 may be more useful as it is international in scope and boasts more than 70 million members. Unlike the other well-known SNS, the user must be 18 years of age to join, which eliminates much of the annoying preteen nonsense. Of course, the investigator can always start looking for professional biographical information in Linked In, which was always intended to be professional in nature.

The investigator needs to guess correctly which SNS the subject is likely to use. Wikipedia offers a very helpful list of SNS. It is a list of major active social networking websites and purportedly excludes dating websites, although this author has found a few there. The list provides the name of the SNS, a description of its focus, how many registered users there are, the requirements for membership, and the Alexa page ranking. On the basis of the information derived from Wikipedia, the investigator can evaluate whether it would be useful to visit a specific SNS and browse for information about his or her subject. Bear in mind that the Wikipedia list is by no means an exhaustive directory of the available SNS. There are other SNS that cater to business professionals. MeettheBoss is for financial services executives, and is international in scope. Partner Up is an online community for small business owners and entrepreneurs in which they come together for business information, support, and marketing. Another "collaboration-type" business SNS is Talkbiznow. Motley Fool maintains a message board for stocks, investing, and personal finance. WiserEarth focuses on the social and environmental movement. XING is a global professional networking site.

Of similar use are blogs. Frequently the researcher can gain insight into the subject's attitudes and behavior by reading his blogs. This author has occasionally found information related to events that would never find its way into the public record or a news article. For example, one blogger concerned about the activities occurring at night inside a pharmacy, wrote in a neighborhood-based blog that she saw Mr. X., a known illicit drug distributor, enter the pharmacy at 11:00 PM and leave 30 minutes later with a bulging manila envelope. Mr. X was never arrested, but this bit of information led to a wider investigation of the subject-pharmacist's activities.

How do you find the blogs that might include articles from or about your subject? There are lots of sites that will search for you, although the best results are obtained if you know the name the subject uses in his blogs. Technorati has a comprehensive searchable list of blogs. Some investigators use bloggerchoiceawards, and Stumble Upon. This author's experience is that these blogs are not geared toward due diligence uses. A good way to find blogs is to try blogs.com, where you will find more information about blogs than you thought possible. You can also try AllBusiness at allbusiness.com, a Dun & Bradstreet sponsored website. It provides blogs for those interested in business and professional discussions, including e-commerce and Internet, finance and accounting, human resources, management and leadership. There are lots more, so take a look.

Don't forget the newsgroups, which are online discussion groups that accommodate everyone. Take a look at groups.google.com, and find one that might contain discussion about the topic or person you are researching. The posts that are found in the Google groups typically remain there for several years, so you may find archival information of interest in one of them.

There are also online communities which are a hybrid of a content website and a message board. The investigator may find people with similar interests through a message board on the site. If you are interested in the activities of a particular company, you may wish to look at.allpm.com, which is a community for project managers. Do you remember chat rooms? They still exist.

Remember though, the information you find at a social networking site or a blog has a 50/50 chance of being true and reliable. Are those good enough odds for your investigative report?

Concept IV: *By using a little search strategy, you can reduce the amount of time you'll need to spend to obtain information.*

This section is going to be basic; many experienced investigators use search strategy automatically. Because of experienced investigators' training, search strategy is intuitive. However, in teaching classes in investigative research, this author is constantly amazed that some investigators cannot articulate the research strategy needed to complete a research study. The elements of any search strategy should include the answers to the following broad questions.

1. What is the purpose of the search? Be specific. Are you trying to (a) confirm information you already have? (b) find an appropriate person to interview? (c) learn about an industry or topic so that

you can write a knowledgeable report about a business? (d) determine the current officer of a business? (e) determine the assets of a business or individual. The list is endless.

2. What do you already know about the information you are looking for? What information can you use to start your research?

3. Where are you in your investigation? Just starting and looking for general knowledge about the company or the industry? In the middle and trying to verify what you may have found in a data aggregator or other secondary source? At the end and trying to draw conclusions?

4. Where do you think the information you need is located? Is the information in a courthouse? A governmental agency? A news article? Is there a geographical delimiter for the location of the information? Are you not sure where it might be?

5. How current does the information need to be? Are you looking for information that has recently been published or do you need archival information?

6. How can you obtain the information? Is it available electronically? Maybe the information is not housed in a source that is available via the World Wide Web.

7. When should you stop searching? This author finds this question the hardest of all.

Answering these questions will assist you in formulating an effective search strategy. The rest of this section will assist you in answering questions four and six above.

KEYWORD SEARCHING

Fortunately, Google and the other major search engines have eliminated much of the aggravation that was inherent in keyword searching during the early Boolean search era. There is no longer a need to learn so much about connectors and the order of the words in the search string, although some search engines still require some connectors. Also fortunately, the major search engines have become so fast that if the investigator submits an inartful search string, it is easily and quickly modified to reduce the number of hits or change the focus. But still, keyword searching still requires some planning. Even if you believe yourself to be an expert keyword search strategist, it doesn't hurt to take a few minutes to review each new search engine's rules for searching. This is particularly true when searching a specific website with its own internal search engine.

If you aren't getting the results you want using one search engine, try another. There are still quite a few general search engines, and they vary in speed, depth of indexing, advanced search features, and presentation of the results. This author's experience is that results had tended to be similar among multiple general search engines, but now each is trying to distinguish itself by improving on the Google model. Some are attempting to attract users by offering "smarter" searches; that is, they are now attempting to provide search results that are more useful to the user by focusing on content, rather than statistical analyses (e.g., number of hits or popularity). If you want to learn about the different search engines, visit Searchenginewatch.com, or for a more communal view, visit Searchengineshowdown.com. Or do a Google search for "search engine comparison."

Consider Bing (bing.com) which is Microsoft's attempt to make web searching easier by eliminating irrelevant hits and organizing results by categories rather than by popularity. As of the writing of this chapter, most of Bing's categorizing efforts are geared toward the consumer and relate to topics such as travel, shopping, health, and local information. However, this author has just completed a comprehensive due diligence and assets investigation with respect to a national insurance company using, in part, both Google and Bing, and must report that the search results were somewhat different in each engine. While the results from both were comprehensive and relevant, Bing brought back more relevant results earlier in the search list. This evaluation is based on limited research and should be considered only anecdotal only. Still, if you're not finding what you need on Google, you might want to try another search engine.

OTHER WAYS TO TRAVEL THE WEB

Rather than using a search engine, you may want to try a subject directory. These are databases of websites organized by category. The categorizing is done by human beings with an understanding of language and the topics of the websites, so increased relevance of the results is probable. The information is organized, evaluated, and indexed by a person—not mechanical software—who ranks the website using predetermined criteria. The user drills down through a series of menus of ever narrower scope to find the information he or she is looking for. This is more akin to browsing in a library. It eliminates the need to accurately develop a keyword search that will find all the relevant websites and eliminate the extraneous ones.

There are two problems inherent in subject directories. First, the information may not be as current as that found with a search engine. It takes time for the indexers to evaluate the websites, and that lengthens the time between directory updates. Second, there is the human factor. Is the indexer correctly evaluating the significance of the website in terms of the needs of the investigator? Consider the problem of indexing case law. Legal experts for a publishing company read all the opinions written in a particular court or jurisdiction, and then determine the import of the court's decision based on the facts of the case. If the indexer does not include or misinterprets a specific finding in his evaluation, that conclusion of the court will not be represented in the index. In effect, that bit of law will be lost as precedent in future decisions. This "human factor" effect is present whenever people categorize information. So, the fact that trained human indexers are creating the web subject directories is both the good news and the bad news.

Subject directories typically are useful when you begin the due diligence research. They may help you determine effective words to use for keyword searching, and help you build a general understanding of the nature of the business or industry you are investigating. Subject directories may be helpful in product information searches. Use a subject directory when you don't know what you're looking for or use it when you need to narrow it down.

The subject directory you need will vary depending on the nature of the due diligence investigation. To find a subject directory, you may wish to look at The Open Directory Project at dmoz.org/. I generally choose the Reference link and start drilling from there. You can also use About.com at about.com. My favorite is the Librarians' Internet Index at ipl.org/. It seems to include more sites that provide professional, financial, and business information. This site also includes a search box at every level so if you are ready to move to a keyword search within a category, you can do so.

Probably the oldest and best research subject directory is The Virtual Chase at Thevirtualchase.com. The researcher can start at the main menu, then drill down to Company Information, Officers and Executives, Public Company Filings, Public Records, Public Opinion, or Companies in the News. If you choose Public Opinion, you will find websites such as Glassdoor.com which may provide you with salary details for employees of specific companies. It also leads you to ResearchBuzz at researchbuz.com, which allows you to search official blogs of politicians, companies, libraries, and more. There are even categories for Special Search Engines and Developing Search Strategies. What more could you ask for?

PREMIUM SEARCH TOOLS

The premium databases are the ones you must pay to use. As with everything else, the adage, "You get what you pay for," applies to information gathering as well. You owe it to your client to manage your time well, thereby reducing the costs of the investigation. Using a general data aggregator will significantly reduce the amount of time you will spend in searching for relevant information. There are literally thousands of premium databases that claim to offer almost every kind of information you would need in your due diligence research. These premium databases are frequently available only to law enforcement, licensed investigators or other professionals who typically have a permissible purpose to use the sometimes confidential information the databases provide.

In terms of backgrounds on individuals, the premium databases are useful for obtaining fairly accurate address histories, which in turn, will assist the researcher in knowing where to look for real property, vehicles, businesses, litigation, or criminal records, to name just a few. Some databases will provide the researcher with dates of birth and Social Security numbers, which not only help to identify the subject, but are useful for determining whether the subject is availing himself of more than one identity. As discussed above, a comprehensive report on an individual will frequently lead the researcher to his business affiliations and associates who may become of interest in the course of the background investigation.

There are two schools of thought about using premium databases first or after exhausting all of the free sources. One side maintains that by using a general data aggregator first, the rest of your investigation can be more focused, thereby maximizing the time spent hunting for information. On the other hand, this also may blind the investigator to avenues of searching that are not included in the database, and there are many. The other side advocates exhausting all the free resources first, and then using the fee-based sources. There is a combination strategy, which this author tends to use most often, which involves moving back and forth from free to fee-based as necessary. Do a general Google or other search engine search for the name of the company and the individuals, to develop an understanding of the nature of the business and industry, and to determine what is freely available with regard to all the subjects. Oftentimes, a general search will bring up news stories published in general circulation newspapers, significant civil litigation, and even some blogs which reference the subjects. Then use one or more premium websites to find any information that the general search might have missed. And finally, return to the appropriate primary source websites to find the images of the original materials you need to document the information you found in the secondary sources, such as the data aggregators.

MORE PREMIUM INFORMATION SOURCES

There are many online business profilers that compile and present data regarding businesses and the individuals associated with them. The size of the business will determine which business data compiler you choose. Smaller businesses typically are not well-represented in large (and expensive) databases such as Dun & Bradstreet, which does a much more credible job with medium-sized and large businesses. For smaller businesses, the researcher may want to use profilers like Manta at manta.com, or Cortera, at cortera.com. Dun & Bradstreet offers a very watered down version of its Business Information Report at allbusiness.com. There are others. This author frequently purchases business credit reports from Experian at experian.com. These may contain a wealth of information in addition to the trade experiences, and give a good picture of whether the company is actually operating or just being used as a shell (perhaps to launder money, but that's a different topic).

News and media searches are essential to every due diligence investigation. There are several comprehensive news databases available from Dow Jones at factiva.com and from Lexis Nexis. There are also news aggregators such as High Beam, which is an excellent fee-based service. High Beam at highbeam.com states that it is ". . . the premier online research tool for business and academic use. Here, you can search more than 80 million articles from the archives of over 6,500 newspapers, magazines, journals, and other publications." This author has had much success with High Beam, especially in finding articles that may not have appeared in newspapers of general circulation.

Another useful premium service is Northern Light at northern-light.com. At its website, Northern Light states, "Northern Light provides strategic research portals for market research, competitive intelligence, business analysis, product development, and technology research. . . ." "A typical strategic research portal from Northern Light might contain one or more repositories of internal primary research, dozens of licensed external secondary research subscription sources, business news, financial analyst reports, government databases, and content acquired from custom Web crawls." Northern Light is expensive, but if the budget permits, it is well worth the fee.

Search Tip: *By using different databases with different fee structures, the investigator can save a great deal of money in data acquisition. For example, when using many of the general news services, the researcher may be required to pay a certain sum to read and print out each article. However, by using the Lexis Nexus Accurint service, the researcher pays per search, and not for each individual article. (Let's try to keep this tip a secret so the fee structure doesn't change. . . .)*

To find government websites that may house the information you need, use a directory of government sources. Use the government directory at usa.gov or the Carroll Directory at carrollpub.com. While there is no guarantee that the links will lead to websites that provide information about specific people or companies, it will at least let you know where a potential source exists.

Use trade association websites to determine if a subject is a member of the group—especially if he claims to be. There are trade groups in every industry from accounting to the Association of Zoos and Aquariums. Some states require medical practitioners to file profiles with the professional licensing board, and then make those profiles available via the web. There are military finders, such as searchmil.com that provides a wealth of information about military facilities throughout the world. These sources are endless, too.

GET CREATIVE

If your subject is an expert in a certain field or industry, use an expert-finder search site to learn about his credentials. Try using Profnet at profnet.com, an "online community of thousands of professional communicators" that will connect you with professional experts. Registration is required but free. Or use AllExperts. Search Forbes for information related to a specific business. The CIA World Factbook has more uses than can be described in this chapter. Check out Refdesk.com, which describes itself as the "Fact Checker for the Internet." Or take a look at Internet FAQ Archives at faqs.org/faqs, which also includes business information. Again, he list is endless.

Take advantage of RSS feeds. RSS stands for Really Simple Syndication, and will allow the investigator to receive constant updates about the subjects she specifies. Most blogs will allow readers to set up a "feed," which will bring blogs regarding the topics you request directly to you the reader's desktop. Setting up RSS is easy. You'll need a feed reader, which you can download for free. Do a Google search for "feed readers" and you'll receive enough sites offering downloads to choose from. If a site has enabled RSS, there will be an RSS icon on its address bar. Click on the icon and follow the directions to set up your feed. Easy enough? The feeds will alert you to news articles, blogs, and many other sources of information related to your search topics, as they become available. The feeds are customized to your specific needs, eliminating the need to wade through all the irrelevant "stuff" that normally comes with electronic research based on keywords and the popularity of the website.

Concept V: *Your job as an investigator is not finished when you collect the information. You must also analyze it and then create a cogent report that is meaningful to the client.*

KNOW WHAT YOU'RE TALKING ABOUT

The investigator should understand enough about the subject's industry to include as much relevant information as possible. That's why this chapter touched on researching the subject company's industry while collecting information specific to the due diligence subjects. The investigator does not need to educate himself in the intricacies of widget development, or the investment strategies in the derivative market. But he or she should be aware that certain information is required in order to give the client a complete picture of the subject(s). At the very least, a due diligence investigation should include basic information such as the company's legal name, its address and telephone numbers, and the location of the branches. It should also include the corporate structure: its parents and subsidiaries and the operations of each. The report should include the executives' names, corporate affiliations, and backgrounds. A bit of company history is always helpful. A survey of civil litigation or criminal records related to the company and its officers should be included. The lifestyle or standard of living of the officers may be relevant. All of this information forms the bare bones of the due diligence report and is probably available electronically using basic searching techniques, free sources, and premium databases.

The rest of the due diligence report depends on the purpose of the due diligence inquiry. Is it for a merger or acquisition? Is it being used by an attorney in a legal matter? Is an insurance company looking for assets? There are as many reasons for due diligence inquiries as there are inquirers. The investigator may need to include assessments of the company by creditors, by its investors, by industry analysts, or by competitors. This is when advanced search skills come into play. For this information, the investigator needs to consult the news reports, trade journals, and the independent business profilers. The investigator needs to know what sorts of reports the company needs to file with regulatory agencies, and whether those reports are considered public domain. More and more information is becoming available electronically and in its original form. As the investigator, it is your responsibility to include those original reports in your investigative analysis.

TELL THE CLIENT WHAT IT MEANS

It is not enough just to collect the information related to the due diligence investigation. The investigator also needs to explain what it means to the client. Of course, it is the client or his attorney who must analyze the meaning of the SEC Form 10-K, or the IRS Form 990 related to a nonprofit, or the effectiveness of the Risk Management Policy of ABC Corp. that you have summarized and appended to the investigative report. But the investigator has a duty to let the client know where the information came from and how reliable it is. The investigator cannot state in his report that the public relations officer of ABC Corp. stated that the widgets that its competitor is producing are defective. What was the context? Was it a marketing opportunity? Was it a news conference announcing the introduction of the ABC Super Widget? Was the statement made at a scientific conference? You can see that the context tells a great deal about the reliability of the information provided. The client needs to know the value of the information you are providing, or the report does not assist him in making his business decision.

Suppose you found a bit of information in a discussion group. Mary Jane from Peoria said that the chief operating officer of XYZ Investment Company was a thief and a liar, and she can prove it. That's the end of her contribution to that discussion. Would you incorporate that piece of data in your client report? Is that information accurate and reliable? Who is reporting that information? What, you don't know? Perhaps you need to consider finding some supporting documentation before reporting Mary Jane of Peoria's analysis of the COO's conduct.

TELL THE CLIENT WHERE TO FIND IT

Include proper citations to the sources of the information. The client may wish to evaluate the validity and reliability of the information you provide on her own. You can make it an opportunity to impress the client with how bright and resourceful you are by including the sophisticated and respected sources you consulted to compile his report. Be sure to use appropriate citation format. Citation styles vary depending on the type of information you are reporting. If you are interested in an overview of this topic, do a keyword search for "electronic source citation style" and you will find thousands of style guides. You may narrow it by searching for "citation styles" and the type of document you are referencing. This will assist you in including all the information necessary for your client to find the source you reference.

CONCLUSION

Part of your responsibility as an investigator is to evaluate the information you provide to the client. This chapter began with the admonition: ALWAYS GO TO THE SOURCE. Why? Because the original document is the only source that can be trusted. There's really no arguing with the primary source, even if it is inaccurate. You must be sure that the information you provide to your client is accurate, reliable, and supportable. Except for the images of primary source documents, everything you obtain electronically should be suspect. Certainly the information derived from social networking sites, blogs, or discussion groups cannot be trusted. News articles are more reliable, but you cannot be sure that the reporter or the publisher is not biased, or that the news article presents the most current facts. Has the article been updated or has the news item been resolved in a way that the publisher thinks will no longer interest the public, and so a follow-up report is never written?

Even the respected Federal Bureau of Investigation National Crime Information Center (NCIC) warns law enforcement officers that a positive response from the NCIC during a traffic stop does not create probable cause for the officer to take action. Instead, the officer is instructed to make contact with the agency that entered the information into the NCIC system in order to confirm that the information is accurate and up to date.

How can you determine whether a fact is truly a fact? Just listen to the political commentary during any campaign. Can you isolate the facts from the rhetoric? This chapter began with the concept that only primary source information can be trusted, and so it will end with it.

Chapter 20

ACCIDENT INVESTIGATION
AND RECONSTRUCTION

David G. Duchesneau

Accident Reconstruction is commonly thought to be synonymous with motor vehicle accidents but, in all actuality, accident reconstruction deals with any type of accident in all areas of settings and industries. Every day, across the United States and abroad, people and machines react unexpectedly, causing thousands of accidents. Every day, accidents claim lives or cause permanent injury.

When an accident occurs, such as motor vehicle, train, construction, pedestrian, lawn mower, golf cart, marine, employee, step ladder, it is not enough to say that something went wrong.

Accident investigation and reconstruction not only help determine exactly what happened, but can also help prevent future accidents from occurring. In short, regardless of what type of accident occurs, all accidents can be investigated and reconstructed to determine the cause of said accident.

DEFINITION OF AN ACCIDENT

BusinessDirectory.com defines an accident as "an unplanned, unexpected and undersigned, not purposefully caused event which occurs suddenly and causes injury or loss, a decrease in value of the resources or an increase in liabilities."

YourDirectory.com defines an accident as "a happening that is not expected, foreseen or intended. An unpleasant and unintending happening, sometimes resulting from negligence that results in injury, loss damage, etc."

The legal definition on Lawyers.com is "an unexpected sudden event that occurs without intent or volition although sometimes through carelessness, unawareness, ignorance, or a combination of causes that produces an unfortunate result, such as an injury, for which the affected party may be entitled to relief under the law or to compensation under an insurance policy."

Black's Law Dictionary, Second Edition, defines an accident as "an unforeseen event, occurring without the will or design of the person whose mere act caused it; an unexpected, unusual, or undersigned occurrence; the effect of an unknown cause, or, the cause being known, an unprecedented consequence of it; a casualty."

WHY ONE NEEDS AN ACCIDENT INVESTIGATOR

With the above definitions of an accident, it is quite obvious why one would want and need the services of a private investigator who has been trained in accident investigation and reconstruction.

First, accident investigation and reconstruction will determine the cause of the accident and help avoid future reoccurrence, whether on a company's, client's, or the homeowner's premises.

Second, accident investigation and reconstruction may reduce liability by determining the cause of the accident and assigning liability for damages and injuries. Thus, a good accident investigator and reconstructionist can assign fault and liability, saving thousands of dollars.

Third, a good private investigator will provide answers as to what caused the accident and sometimes, just knowing what really happened, can bring a sense of closure. An accident reconstruction will provide what really happened in any specific situation.

Fourth, an accident investigation and reconstruction will gather evidence that can be used in court. If one is attempting to assign fault, negligence, and/or liability, only a qualified accident investigator can gather and preserve the evidence needed to solidify a court case. This truth holds for all types of accidents, motor vehicle, industrial, pedestrian, bicycle, or any unique accident that may have occurred.

Depending on the nature of the accident, a private investigator trained to conduct accident investigations visits the accident site and collects evidence. In the case of a motor vehicle accident, measures the skid marks and gouges on a roadway, inspects the vehicle and tires for any possible defects, photographs the accident scene, interviews witnesses and those involved in the accident. The investigator will reconstruct the accident to determine the factors involved in the cause of the accident. Whatever type of accident that is being investigated, the common denominator is a qualified accident investigator. Only a good and experienced private investigator will be able to obtain the evidence needed to properly reconstruct the accident.

The first step that a private investigator will do in any accident reconstruction is request a copy of the accident report, either from the police jurisdiction that initially covered the accident or from the insurance company.

MOTOR VEHICLE ACCIDENTS

Motor vehicle accidents are the most common type of injury producing incidences in the United States. The main issues in litigating motor vehicle accidents involve vehicle speed, seatbelt usage, airbag deployment, vehicle component failure, roadway design, occupant biomechanics, rollover, visibility, weather, road hazards, poor illumination, and any other contributing factor that may have caused the accident.

Motor vehicle accident reconstruction is the scientific process of investigating, analyzing, and drawing conclusions about the causes and events during a vehicle collision. Reconstructionists are employed to conduct an in-depth collision analysis and reconstruction to identify the collision causation and all of the contributing factors in different types of collisions, including the role of the driver, vehicle, roadway, and the environment. The accident reconstruction provides rigorous analysis that an expert witness can present at a trial. Results from accident reconstructions are also useful in developing recommendations for improving the safety of roads and highways, as well as future motor vehicle designs.

Scene inspections and data recovery involve visiting the scene of the accident. The investigator takes photographs of the scene from all angles, as well as measurements of the roadway, including the break-down lanes and guardrails. The speed limit is recorded and the investigator will look for any physical evidence, such as skid marks and gauges, resulting from vehicle damage. This evidence will be photographed. The length of a skid mark can often allow calculation of the minimum speed of the vehicle prior to impact. Vehicle speeds are often underestimated by a driver, making an independent estimate of speed essential in accidents. Accident reconstructionists are relied upon to determine the distance that a vehicle traveled before coming to a complete stop. The length of the skid marks can determine the speed the vehicle was traveling at the beginning of the skid. An investigator can accomplish this with considerable accuracy, based on knowledge of the physical principles that are involved, including available information relating to the friction of tires on various types of road surfaces. Eyewitness statements are crucial and inspection of the roadway is vital, especially when traction has been lost due to black ice, diesel fuel contamination, or road debris.

Reaction time is when a person becomes aware of a dangerous situation and the time-interval elapsed before defensive action is taken. This time has been found to be approximately 0.7 seconds for most people, regardless of background and training. Driver reaction time is the time taken by a driver after perceiving a hazardous situation and taking preventive action. Thinking or mental reaction time is the time required for the driver to decide what to do, while muscular reaction time is the time required to set the vehicle controls in motion. The thinking and reaction times vary considerably, depending upon how complicated a decision is. The 0.7 second reaction time applies only if the person knows what to do to avert the danger. In the case of an impending collision, the use of brakes to slow the vehicle is well known and, in fact, is ordinarily habitual, so that there is no delay, other than the reaction time itself, in applying the brakes when necessary.

Airbags are credited with reducing numerous injuries and saving many lives during motor vehicle accidents; however, there have been incidents where airbags have not functioned as intended, and have even caused injuries, such as explosive powder burns, detached retinas, child suffocation, and impact death. In other cases, airbags have not deployed when they should have, or even deployed unnecessarily, thus causing a motor vehicle accident and resultant sequellae. Many malfunctions do not occur in the airbag modules but rather in the electronic device that detects a collision and signals if and when an airbag should be deployed. Therefore, the accident investigator will inspect and photograph the vehicle for any type of damage and air bag deployment. The investigator will inspect the brake lights to verify whether or not the brakes were used at the time of the collision.

FALLS

Second only to automobile accidents, falls are the leading cause of injury and death. Of these, statistics show that accidents due to slipping form a large proportion of falls. Slips and trips occur on floors, streets, walkways, stairs, curbings, basically in any location that a person may move about. Although both slips and trips results in falls, they are quite different. A slip is associated with insufficient resistance between the person's foot and the walking surface, while a trip involves much more resistance than the victim had anticipated. A third type of fall occurs when a person has a loss of balance. This can occur when an individual expects a surface to provide support, but it does not.

The accident investigator will document, photograph and take measurements of the area of the accident (fall). Eyewitnesses will be interviewed and records will be checked to ascertain if any falls occurred in the past. A diagram will be drafted of the accident area.

PEDESTRIANS AND BICYCLES

Pedestrian and bicycle accidents account for thousands of injuries and deaths annually. Even though pedestrians and bicycles move differently, they share important characteristics, as they both have little protection during a roadway collision with a motor vehicle. In many instances of accident, the visibility of pedestrians and cyclists to drivers, and vice-versa, is a major factor in the cause of the accident.

In reconstructing these types of accidents, the investigator documents the accident scene with photographs, measurements, and diagrams, as well as interviewing the victim(s), the operator of the vehicle, and any eyewitnesses.

GOLF CARTS

According to the Consumer Products Safety Commission (CPSC), there are approximately 10,000 golf cart-related accidents requiring emergency room treatment in the United States annually. The majority of these accidents are related to either braking, cart rollover, or passenger ejection. These problems are common to golf carts due to their open design, lack of seat belts, poor braking capabilities, and uneven terrains. While industry standards prohibit golf carts from exceeding a maximum speed of 15 miles per hour, rollovers and ejections still occur, due to sharp turns, steep inclines, mechanical failures, and driver error. Most golf carts are equipped with rear brakes only, thus limiting their stopping ability.

If an insurance claim is made and a private investigator is retained to investigate and reconstruct these types of accidents, the same protocol should follow, i.e., interviewing the victim(s) and eye-witnesses, photographing and diagramming the accident scene, as well as a thorough inspection of the golf cart.

LAWNMOWER ACCIDENTS

Statistically, there are approximately 180,000 lawnmower accidents annually. There are two (2) basic types of lawn mowers, the walk behind, which can be either pushed or self-propelled, and the riding. The leading cause of lawnmower accidents is contact with its rotating blade. While the danger from this may seem obvious, it is an established fact that people will, and do, place their hand and fingers near the blade, generally in an attempt to clear away an obstruction. Another cause of lawnmower accidents is the throwing of objects by the blade, such as small stones. These objects can, and will, travel in all directions, causing injury to nearby persons, including the operator. The operator or a nearby person may slip, causing a foot to enter under the skirt of the mower and contacting the rotating blades. Burns occur as a result of touching a hot surface of the engine's exhaust system. In addition, fires are caused by a gasoline leakage or vapors ignited by a spark from the ignition system. Riding mowers can cause injuries due to their instability, increasing the propensity of the mower to overturn under certain conditions. Due to the operator's limited visibility, as well as the noise generated by the mower, a riding mower may also be subjected to a higher incidence of backing-over accidents, due to the limited ability to hear the cry of a person behind them. If an accident occurs and a claim is made, the Claims Adjustor often retains the services of a private investigator to reconstruct a lawn mower accident. The investigator documents the accident with photographs, interviews the injured person(s) and witnesses, and conducts a complete examination of both the mower and the area where the accident occurred.

LADDERS

According to the Consumer Product Safety Commission (CPSC), there are over 100,000 ladder accidents annually in the United States requiring emergency room treatment. Approximately 85 to 90 percent of these accidents involve falling off the ladder and 8 to 9 percent of these injuries are serious enough to require the victim to be admitted to a hospital. Most accidents are from user misuse, such as an improper extension ladder lean angle against a wall causing it to slip outward, use of a damaged ladder, or failing to lock a stepladder's spreaders. Many ladders fail due to design or manufacturing defects, as well. Many are designed too flexible and some extension ladders are equipped with inferior rung locks. In addition to posing a severe health concern, these accidents have significant loss-of-wages and high medical expenses. If an injury claim is made and the insurance adjustor retains a private investigator, the investigator takes photographs, inspects the ladder, interviews the victim(s) and witnesses, and documents the injuries.

SUMMARY

Any and all types of accidents have the potential to be investigated and reconstructed by a private investigator. Proper and factual documentation is the key factor in any investigation.

In the private sector, accidents are investigated and reconstructed after the fact, relying on investigative experience and knowledge to gather and document facts as accurately as possible, factual, clear, concise, to the point, and without prejudice or conjecture.

An accident reconstructionist provides an expert opinion and detailed analysis regarding different types of accidents, giving reports to insurance claims adjustors or attorneys as part of a defense in litigation, and providing expert testimony in court, if needed. Many attorneys and law firms value the assistance of accident reconstructionists in preparing trial documents and court exhibits.

Chapter 21

EMPLOYEE THEFT

JEFFREY STEIN

Employee Theft is one of the largest problems businesses have today. According to the American Society of Employers, the FBI previously called employee theft the fastest growing crime in America. Here are some devastating statistics that will be helpful when deciding if conducting employee theft investigations is an area that you would like to focus on.

The following statistics are also important talking points when discussing your client's needs and concerns. Giving you the ability to inform them why they need a licensed professional investigator who is a subject matter expert in employee dishonesty to assist them with this growing epidemic.

The American Society of Employers reports that 20 percent of every dollar earned by an American company is lost to employee theft–$53.6 billion per year.

Fifty-five percent of perpetrators are in the highest-level positions and the average length of time it takes for one to be caught was 18 months.

The U.S. Chamber of Commerce estimates one-third of all corporate bankruptcies are a result of employee theft.

The U.S. Chamber of Commerce estimates that 75 percent of employees steal from the workplace and that most do so repeatedly.

According to research conducted by the Association of Certified Fraud Examiners (ACFE), U.S. organizations lose an estimated 7 percent of annual revenues to fraud. Based on the projected U.S. Gross

Domestic Product for 2008, this percentage indicates a staggering estimate of losses around $994 billion among organizations, despite increased emphasis on antifraud controls and recent legislation to combat fraud.

WHO

Before we focus on the "How To" investigate employee thefts and frauds, you first need to understand who steals, how, and why. Does the "why" really matter? Yes, it might help you identify the "who," based on the why. It will also be helpful to know the "why" during the interview process to help you receive the verbal and written admission.

What does the employee who steals from their employer look like? What is his or her position within the organization? What is his or her salary?

The answer is, it could be anyone, it does not matter what race, religion, sex, nationality, or what his or her financial status maybe. All levels of employees from the first level associate to the CEO are involved. We have all read in the news about executives who have stolen one way or another from their employer, shareholders, or trusted client; and if you read the local police blotters, you may learn about other levels of employees who have stolen from their employers. When beginning your due diligence into investigating employee thefts and frauds, keep an open mind and do not rule out anyone until you have sufficient evidence that identifies the actual perpetrator.

As we discuss employee theft, everyone knows that it is common in the retail world. Does employee theft happen in other business too? Yes, although it is very common in retail stores, restaurants, bars, and warehouses, any and all businesses are potential victims. Here are some examples:

- Doctor's office—nurse steals money from the daily deposit comprised of the co-pays from the patients.
- Director of Operations at the same doctors office, after being briefed on physical security procedures to help reduce and eliminate thefts from occurring at the workplace, was later identified as embezzling over $65,000 from the bank deposits.

- Executives falsifying their expense records to inflate their expense payments and or conceal personal trips.
- Car Dealership–office employee identified manipulating customers' credit card payments and transferring the credits to her own personal credit cards.
- Automobile Mechanic–stealing customer's personal belongings and money from their vehicles.
- Gas Stations–employees pocketing cash sales.
- CEO of a major retailer fabricated his resume.

The list can go on and on from sales associates, store managers, secretaries, executives, blue collar workers, white-collar workers, CEOs, etc., where there is a will, there is a way.

WHAT

The items that employees generally steal fall into two categories–tangibles and intangibles.

Tangibles include inventory and all other assets owned by the employer. For example, a clothing stores inventory includes all of their items on hand and for sale as well as the store's computer and other physical assets. Copper theft is on the rise and is another example. Copper can be stolen from refrigeration units, rooftops, plumbing stores, etc.

Intangibles include money, time, and information. For example, employees who steal time by saying they are working and getting paid for their time when they are really surfing the Internet for five hours of the day. With social networking sites like Facebook, employees are spending more and more time on such sites than performing their daily job functions. Another example is the sales associate who claims to be making sales calls but instead is spending the day at the beach. Embezzling is another common intangible method of stealing from a company and its customers and shareholders.

WHY

We are going to expand on some of the ways employees cause loss to their employers and how to investigate them, but before we do, let us briefly talk about why the "why" could be an important part of the investigative process.

There are many reasons employees steal from their employers. Learning as much as you can about the employees, their personal lives, families, financial status, health issues, personal troubles, drug addictions, gambling addictions, etc. may help you with your investigation. Dishonest employees steal for various reasons including, but not limited to, need, vindictiveness, drugs, greed, and financial problems.

Those are some of the more common reasons adults steal from their employers. Peer pressure, money, greed and fitting in are also some common reasons for the younger adult. However, there are even more reasons that can come in to play: for example, the young mother stealing money to give to her child for lunch money because her husband is an alcoholic and uses their hard-earned money on his alcohol and gambling problems. Another example is the store manager who conceals losses during the store's inventory so he can receive a bonus and or keep from being terminated because of poor shrink results.

When conducting due diligence, in the early stages of your investigation, the more you are able to learn about the employees the more it may help you identify the motive and lead you to the "who." So the why may help to point you to the who, but it is also a valuable tool to utilize when conducting your investigative interview to help you relate to your suspect and to assist in the admissions. During the interview process, an experienced interviewer will utilize this information to help receive the verbal and written admission from the subject.

HOW

How do employees steal from their employers? An entire book could be devoted to the "How" and probably by the time it was published, another book could be published with even newer ways that surfaced since the previous book. In the past, I have recovered how-to-steal manuals from both employees and shoplifters. You can even find them available on the Internet. There are common methods, unique methods, and, of course, where there is a will there is a way. Therefore, let's discuss a few of the methods that professional investigators may encounter. These can also be useful for the investigator to share with his or her clients.

Most thefts start out small, where the employees test the waters. Once they get away with the initial theft, they continue and while they continue both the frequency and the dollar amount of the thefts increases. Dishonest employees do not even realize how much they may have stolen from their employer until they are confronted and the evidence is presented to them. In some cases, a paper trail of their crimes is established and also through admissions and analyzing the patterns, frequencies, and theft items. It is only then where the employee learns of the actual dollar amount of loss that they caused their employer.

When thefts are not identified and the bleeding continues, they can end up in the thousands or tens of thousands of dollars. For example, if supervisor at the local golf course stole five dollars a day from the daily funds for five days a week, for 50 weeks out of the year over a course of 15 years, he would have stolen $18,750. Of course, five dollars is a small amount, but just imagine how quickly the losses add up, especially when an employer has multiple employees stealing from them and no checks and balances in place to identify these losses.

Another example of how losses add up when an employer lets their guard down involved an investigation of a manager of an independently owned gift shop. The business owner had received an anonymous tip that the employee (store manager) was selling stolen merchandise on e-bay. During the investigation, merchandise was purchased on e-bay by the investigator. The only thefts that were known then involved the stolen merchandise and because of some accounting issues, there was also some concern that instant lottery tickets that were sold from the store may also have been compromised. Through a detailed investigation and thorough investigative interview, the final admission from the dishonest employee was theft over $35,000 during a five-year period.

Tangible and intangible items are often stolen over a period of time with the amount and frequencies increasing each time they get away with it.

Merchandise is often concealed on a person, in bags, briefcases, purses, and backpacks. Another common method is for the employee to conceal merchandise in the garbage and retrieve it later after the business closes or before it opens. This writer has seen and investigated stolen merchandise that was being concealed in wax buckets and floor-cleaning machines, after being put in plastic bags, so the merchandise was not ruined. The cleaning company then walked right past security carrying what was thought to be empty wax buckets while the large floor cleaning machinery was being pushed out with stolen merchandise in it, too. In the retail industry, fraudulent refunds and voids are a very common method for employees to steal money by concealing their thefts through these fraudulent transactions.

Regardless of the item, no matter what it is, there is always a market for it. Therefore, do not down play someone stealing odd or unique items. Most merchandise has a market somewhere; like the old expression, one person's junk is another person's treasure. Items can be fenced through various venues.

Listed below are some additional examples and methods of stealing either tangible or intangible items:

- Under ringing merchandise, also known as sweat hearting
- Theft of cash or bank deposits (often fictitiously reporting a burglary or robbery)
- Theft of time
- Fraudulently writing and/or accepting bad checks or credit cards
- Being paid to accept stolen credit cards
- Padding of inventory
- Embezzling
- Setting up a fake employee–payroll fraud
- Creating and paying a fake company or vendor
- Eating or drinking the profits
- Failure to ring a cash sale and pocketing the money
- Expense fraud (fraudulent expenses and either stealing the money or merchandise)
- Employees' theft from their employers' clients and customers
- Workers Comp (sick time, etc.)
- Office supplies
- Using employer's phone to make long-distance calls
- Using employer's postage
- Using employer's carries to ship personal items (UPS, FedEx, etc.)
- Proprietary information
- Stealing customers' data bases

The list goes on and on and so does the potential list of clients that you can offer your services to combat these ongoing and growing problems.

CONDUCTING THE INVESTIGATION

What to do first? Find out what the client's objectives are. What do they suspect? Who? Why? When? How much is their known loss?

You should also know your local, state, and federal laws prior to conducting the investigation and interview process.

Now it is time to roll up your sleeves and conduct your due diligence. No rocks should be left unturned during your investigation. It is very common to identify more than one dishonest employee when called into an investigation involving employee dishonesty as well as identifying thefts and frauds that the client was not even aware of.

At this stage of the investigation, if it is possible, I do not recommend letting anyone know that an investigation is ongoing. The reason for this is that when it is time to interview the subject, it is always best to catch him off guard, so he does not have time to prepare and concoct an excuse, explanation, fictitious reason, or alibi for the crime you are investigating. You also do not want the suspect to flee.

If it is known that an investigator is present, fact-finding interviews can be conducted when appropriate. Otherwise wait until all of your due diligence has been completed prior to conducting any fact-finding or integrity interviews.

Next, it is important to conduct an overall assessment of the company's policies and procedures, if they have them. If they do not, that is another service you can provide for them after your investigation is concluded.

Review the general ledgers and profit and loss statements (P&Ls) as well as inventory records if they are available, employee files, absentee records, exception reports, etc. You are looking for patterns and or irregularities.

You want to identify the following:

- Who handles the money and record keeping for the organization? Is it the same person?
- Are there any checks and balances in place?
- Do any of the documents look altered?
- Have they been changed, crossed out, white out used to change the documents, etc.?
- Missing deposits?

- Are there excessive refund or void transactions?
- If excessive refunds and voids are identified, are there any patterns; for example, same name being used repeatedly, similar addresses?
- Are there company documents that are now missing?
- Are there excessive credit memos?
- Is the general ledger out of balance?
- Do the deposits match the amount deposited into the bank?
- Are duplicate payments found in the ledger?
- Are there excessive paid outs for supplies?
- Are there excessive cash transactions found in expense accounts?
- Is the company's inventory shortage higher than the rest of the company?
- Is the company's inventory shortages lower than the rest of the company? This is often overlooked.
- Is it too good to be true? Conduct an inventory validation audit.
- Are the employee time sheets altered?
- Is there actually a real, live employee for each employee receiving a paycheck?
- Are there frequent shipments to a particular address?
- Are you able to confirm what products were sent to what address?
- Were they legitimate shipments?
- Are invoices purposely not voided out to avoid duplicate payments?
- Are all documents and invoices the original?
- Are the employees signing for the proper amount of boxes indicated on the shipping logs?
- Are sales being manipulated to win prizes or contests?
- Verify employee records, resumes, college degrees, and other licenses that the employee indicated they hold.
- Any changes in employee's family life, i.e., divorce, marriage, children, death in family?
- Does the employee frequently call out sick or do they not call out at all even when they are sick?
- Have there been excessive internal or external complaints rendered upon an employee?

If at any time in your review of the general ledgers and profit and loss statements you find that you are either not capable of reviewing this information or find evidence pointing to manipulation of the books, white-collar crimes, or other thefts and frauds, you may want to consider bringing in a forensic accountant. Having a forensic accountant review the information, so it will be well documented for civil or criminal cases as needed, and would be strongly recommended at this stage of the investigation if it were needed.

We all must acknowledge in our career as professional investigators that we are notexperts in every category and we do not do our clients justice by not bringing in the best subject matter expert, investigator for the assignment as needed.

Do you have legal access to the employee's computer, emails, and employment files? If so, examine them at this time. A computer forensic expert should be called in to review the hard drive and any other computer hardware for any evidence that may be helpful in your investigation, including looking for policy and procedure violations. An example would be pornographic information on a work computer. In addition, during this review, the computer forensics expert can identify if the employee has been spending excessive amounts of time on the Internet and social network sites when they were on the company clock.

Once you have reviewed the records that are available and interviewed the client who hired you, you will need to determine what the next course of action is. Do you need to conduct surveillances? Install covert equipment? Conduct mystery shops? Place an undercover operative in the organization?

What background checks and further research needs to be completed on any of the employees? Did you check to see who has an arrest record?

Review and research Internet findings on the company, employees, suspects, etc. If merchandise was stolen, search the Internet for the stolen merchandise; research craigslist, e-bay, pawnshops, etc.

When searching craigslist, you can use this site to better optimize your search: http://www.searchtempest.com/; another good site (fee) for conducting craigslist searches is http://www.adnotifier.com/

Are there any anticompany forums or websites on the internet about the company you are working for? You would be surprised about how many forums and websites are created on individual companies by disgruntled employees. On these forums, they sometimes post crimes that they have committed as well as reveal crimes or policy violations committed by other past and present employees.

Another site to review is http://www.youtube.com/. Search youtube .com for the company you are working for, products, employee names and anything else that may be relevant regarding the investigation. I have investigated several thefts, frauds and policy violations for companies, where their employees posted videos on youtube.com documenting their crimes and policy violations right there on the Internet for everyone to see. Again, do not leave any stone unturned. The evidence may be right at your fingertips.

Did you verify and reconcile the employee's past work experience, resume, college degree, military and any professional license that he or she may have claimed. There are several different studies that have been conducted and some say as high as 60 percent of resumes contain fabricated information. In 2006, a reporter was doing a story on the CEO of a major U.S. company, and during the reporter's due diligence, found that the CEO had falsified his resume that happened to be posted on the company's website. Several articles were written on this high-profile scandal at the time, including *USA Today,* which wrote: "Edmondson had claimed that he received degrees in theology and psychology from Pacific Coast Baptist College in California, which moved in 1998 to Oklahoma and renamed itself Heartland Baptist Bible College. The school's registrar told the *Star-Telegram* that records showed Edmondson completed only two semesters and that the school never offered degrees in psychology. The school official declined to comment to The Associated Press." After this incident surfaced Edmondson quit his post as CEO and acknowledged inconsistencies with his resume.

There are several ways in which employees can ascertain fraudulent information about their experience, work history and education. There are resume mills, diploma mills and now even companies that will provide verbal verification of fictitious employment history for candidates for a fee. Google any of these categories and you will find various information about each deceptive method out there.

Today, diploma mills are high-tech operations that earn more than $500 million annually according to estimates made by John Bear, the author of *Bears' Guide to Earning Degrees by Long Distance.*

- Verify the information on the resume. This can be outsourced or through good old fashion detective work. Make phone calls to verify the information. Employers and Universities will not give you details, but they will usually confirm dates of employment, position and Universities will verify degree obtained and date. You can also conduct advanced internet research. A professional site that is handy for conducting employment information is www.linkedin.com. This is a professional networking site, not a social site, but if utilized properly you can data mine this site for valuable information. Also, inform your client not to be shy about asking their candidates for Proof of Degree–ask the applicant to provide proof of their degrees as well as providing transcripts from each school they attended.

Based on your findings, you will now determine what your next steps are in the investigative process. If you clearly identified the subject and based upon the crime, evidence, and client's wishes, you will conclude your investigation and provide your report to the client, interview the subject, or provide the appropriate law enforcement agency with your findings.

If you are still not sure who the dishonest employee is, at this stage you may want to begin conducting fact-findings interviews. Each case is different and you will need to determine who should be interviewed and in what order. This is a crucial stage in the investigation. If the subject has not yet been identified and you are not an experienced interviewer, you should find an investigator who is experienced in employee interviews. Conducting fact-finding interviews and integrity interviews is an art that is learned over several years of experience and training and cannot be learned in one day or by taking one class. If the interviewer is not prepared and experienced, the entire investigation will be jeopardized and the subject may never be identified.

Please note there are also other methods that can be conducted prior to or simultaneously as the interviews are being conducted. One of them is statement analysis, where all employees can be given a list of questions to be answered in writing or by having them complete a written statement about the incident in question. The statements can then be forwarded to the expert on the subject who can analyze the statements and provide you with some additional findings for you to move forward with your interviews/investigation.

In this section, we are not going to get into the details of interviewing or statement taking as that is beyond the scope of this chapter. However, it is recommended that if you have a witness present during an interview, he or she should take notes during the process while the interviewer focuses on interviewing the employee.

EXTERNAL THEFT–SHOPLIFTING

It is important that we discuss shoplifting in this chapter or we would be doing a disservice to you as an investigator. It is important to understand how widespread shoplifting. Even though employee theft is responsible for 60 percent to 80 percent of a company's losses, shoplifting has been on the rise and goes hand in hand with employee theft at times.

Again, who steals? It can include people of any race, religion, sex, nationality, or financial class as well as customers, visitors, guests, vendors, and, of course, as we are aware, employees.

There are several classifications of shoplifters:

Opportunist: This typically the average person who normally would not steal, but an opportunity presented itself. An example is the person who is waiting in a long check-out line and puts an item in his or her bag or pocket and then gets impatient or aggravated while waiting and leaves the store without paying for it, stealing it. Alternatively, there is the person who is carries an item in the store, like a pair of sunglasses, and accidentally leaves the store without paying for the item. In most jurisdictions, that alone is not shoplifting; it is part of the shoplifting statute (leaving the store). However, the other part is usually "Intent." Therefore, when the customer leaves the store with unpaid merchandise, that act alone may not be shoplifting, as it may truly have been an accident. However, when the individual realizes he still has the unpaid merchandise and has the opportunity to return to the store but does not, then the intent comes in to play. When this occurs, the individual has now shown intent and it becomes shoplifting. This is could be considered an example of the **opportunist**.

Amateur: A person who steals every now and then would be considered an amateur. An example would be teenagers and young adults who either have financial needs, or peer pressure or want to maintain a certain social status by wearing items that they may not be able to afford. Some drug users may fall into this category, too. They may need to steal something so they can sell it on the streets for some quick cash. However, they can also fall into some of the other categories as well.

Professional: The professional either steals to supplement his or her income or it is his or her only means of income. Professionals can act alone or commonly they shoplift in large groups.

The professional category and ORC (Organized Retail Crimes) are often well prepared and have an army of folks who all have assigned responsibilities during the thefts of merchandise. Some create distractions, others just carry the merchandise from one spot in the store to another, while others commit the crime and others serve as lookouts.

Organized Retail Crime (ORC): Organized retail crime has become so large and popular that the FBI has a dedicated task force to investigate ORC groups and many retailers have begun to deploy special investigation units that solely investigate ORCs. These groups have many different levels in their organization and are primarily run by large gangs and terrorist and other violent and serious organized crime lords.

Organized retail crime refers to professional *shoplifting*, cargo theft, retail crime rings and other *organized crime* occurring in retail environments. One person acting alone is not considered an example of organized retail crime. The FBI has estimated that the losses attributed to organized retail crime could reach as much as $30 billion a year. These criminals move from store to store and even city to city. Working in teams, some create distractions while others steal everything from infant formula to DVDs. Often, they are stocking up on specified items at the request of the organized crime leader.

According to Brian J. Nadeau, former program manager of the FBI's Organized Retail Theft Program, "These aren't shoplifters taking a pack of gum. These are professional thieves."[1]

HEALTH AND SAFETY CONCERNS

Gangs consistently steal high-value merchandise that can be easily hidden, such as medications, infant formula, razor blades, apparel, camera film, batteries, DVDs, CDs, and smoking cessation products. Thieves resell infant formula and pharmaceuticals, among other things, after not storing them correctly–or after altering expiration dates. Unsuspecting consumers face serious health and safety risks.

NOTABLE CASES

In Florida, in early 2008, a single shoplifting investigation turned up a massive organized enterprise. Operating for at least five years, criminals had stolen up to $100 million in medicine, health and beauty goods.[2]

Texas FBI agents pulled over a rental truck, leading them to $2.7 million in stolen assets. The goods included $1 million in stolen baby formula that was stored in rodent-infested garages with no temperature control.[3]

CURRENT LEGISLATION

On July 15, 2008, Reps. Brad Ellsworth (D-Ind.) and Jim Jordan (R-Ohio) introduced the Organized Retail Crime Act of 2008[4] that would make it a felony to engage in activities that further organized retail crime. Specific and narrow obligations upon on-line marketplaces known to be used by high-volume sellers of stolen merchandise are also included to benefit legitimate online businesses. According to Rep. Ellsworth, "The bill will provide law enforcement officers and retailers with the tools they need to reveal the cloak of anonymity and bring these criminals to justice; while at the same time, preserving the online marketplace for law-abiding citizens."[5]

On August 1, 2008, Sen. Dick Durbin (D-Ill.) introduced the Combating Organized Retail Crime Act of 2008 that would give law enforcement the ability to prosecute, among other things.

Summing up external thefts, although they are a small percentage of the total shrinkage that is a result of internal and external thefts, you do need to understand that there are also **Kleptomania's**. Of all reported shoplifting, less than 5 percent are actually committed by kleptomaniacs.

Kleptomania (from Greek: κλεπτειν, kleptein, "to steal," and μανια, "mania") is an irresistible urge to steal items of trivial value. People with this disorder are compelled to steal things, generally, but not limited to, objects of little or no significant value, such as pens, paper clips, tape, and shoes. Some kleptomaniacs may not even be aware that they have committed the theft.

Kleptomania was first officially recognized in the U.S. as a mental disorder in the 1960s in the case of the state of California v. Douglas Jones.

Kleptomania is distinguished from shoplifting or ordinary theft, as shoplifters and thieves generally steal for monetary value or associated gains and usually display intent or premeditation, while kleptomaniacs are not necessarily contemplating the value of the items they steal or even the theft until they are compelled without motive.

This disorder usually manifests during puberty and, in some cases, may never stop and lasts throughout the person's life. People with this disorder are likely to have a comorbid condition, specifically paranoid, schizoid, or borderline personality disorder.[6] Kleptomania can occur after traumatic brain injury and carbon monoxide poisoning.[7,8]

Kleptomania is usually thought of as part of the obsessive-compulsive disorder spectrum, although emerging evidence suggests that it may be more similar to addictive and mood disorders. In particular, this disorder is frequently comorbid with substance use disorders, and it is common for individuals with kleptomania to have first-degree relatives who suffer from a substance use disorder.[9]

RELATIONSHIP TO OCD

Kleptomania is frequently thought of as being a part of obsessive-compulsive disorder, since the irresistible and uncontrollable actions are similar to the frequently excessive, unnecessary, and unwanted rituals of OCD. Some individuals with kleptomania demonstrate **hoarding** symptoms that resemble those with OCD.[10]

Prevalence rates between the two disorders do not demonstrate a strong relationship. Studies examining the comorbidity of OCD in subjects with kleptomania have inconsistent results, with some showing a relatively high co-occurrence (45%–60%)[11,12] while others demonstrate low rates (0%–6.5%).[13,14] Similarly, when rates of kleptomania have been examined in subjects with OCD, a relatively low co-occurrence was found (2.2%–5.9%).[15,16]

Every year Jack L. Haynes International, Inc. releases their annual retail theft reports. Below are the results from the 2009 survey. These numbers are extremely enlightening, educating and informative to all professional investigators.

Highlights from Jack L. Hayes International, Inc.'s 21st Annual Retail Theft Survey

Employee Theft: One out of every 30 employees was apprehended for theft from their employer in 2008. *(Based on comparison data of over 2.1 million employees.)*

Apprehensions: Survey participants apprehended 72,120 dishonest employees in 2008, an increase of 3.01%. This was the 5th straight year of employee apprehension increases.

Recoveries: Dollars recovered from dishonest employee apprehensions totaled over $69.8 million in 2008, an increase of 9.90%. This was the 5th straight year that dishonest employee recovery dollars increased.

The average dishonest employee case value in 2008 was $969.14, a 6.7% increase over 2007's average case value ($908.33).

DISHONEST EMPLOYEES			Difference	
	2007	2008	#/$	Pct.
Apprehensions	70,015	72,120	2,105	3.01%
Recoveries	$63,596,599	$69,894,691	$6,298,092	9.90%
Avg. Case Value	$908.33	$969.14	$60.81	6.70%

Why do companies not pursue or invest in investigating their employee theft issues? Many of them either do not understand how big a problem they really have until it is too late or they put their head in the sand hoping the problem will go away. As you will discover in many cases, the client will call you when their losses have become so large, that they no longer can avoid the problem if they want to continue to stay in business. They also do not want to spend money. So we as professional investigators must educate our clients and the public that there is a return on their willing to invest in quality professional investigators to conduct background checks, investigations, physical security assessments, risk analysis, and many more specialties that can save them thousands of dollars in the long run. Dishonest employee investigations will never go away. As long as there are employees, there will always be dishonest employees who will steal from their employer. Once you are able to close an employee theft investigation, you have the insight at that stage to advise and consult the client on ways to prevent and deter thefts from reoccurring. You have the opportunity to write policy and procedure manuals for them and guide them on other investigative and preventive measures, all of which can lead to additional legitimate billable hours.

Prevention is the best medicine for any business owner. However, when all else fails, you need to be available and knowledgeable in identifying the loss and investigating and concluding the case as needed.

REFERENCES

1. Federal Bureau of Investigation–Press Room–Headline Archives.
2. Multimillion-dollar Theft Ring is Broken | theledger.com | The Ledger | Lakeland, FL.
3. Retailers Organize Against Crime | Security Management.
4. http://frwebgate.access.gpo.gov/cgi-bin/getdoc.cgi?dbname=110_cong_bills& docid=f:h6491ih.txt.pdf
5. The Online Office of Congressman Brad Ellsworth–July 15, 2008: Ellsworth, Jordan Introduce Bill to Fight Organized Retail Crime, Protect Online Consumers. Retrieved from http://en.wikipedia.org/wiki/Organized_retail_crime
6. Grant, J. E. (2004). Co-occurrence of personality disorders in persons with kleptomania: a preliminary investigation. *J. Am. Acad. Psychiatry Law, 32*(4): 395–398.
7. Aizer, A., Lowengrub, K., & Dannon, P. N. (2004). Kleptomania after head trauma: Two case reports and the combination treatment strategies. *Clinical Neuro*
8. Gürlek Yüksel, E., Taskin, E. O., Yilmaz Ovali, G., Karaçam, M., & Esen Danaci, A. (2007). Case report: Kleptomania and other psychiatric symptoms after carbon monoxide intoxication (in Turkish). Türk psikiyatri dergisi = *Turkish Journal of Psychiatry, 18*(1): 80–66.

9. Grant, J. E. (2006). Understanding and treating kleptomania: new models and new treatments. *The Israel Journal of Psychiatry and Related Sciences, 43*(2): 81–87.

10. Grant, J. E., Kim, S. W. (2002). Clinical characteristics and associated psychopathology of 22 patients with kleptomania. *Comprehensive Psychiatry, 43*(5): 378–384.

11. Presta, S., Marazziti, D., Dell'Osso, L., Pfanner, C., Pallanti, S., Cassano, G. B. (2002). Kleptomania: Clinical features and comorbidity in an Italian sample. *Comprehensive Psychiatry, 43*(1): 7–12.

12. McElroy, S. L., Pope, H. G., Hudson, J. I., Keck, P. E., White, K. L. (1991). Kleptomania: A report of 20 cases. *The American Journal of Psychiatry, 148*(5): 652–657.

13. Baylé, F. J., Caci, H., Millet, B., Richa, S., Olié, J. P. (2003). Psychopathology and co morbidity of psychiatric disorders in patients with kleptomania. *The American Journal of Psychiatry, 160*(8): 1509–1513.

14. Grant, J. E. (2003). Family history and psychiatric comorbidity in persons with kleptomania. *Comprehensive Psychiatry, 44*(6): 437–441.

15. Matsunaga, H., Kiriike, N., Matsui, T., Oya, K., Okino, K., Stein, D. J. (2005). Impulsive disorders in Japanese adult patients with obsessive-compulsive disorder. *Comprehensive Psychiatry, 46*(1): 43–49.

16. Fontenelle, L. F., Mendlowicz, M. V., Versiani, M. (2005). Impulse control disorders in patients with obsessive-compulsive disorder. *Psychiatr Clin Neurosci, 59*:30–37.

Recap of Internal and External Statistics by Jack L. Haynes International.

INDEX